"Honest and solid as a hockey player, Sittler the writer is no less substantial. His book gets into the tough corners, too." – Jim Kernaghan, *London Free Press*

"What Sittler has to say about hockey and its cast of characters is often riveting." – *Books in Canada*

"The authors know the kind of anecdote readers want, and the story of Punch Imlach's destruction of the team is engrossing." – Paul Quarrington, *The Globe and Mail*

"Detailed, analytical, and affecting ... Sittler is honest about the pain of facing his hockey career's inevitable end." – *Quill and Quire*

"Sittler is blunt. He skewers Ballard and Imlach on what he considered terrible trades and shabby treatment ... If that's what you're looking for in this book, you'll be satisfied. There are lighter moments, but the book keeps heating up." – *Calgary Herald*

D0789460

CHRYS GOYENS is the co-author of *Lions in Winter*, a history of the Montreal Canadiens, and author of *Robinson for the Defense*, a biography of Larry Robinson. He has worked in radio as a news reporter and talk show host in Montreal and has been Quebec correspondent for the *Toronto Star*, the editor at *Sporting Life*, and has contributed several articles to *Sport Magazine* in the United States.

ALLAN TUROWETZ, co-author of *Lions in Winter*, lectures in courses on the Sociology of Sport at Concordia University in Montreal. He was team sociologist to the Buffalo Sabres Hockey Club in 1978, to the Hartford Whalers Hockey Club in 1979 and to the Canadian Men's Basketball team in 1980. A former radio talk show host, he is now the President and owner of T.B.A.

DARRYL SITTLER & CHRYS GOYENS
WITH ALLAN TUROWETZ

Sittler

M&S

An M&S Paperback from
McClelland & Stewart Inc.
The Canadian Publishers

An M&S Paperback from McClelland & Stewart Inc.

First printing September 1992
Cloth edition printed 1991

Published by arrangement with Macmillan Canada

Canadian Cataloguing in Publication Data

Sittler, Darryl, 1950-
Sittler

"An M&S paperback."
Includes index.
ISBN 0-7710-8080-8

1. Sittler, Darryl, 1950- . 2. Hockey players - Canada - Biography.
I. Goyens, Chrys. II. Turowetz, Allan, 1948- . III. Title.

GV848.5.S58A3 1992   796.962'092   C92-094665-8

Cover design by Stephen Kenny
Front and back cover photographs © Graig Abel

Articles by Jim Kernaghan and Frank Orr reprinted with permission —
Toronto Star Syndicate

Printed and bound in Canada

McClelland & Stewart Inc.
The Canadian Publishers
481 University Avenue
Toronto, Ontario
M5G 2E9

Contents

FOREWORD

It was the summer of 1974, at the end of my fourth season, that Toronto Maple Leafs GM Jim Gregory and I were talking, kibbitzing really, in his office on the second floor at Maple Leaf Gardens. He made some joke about trading me.

"You can't trade me, I've got a no-trade contract," I replied, a trifle smugly. This was a major concession by the Maple Leafs in my last contract negotiation. My major concession was that I hadn't gone to the World Hockey Association Toronto Toros, who were throwing a lot of money around.

"No you don't."

"Yes I do."

"No you don't."

"Well, Jim, that's real easy to check," I said. "We'll get on the phone to Eagleson right now and check this out. I wouldn't have signed the deal if I didn't believe it was a no-trade contract. I have a lot invested in this team and this city and I want to play my whole career here. If that isn't possible, I want some say in where I'll be going."

"You don't have to call Al. Let's talk to Harold."

We moved the conversation across the hall to Harold Ballard's office where The Boss was sitting behind his desk.

"What's wrong?" he growled. Ballard always anticipated the "best case" scenario.

I spoke up. "I thought I had a no-trade contract, I believe I do, and Jim Gregory is telling me I don't."

"Whattayamean a no-trade contract," he boomed. "Dontcha have any confidence in your ability?"

"I've got all the confidence in the world in my own abilities, Harold. But if the Boston Bruins offered Bobby Orr and Phil Esposito for me, I'm sure you'd make the deal."

He wasn't going to be mollified by common sense, and you could almost see the delicious thoughts of Orr and Espo in blue-and-white scrolling across his forehead, like on the electronic newsboards they have outside buildings to bring the latest news bulletins to passersby. Those thoughts danced right out, exit stage left, when he had an agonizing thought of what he might have to pay these guys.

Harold was nothing if he wasn't practical. He turned back to me.

"Ya might think I'm whistling Dixie here but it would take both of those guys to move you outta here."

"Yeah, you're right," I countered.

"I know," he smiled.

"I do think you're whistling Dixie."

His face changed expression for a second or two, the look of a kid with cookie jar right up to the elbow. Figuring quite rightly that I didn't mean too much disrespect, and not anxious to have a blow-up in his office over the issue, he got up and came around the desk.

Harold put one arm around my shoulder. Buddy to buddy. Blood brothers who share the same uniform. Forever together.

"Brian, we wouldn't trade you for love or money."

He thought I was Spinner Spencer.

Gregory, always quick on his feet, jumped right in to rescue The Boss.

"Harold, it's Darryl!"

Harold was already lying. Or his memory was locked firmly on the Maple Leaf Gardens balance sheet, and he had trouble remembering exactly who was in white-and-blue on any given night—unless, of course, that player had recently asked for more money. Brian Spencer had been left unprotected by the Maple Leafs and claimed by the fledgling New York Islanders in the 1972 Expansion Draft.

The ancient Chinese had a curse: "May you live in interesting times!"

For myself, and all of the rest of the Maple Leafs "family", life with Harold Ballard was always interesting times.

ACKNOWLEDGMENTS

Sometimes it takes a forum such as this to be able to tell certain people what they mean to you. This book is dedicated to the people who really count, and have always counted, in my life.

To my wife Wendy, thank you for the love, support and patience you have shown me throughout the twenty years of our marriage, for our three wonderful children and for having chosen to be the dedicated mother and wife that you are. And also for representing the real backbone of our family, always being there for all of us throughout our busy lives. Your strength, your great sense of humor, your spark and gentle sensitivity mean so much to me.

To Ryan, all my pride in what you have accomplished so far, and all of my support for what you will accomplish later on. Your special talents, your hard work and outgoing personality will always serve you well. I look forward to giving you love and support in reaching your goals of graduating from university and someday playing in the NHL.

To Meaghan, for the bright smile and warm personality that make you very special. Your determination and strength of character will help you to achieve whichever goals you choose to pursue in life. Always know that you have my love and encouragement. I'll be there when you skate onto the ice at the 1998 Olympics.

To Ashley, thank you for your happy-go-lucky personality and great sense of humor. You are quite a character. Your big brother and sister got "more press" in this book because they were around more when Dad was playing in the NHL. But you're just as special in every way. I look forward to giving you my love and support as you try to fulfill your wishes and dreams. I'm proud of you.

To my mother, for teaching me what responsibility and hard work are all about, and for the many long hours you put in helping a boy fulfill his dream.

To my (late) father, for your quiet, unstinting encouragement throughout my life, for the closeness we shared and for being my friend. I miss you.

To Alan Eagleson, my gratitude for your friendship, direction and counsel over the years. To friends and financial advisers Graeme Clark and George Lyon, many thanks.

To Ronald McDonald House, Sick Kids Hospital, Terry Fox and the Canadian Cancer Society, Ontario Head Injury Association, Special Olympics, Easter Seals, Big Brothers and other organizations which have had a great impact on my life and which have provided me with lasting memories, thank you for getting me involved.

Thanks to minor hockey coaches and supporters, the London Knights, the Toronto Maple Leafs, the Philadelphia Flyers and the Detroit Red Wings. And especially to may teammates and linemates, for the support and friendship they provided and the memories we share of playing the game we love so much.

Thanks to the media, for the support and understanding through the ups and downs of my career; you have been very fair and I appreciate that.

And to my fans, thank you for just being there, then and now, and for giving me the opportunity to entertain you with the skills and talents I was blessed with. My hope is that the Leafs will soon be a hockey team that you can again be proud of.

And most of all, I would like to acknowledge God for the life He has given me. I will continue to place my trust in Him.

1

Lordy, lordy . . . Darryl's forty!

IT IS SOMETIME after 7:00 a.m. on Tuesday, September 18, 1990. I'm stirring from sleep in the main bedroom of our cottage on Lake Simcoe just outside Orillia, Ontario. A gorgeous late-summer sun streams in through the bedroom window; the first day of the rest of your life, as the poet once said, beckons with golden wings. This morning has special significance for me because this is the first day in the fifth decade in the life of Darryl Glen Sittler, former hockey player.

If that doesn't make it special enough, my eyes open to a strange sight never witnessed at any time during my first four decades. Hovering directly overhead is a dark, black, box-like device with blonde hair sticking out of it in all directions.

I try to shake the sleep from my eyes and focus. Just then, the apparition speaks.

"Darryl Sittler is forty years old today! Happy Birthday!" It's my wife Wendy, which explains the long, blonde hair. The curious black device turns out to be the family video camera, its lone eye staring coldly at me as I struggle to wake up. "Oh geez," I think, "something's up! I wonder what deal Wendy has lined up for today—she owes me big considering the nasty trick I pulled on her thirty-fifth birthday."

Still puzzling over the directions this day will take, I prepare to answer nature's call, leaping out of bed and heading towards the washroom. Wendy, a notorious late riser—I'm usually up and about doing things at the crack of dawn, hours before she is—also leaps out of bed and follows me across the living room, videotape rolling. It must be something special to get her up with the birds.

"So what do you think your fortieth birthday will bring?" she asks coyly.

"No idea."

"I just want you to know that at 9:30 I want you fully dressed and ready to go, to start off your Big Fortieth."

"I'm working today." I have a lot to do around the cottage, season-ending puttering which translates into cleaning up after my two daughters and son. Maybe I can still escape.

"Okay, but you wanted a party." Wendy's all sweetness and light.

I'm thinking, darn, she's not fighting hard enough; if she had something spectacular lined up, she wouldn't buy that weak alibi.

"I don't want a party," I complain, knowing full well that I'm in for something. A few years earlier, on my wife's thirty-fifth birthday, I had arranged a special surprise. Her birthday is July 2, right in between the Canadian and American national holidays, usually a time when the whole family can get together on one side of the border or the other. This is especially convenient because although we live in the Buffalo, New York, suburb of East Amherst, Wendy's family is in London and mine mostly lives in and around Kitchener.

On that occasion, we were staying at my in-laws' cottage. Wendy and I had gone away for the weekend two days before her birthday. I had planned to spring the surprise party upon her return—our absence would make it easy for her family to help with all of the party arrangements. When we got back, everybody would be there waiting. They even had had a huge banner made to hang across the street, which is on a cul-de-sac. It's hard to ignore a street-wide birthday banner (even though her name had not yet been inserted on it), so to cover its real purpose, I told her that our neighbor Glenn Harding's birthday was July 4, and we were coming back a little early to participate in a surprise party for him.

Wendy has a great sense of humor, and she wanted to make a splash for "his" birthday. She put together a special outfit—a frilly slip and a little garter belt on the leg—and she planned to slink in like the French maid of fantasy—give Birthday Boy a kiss while he still was dazed from the shock of it all, say something sexy in an outrageous French accent, then leave and get changed to rejoin the party.

Now, Wendy is a modest person and wouldn't think of parading through Orillia in such an outfit, so she kept her street clothes on until we were about a half mile from the cottage, then she changed into her little outfit. I took advantage of this opportunity to pop into a convenience store and phone ahead to make sure that everything was ready.

When we drove around the corner onto our street, everybody was there—family and friends—a huge banner saying HAPPY BIRTHDAY WONDERFUL WENDY—and video cameras rolling. For the longest time we weren't sure that she would get out of the car.

Naturally, the love of my life vowed revenge.

As my fortieth birthday approached, I wondered if she was going to do something similar. I didn't really want her to, because when I'm not on the road on business I'm the essential homebody, and something quiet with the kids would suit me just fine. I had lined up my business schedule to leave the day of my fortieth free. My son Ryan had a hockey game that night in Buffalo and I wanted to go to that, with maybe a quiet dinner before. I was in Toronto on business the day just before my birthday, and when I called home, Wendy suggested that we stay overnight at the cottage. I agreed, wondering why she wanted me up there. I suspected she was planning a surprise party at the cottage with the Orillia gang.

We agreed to meet at Bill and Sue Swinimer's; Bill is the CEO and founder of Uniplast Industries, a company I do some representational work with. When I arrived that Monday night, I half expected family and friends to jump out from behind the bushes yelling, "Surprise!"

Nothing.

I spent part of the evening surreptitiously checking under tables and behind curtains for the surprise, to no avail. Later I discovered that Bill and Sue were in on it, and were probably giggling inside as they pretended not to notice my "subtle" attempts to track down my surprise party. Wendy arrived from Buffalo at about eleven and still nothing happened. Ditto back at our cottage.

As we drive off at 9:30 on the fateful day, Wendy can hardly contain herself: "Where do you think the party is now?"

"What could be so special in Orillia at 9:30 in the morning?. There's probably a 'lordy, lordy look who's 40!' banner across the main drag." I'm trying to be nonchalant as I give my chauffeur-for-a-day her itinerary—starting with the Tim Horton's for my regular large coffee and muffin. Maybe the doughnut shop will be surrounded by birthday flamingos or penguins?

Hold the press. There is no banner across the main street; as far as Orillia is concerned, Darryl Sittler's fortieth birthday is not an event of civic importance. Tim Horton's is remarkably flamingo-free. We park outside the store and Wendy follows me inside, video camera rolling. Aha, maybe the gang is inside? This Candid Camera business is starting to get embarrassing.

Nothing and nobody, except a few regulars filling up on muffins, apple fritters and extra-large coffees. As I order my traditional "large-coffee-and-muffin-to-go" at the counter, the camera is recording each word of this momentous occasion for posterity.

"And a big chocolate milk for the lady with the camera," I say real loud, nodding in my wife's direction. The girl at the counter giggles, and at this point I'm starting to get a little paranoid: is everybody in Orillia in on it except me?

Back out in the parking lot, Wendy sets the camera on the roof of the car and says, "Wait right there!" She circles the car and pulls a blindfold out of her pocket. Seconds later, I'm functionally blind with the bandanna snugly set over my eyes. She laughs as we drive off, me blindly sipping coffee and chewing on a muffin, and she shamelessly milking the moment with a "Little does he know this could be his last meal . . ."

I have a few moments to reflect, however. What could she do to me that's so bad that I need a blindfold?

We drive north out of Orillia, a fact I know only because Wendy tells me so. However, that apparently is the only fact she knows, too, because she has to stop and ask for directions at a gas station. Rather than simply rolling down the window, she gets out of the car and closes the door so I can't hear what she is saying.

Which is, as I discovered later, "Do you know where the Coldwater Parachute School is?" The people at the station hear this, take one look at me sitting blindfolded in the front passenger seat, and immediately break out laughing. Of course, I am oblivious to the fact that I am giving everybody such a good time.

We drive off, with a little more purpose this time. About a half hour goes by before the car finally pulls up. "Stay there." She comes around to the passenger side to let me out of the car, video camera going all the way. I am then led by the arm about thirty yards or so and, finally, the blindfold comes off.

I am standing in the middle of a field, in front of an old hulk of a school bus with a big Happy Birthday banner on it. Three of my friends are there . . . Dave Baker, Tom Hussey and Bill Swinimer, and Bill has his own video camera going and Dave is chuckling incredulously: "You mean she blindfolded you and then had to start asking people how to get here because she left the instructions at home?"

An auspicious beginning, to say the least.

Another fellow comes up to me and introduces himself. The old cleaned-out school bus, it turns out, serves as the office for the Coldwater Parachute Club.

"I'm your parachute instructor. You'll be jumping out of a plane at 3,000 feet at 2:30 this afternoon."

In real good Canadian, "like get serious, eh?"

I turn to Wendy. "You got me!" Okay folks, the joke is over, let's go home.

Everybody starts talking at once. No joke, they fully intend for me to jump out of a moving airplane, more than half a mile up, protected only by a pound or two of silk or miracle-fiber nylon.

Wendy is in her element. "I thought you had a lot of friends until I started calling them up and told them what your birthday surprise was going to be. I asked them if any wanted to jump with you." Dave Baker, apparently, was the only one to say yes.

Never did trust your judgment, Dave.

Dave, who's fifty-three, is the owner of a car dealership in Richmond Hill whom I've known for years; he had said yes, without really thinking about the magnitude of what we were going to do there that day. It starts sinking in when they put the blue jumpsuit on him and hand him his black-and-red parachute. I get a black jumpsuit and a red-and-white parachute.

"Just my luck it won't open because it's the wrong colors," I think to myself, the eternal blue-and-white boy from St. Jacobs, Ontario. Then again, I ended my hockey career in the red-and-white of Detroit; maybe I'll end it all in the red-and-white of a parachute?

Dave and I spend most of the morning taking jumping instruction and having a good time together, while Wendy, Tom Hussey and Bill Swinimer hang around, Swin and Wendy merrily filming. Tom Hussey is another good friend from Orillia; comptroller of Uniplast Industries, Bill's company. It turns out to be a fun time, although both Dave and I share a few sobering thoughts when we have to fill out and sign a disclaimer form that starts: "In case of accident, please notify . . ."

"You won't have to go far," I say, pointing at Wendy.

Dave has the best line, as usual: "When I told my kids last night what I was going to be doing today, they looked at each other exclaiming, 'Holy smokes, this time tomorrow night, this could be all ours!' I found that to be real encouraging."

The amazing thing about the events of the day is that, up until a week before, Wendy had no idea what she was going to do. I hate to imagine what might have happened if she really had had the time to apply herself. In turns out that the major problem was finding a parachute club that would accept, train and jump two rookies on a weekday. Skydiving clubs are hives of activity on weekends and daily throughout the summer, but off-season weekdays are very quiet.

I can also imagine her post-mortem with my insurance people: ". . . and the next thing we knew, the chute failed to open. How much do I get?"

"Not a cent, ma'am. There's a rider stipulating that skydiving and alligator wrestling are not covered. Ever. Awfully sorry to hear about it, though."

Anyway, Dave Baker and I are it. Nervous as I am, I'm also excited about the jump. I remember mentioning to Wendy three or four years ago that I might like to go parachute jumping at least once in my life, just to experience it. Wendy's memory also, it seems, was operating at 100 per cent capacity. It turned out to be a natural fit because she always wanted to do something unforgettable for my fortieth birthday.

During a brief lull while Dave is suiting up I have a sudden flashback: today is exactly twenty years and one week after I walked into my first Toronto Maple Leafs training camp. Yes, Virginia, there is life after hockey. It just might be a lot shorter than originally planned.

I think of all these things now as I perch near the open door of the rickety little Cessna that had no business taking five adults up to 3,000 feet. Suddenly, I'm watching Dave's red-and-black chute opening several hundred feet below and behind me, wondering if somewhere above or below, that noted horse player Punch Imlach is watching and calculating the odds on the chute malfunctioning. Or maybe Punch and Harold are together, making book. "Think he'll choke, Harold?" "Nah, he'll jump okay, but after he lands and breaks his leg, he'll blame it on us to the press! You can take that to the bank!"

Our instructor, a second professional parachutist, and Bill Swinimer have accompanied Dave and me upstairs. Swin was along to record the great moment; but the battery on his camera proved to be deader than a doornail. The only shots we eventually got were of these two specks floating down out of the sky, slowly getting bigger and bigger, from Wendy's camera on the ground. It could have been anybody.

The experience will stay with me a long time. There is nothing to compare it to. No matter how you rationalize it, or how they train you, nothing really prepares you for standing half-in, half-out of an airplane, getting ready to push off at 3,000 feet. Your heart stops, everything happens so fast.

Suddenly you're out and dropping. They've told you the parachute will open after you've counted "one thousand, two thousand, three thousand, four thousand". If, by then, it hasn't opened, you're supposed to look above you to check the chute. Then you go for the reserve.

I haven't reached "four thousand" when I feel the tug that tells me that mine has opened perfectly, and I'm able to concentrate on looking down, instead of up. That's because the next step is to search for a guy on the ground holding a sign with a directional arrow on it; he points it in the direction where you should steer your chute because he knows the wind direction and your safest route down.

It's a perfect day for jumping; there isn't a cloud in the sky and it's warm with barely a breeze. When I land, I roll around a little bit. I try to come in standing up, but a little gust catches the chute and puts me back on my rear end. I get up, heart pumping wildly, a little voice inside saying, "Pay up, Punch!"

Dave has landed before me, giving him much more time to prepare a memorable line. As we receive the official certificates documenting our first jump, he deadpans, "I've had better jumps, but this is the first time I've ever gotten a certificate for it."

Wendy is right. I would never forget my fortieth birthday. And I don't realize that the day is only half over. After all of this excitement, we return to the cottage to get changed. The plan is to head back to Buffalo to catch my son's hockey game. We'll have time to stop somewhere for a bite to eat and decide on the Porto Fino, a great Italian restaurant in Mississauga that we've enjoyed over the years.

The owner, Joe Corrente, is a very warm and receptive guy, and greets us at the door. I once gave him a Sittler family portrait taken the night of my induction in the Hall of Fame to hang in his lobby. As we enter, I notice it is off the wall—a "collector" probably removed it, a depressing thought. Joe guides us through the restaurant into the back, and then we detour toward the banquet area. I still haven't twigged to it, and I meekly follow him through the door.

"Surprise!"

Gotcha No. 2. About fifty of my friends are here. Ryan's hockey game in Buffalo is now out of the question—he's probably known all along that I won't be there tonight.

Smiling faces are everywhere: one of the first I see is Lanny McDonald, the best friend I made in hockey . . . Jim McKenny is there . . . Billy Watters . . . Paul Henderson . . . Jim Gregory . . . Ron Ellis . . . Dave Burrows . . . Mel Stevens . . . Gary Sabourin . . . my brother Tim . . . Tom Hussey, Dave Baker and Bill Swinimer who had been with me during the day and kept real quiet . . . as well as groups from Buffalo, Orillia and Toronto, people I have met and grown to like before, during and after my hockey career. Better yet, people I had never expected to see all gathered in the same room.

I turn to Wendy for the second time that day, "You got me!"

Bill Watters emcees the evening in a very casual style. He has everybody introduce themselves and describe how they are associated with me or have come to know me—a unique way of telling my life story, through the eyes and experiences of others. Many of them, obviously, haven't met each other prior to this occasion, as they have come to know me from different circles, or my various travels.

Wendy has also arranged to have those friends who couldn't be here send videos: Tiger Williams and Garry Monahan and their wives out in Vancouver have done one, as has George Lyon, my friend and stockbroker from Minneapolis. Greg and Lori Smith (I played with him in Detroit), have sent one up from Washington where they live; Roger Neilson and Colin Campbell from the New York Rangers also have sent one, as have Bruce and Elaine Selig and family, friends from New Jersey.

And even though Jack Valiquette is at the party, he and the boys from Orillia have put together a tape that is very funny.

The winning tape, however, is home-made. With the tune of my favorite country singer, Willie Nelson's "On the Road Again" as the score, it shows my family at home without me. All of my children are shown leaving home and going off to various special events. They all have a Happy Birthday message for their dad, and show that they, too, can be busy and On the Road Again, just like the old man. The closing credits inform all that the tape is brought to us by Wendy

Productions. Producer, Director, Cameraperson, Writer, Arranger and Technical Expert . . . Wendy. (With a little help in the music department from Willie the Outlaw.)

Wendy also has asked the people in attendance if they want to say something special, read a poem, bring old pictures, tell old stories—and we've got all that on tape.

A special moment comes when I am presented with a Leafs blue away jersey with the number 27 on the back, which I put on. Doug Kelcher takes us on a historical romp, to the theme of a "few years in the life of 27", touching on its history, the sweater's current owner, and hockey in general. As the story unfolds, I am prodded this way and that, now facing the audience, now with my back to them, a lot like a prize Holstein being trotted out at a farm auction.

The first time I turn around, the NHL-approved name bar announces the sweater's current owner to be (John) KORDIC. (He has since handed off to Lucien Deblois.) Each time my back is displayed to the audience, a different name appears above the big 27. A layer down we find, (Doug) SHEDDEN, who had worn the number for a single game. More digging into the history of Maple Leafs 27 turns up the name (Dave) SEMENKO and under that, ironically, a player drafted by Toronto in a choice obtained by the Leafs from the Flyers in the trade for me, (Miroslav) IHNACAK.

After the Ihnacak name bar comes off, only one name remains: SITTLER. On this solemn occasion they have chosen to forget that other illustrious name that made the number 27 famous before my arrival on the scene in 1970.

I am back in Toronto travelling blue. However, the sweater isn't complete. Bill Watters calls up Jim Gregory, the Leafs general manager during the first eight years of my career.

"For every hero story, there's a tragedy," Jim begins. "There were a few hero stories with Darryl and I don't remember his sweater being like that." I remember it being like this, he concludes with a flourish, placing a white velcro "C" on my chest.

This is the way we all remembered it, Jim. The last time a "C" came on or off my sweater, nobody was laughing.

There are other special presentations, including one by Jim McKenny. It is fitting in that it commemorates a media trip we'd made to the Goofy Games at Disney World. None of the Leafs is more qualified to participate in the Goofy Games than the man we all called Howie. More on him later.

Another former teammate had a special present for me. When I was a rookie, Gary Sabourin was a stalwart with St. Louis Blues, a hardnosed up-and-down winger who was respected throughout the league. He finished his career with Toronto in 1974-75 and I always enjoyed his company, especially his imaginative and enthusiastic contributions to dressing room humor.

During a game in my rookie year, I tried to line him up against the boards and lost my balance. He knocked me on my seat. I was lying down there, looking up, when he skated over, a stern look on his face, and counselled, "Ya better eat another sack of potatoes if you wanna try that, kid!"

His gift to me at my fortieth birthday party was a sack of potatoes.

What a memory, to be able to remember an obscure little incident that took place in a nameless, numberless game two decades ago! I'm getting misty-eyed.

Sabby senses my unstated question, and breaks into a broad grin: "Heck, Sitt, I told that to *all* the rookies!" Sheesh, he probably cruises the countryside looking for the fortieth birthday parties of all former NHLers, dispensing spuds all the way. Maybe he moonlights as a secret agent for the PEI Potato Marketing Board.

I am reminded of a typical story about Sabourin. I've always enjoyed fishing and Sabby is a self-confessed Master of the Rod and Reel. Early in my career, he had a place in a little northern Ontario town called Britt, right on Georgian Bay, north of Parry Sound, old stamping grounds of the greatest hockey player who ever lived. I had heard more than once that Britt, the nearby Magnetawan River and Georgian Bay were fishermen's paradises for the serious angler, no amateurs need apply. Whenever Sabby could get away, he'd go pickerel fishing in the spring.

He had invited Wendy and me up there and we arrived after ten on a Friday night, after a four-hour drive from Toronto. It appeared that Sabby might have had a beer or two in anticipation of our arrival. The salutations dispensed with, Wendy and I were getting our bags stowed away when he came over to me: "Come on, let's go. We're goin' fishin'!"

"Geez, Sab, it's almost eleven o'clock at night. Ain't Georgian Bay closed at this hour?"

"No problem, I know where I'm goin'. We'll go out, troll a little tonight, put the tent up and first thing in the mornin', we'll be right there. We'll step right out of the tent and commence to fishin'."

This was his home turf, so he could make the rules. Into the boat we climbed, and off we went, me holding onto this big flashlight for dear life because it was pitch black, cold and windy.

You don't know how black night can get until you are way up north. There's no reflected glow of a nearby big city somewhere on the horizon. Up is black, down is black, sideways is black. Unless there's a full moon. There wasn't.

We were tooling along the Magnetawan River in this cedarstrip boat with its 25 h.p. motor and the next thing you know, Sabby had navigated us off the main channel, and we were snaking in and out of a group of islands.

Thunk! We lurched to a sudden halt. Sabby had run the boat up against something. I shone the flashlight down and discovered a very big rock. Damage inspection showed that we were luckier than we were smart, no hole. I got out, pushed us off and jumped back into the boat.

"Sab, that's a lesson, slow it down."

"Awright." He sounded a bit miffed.

He slowed right down and we began to troll. When you troll for pickerel, you've got to cut the engine down to a very low idle. This caused Sabby to have problems with the motor, as it kept stalling on him. He pulled the cord, nothing happened. Pulled it again. Same result. Finally it sputtered to life.

Sabby always had a quick temper. He was cursing and swearing and I was doing my level best to help, sitting up front and giving him the gears about the big fisherman from northern Ontario who couldn't show a city boy from Toronto anything. The motor stalled again. He tugged on the cord and nothing happened.

That did it.

"Blankety-blank cheap outboard!" Sabby gave it a little more gas and went to start it again. Unbeknownst to him, it was still in gear. He yanked, the engine caught, the boat surged forward, and Sabby, obeying the laws of momentum (the boat's) and inertia (his), toppled backwards right out of the boat. Splash.

Did I remember to describe how dark it really was? I hustled to the back of the boat as it skimmed across the river, grabbed the outboard, and started circling, trolling for Sabourin, the flashlight playing out across the water and on other weird shapes in front of the boat. He was out there somewhere all right, but in that pitch black and all, I could be getting closer to him, or farther away. I was fully conscious of the fact that the next thump I heard might be the boat hitting a rock, or Sabby's head. Right about then there wasn't much difference between the two.

Finally I found him, shut off the motor, and had to grab him by the seat of the pants with both hands to pull him into the boat, as we drifted gently down the Magnetawan. He'll never live that down.

Our wives thought we'd gone for the night so they had retired long before we showed up at about two in the morning, Sabby soaking wet but feeling no pain. We never did pitch the tent, come to think of it.

Back at my surprise party, we view several of the tapes. Tiger and Garry's tape has everybody in stitches. Garry Monahan had played in Japan for three years at the end of his career. A Japanese friend of Tiger's back in Vancouver, who's a lawyer, came on and introduced himself: "Hi. I'm Garry Monahan, remember me?" and he goes on to say that he played in Japan for a while, and isn't it great to be back home in Canada. Then he starts interviewing Tiger. There was a distinct possibility that the guys enjoyed a few cocktails while they were filming their masterpiece. Monahan came in at the end of the thing, playing the Purolator Courier who had to get this tape off to Wendy Sittler in Orillia, Ontario.

We finally wound down the festivities in the wee hours.

In retrospect, what strikes me every time I look at the videotape of the day's events, is the real cross-section of people who have become part of my life, including many who never knew me during my hockey days.

You know how it is with friends? You might not have been able to get together in the same place for three or four years, or even longer, and yet when you finally do get together, the time gaps become unimportant. You might all look a little older, your kids have shot up like weeds, but it's like you've never really been away. That doesn't happen with a lot of people, but it does with those you're close to. It's nice when you have that relationship with people. It's something you don't give a lot of thought to until it's there; you're all in a room together and it feels right.

What stays in my mind about the party was that I really felt good for Wendy. She probably had been very apprehensive about the party, about whether she could pull everything off, and it went so great, right through the day. I felt terrific about that aspect of it. People could sense the strength of our relationship, and the happiness in our lives.

I have been out of hockey for more than six seasons now. In my travels across Canada and the United States in the last half-decade, I've often been asked if there's life after hockey.

"Yes," I reply, "especially if there was a lot of life before hockey."

This book will go a long way to explaining that answer, and how I got here from there.

2

Halls of Glory

HERE'S A QUICK trivia question for you: Name the only hockey player in the history of the National Hockey League to be inducted into the Hall of Fame along with his agent.

A hint? His initials are D.S.

On October 3, 1989, R. Alan Eagleson and I were enshrined in the National Hockey League Hall of Fame in a special ceremony at the Toronto Convention Centre. Joining us that night were Father David Bauer, the original founder of the Team Canada program, former Red Wings great Herbie Lewis, and Vladislav Tretiak, the fabulous Soviet goaltender, as well as journalists Claude Larochelle and Frank Orr, and the late broadcaster Dan Kelly.

The Eagle made it in the Builders' category, and I, of course, was selected in the Players' category. I know for a fact that this was the first and only time a player and his agent have entered the pantheon of prestige together for the good reason that R. Alan was the first agent ever selected.

If Punch Imlach only knew, eh?

"I couldn't be more happy than to share an induction ceremony with my friend Darryl Sittler," Alan said during his acceptance address. "The Players' Association started in '67 but it originated in '66. Bobby Orr, that summer, put his faith in me and wanted to turn professional."

He paused. "And after that was accomplished, Carl Brewer put his faith in me and wanted to turn amateur." That got a rise from the audience, and Alan continued.

"Having accomplished those two goals, the Springfield Indians went on strike and put their faith in me and we worked on Eddie

Shore's retirement." In this throwaway line, he understated his case about leading the revolt against Shore, who ran his hockey teams like a concentration camp. Don Cherry may dine out on a lot of Eddie Shore stories these days, but in the 1960s Shore hurt as many hockey careers as he helped. Guys like Bill White spent a lot more time in the American Hockey League than they needed to, and were only rescued by the 1967 expansion. Shore had a way of keeping his best players, whether the National Hockey League wanted them or not; he even had NHL executives running scared. Shore was considered an untouchable until the Eagle came along. The real veterans in the audience knew what Alan Eagleson meant about "Eddie Shore's retirement."

The laughter had died down, and Eagleson turned solemn in reference to the very emotional year he had just come through. A competing player agent, Rich Winter, and Ed Garvey, former executive director of the National Football League Players' Association, had spearheaded a movement to oust Eagleson from the NHLPA. It was their contention that he had too much on his plate and that Alan was in conflict as an agent, head of the NHLPA and chief international hockey organizer and negotiator for Hockey Canada. They wanted him to step down voluntarily. If he wasn't going to do that, the association itself should reject him, they said, as they forced a vote on the issue.

At the invitation of New York Islanders' Bryan Trottier, president of the NHLPA and an Eagleson supporter, I had attended the session in Florida where Alan won his case with the support of veterans like Bobby Smith of the Canadiens, Mike Gartner of Washington, Mike Liut of Hartford, Lanny McDonald, Doug Wilson of Chicago and a number of other representatives. It was not unusual for a former NHLPA executive to attend as a senior observer and contribute to such meetings; Tony Esposito had done so for years and withdrew only after he joined management ranks as general-manager of the Pittsburgh Penguins. I did my best to remind the representatives not only of what Alan had done in the past, but also of the kinds of things he was in a position to do in the future because of the high esteem in which he was held by management and the league owners.

The Eagle mentioned that personal trial in passing, that evening. "In the twenty-eight years in which I've been involved with players, this is indeed a highlight. Somebody asked me earlier today if I ever dreamed of such nice things happening on an event such as this. I said, 'Well, over the last six months, I wondered if hockey had become a nightmare rather than a dream.' It all worked out well, thanks to the support of the players."

There was an emotional lead-in to my own induction, as well. Shortly before I was informed that I had been accepted into the Hall in June, Wendy's mother, Eve Bibbings, took a vacation to her native country, England. A dreadful telephone call came on a Sunday morning: Eve had suffered a debilitating stroke and it was not certain if she would survive. We needed airline tickets and passports immediately. Alan took care of the passports and his friend Aggie Kukulewicz of Air Canada, the man who has acted as Hockey Canada's Russian interpreter for two decades, handled the tickets. Wendy's sister Diane Sawchuk flew out on the first flight on Monday, and Wendy and I followed with her father two days later.

Nothing could have prepared us for the shock of our first impression. This woman normally was a human dynamo, a true ball of fire, always on the go, always demanding that people in her circle of friends and acquaintants sit up and take notice of her. The person lying in bed, drifting in and out of consciousness as we all expressed our concern, bore little resemblance to my lively second mother.

Deep down, however, this still was the Eve we all knew and loved. "Tell Eagie that I'll be there in my tux," she said.

Eve Bibbings was true to her word; wheelchair-bound, she was part of a huge Sittler family contingent at the Toronto Convention Centre that night. We put her up in a room at the adjoining L'Hotel, which would provide easy access to the ceremonies for her. It was her first time out in public since the stroke, and we were all very proud of her.

I don't think my eyes were dry all night as I took in the proceedings and the anticipation of my own induction grew. Earlier in the day, however, I received the usual stone-cold dose of reality, compliments of my NHL alma mater and its dean of admissions. The sorry state of affairs with the Toronto Maple Leafs hockey club and its past heroes may be best summed up in a little "numbers" game. When I was selected to the Hall, I became Toronto's second No. 27 to receive such a high honor, following the incomparable Frank Mahovlich in that role. And yet our shared number by no means represents the most storied sweater number in Maple Leafs–Hall of Fame history.

In truth, I should never have worn 27; the Leafs should have found a way to recognize Frank Mahovlich's greatness and contribution to the team over the years, even if he was traded first to Detroit, and later to Montreal. The point I make here has to do with an absence of tradition in Toronto, not a negotiation for a sweater ceremony on my part.

NHL teams have retired more than forty sweaters, withdrawing those numbers from active use in honor of the great players who have worn them. Boston Bruins and Montreal Canadiens lead the NHL with seven numbers retired each. And two NHL players, Bobby Hull and Gordie Howe, have had their number 9 retired by more than one team—Chicago and Winnipeg for Hull, Detroit and Hartford for Howe.

How many teams have had more than one player who wore the same sweater number named to the Hall of Fame? None as often as Toronto, because for some reason that has escaped the most ardent followers of the team, team management has steadfastly refused to honor their stars with sweater retirements or recognize them with any other such ceremonies. No. 9 offers the best case in point in that five Hall of Fame inductees have worn it at one time or another in their career—Andy Bathgate, Charlie Conacher, Busher Jackson, Teeder Kennedy, and Norm Ullman. Some of these players, among them Conacher (6), Jackson (11) and Kennedy (10), also wore other numbers in Toronto.

Other shared numbers among Toronto Hall of Fame members include No. 10 (Syl Apps, Teeder Kennedy, George Armstrong and Joe Primeau), No. 7 (Frank Nighbor, Joe Primeau, Tim Horton, King Clancy and Max Bentley), No. 4 (Red Kelly and Hap Day), and No. 12 (Ace Bailey, Gord Drillon and Babe Pratt).

Even the famed No. 6, retired after Ace Bailey's famous career-ending accident in 1933-34, was worn by two other players in Toronto in later years: Charlie Conacher and Ron Ellis. Only Bill Barilko's No. 5 was never worn after it was retired, following his death in a plane crash.

Why retire a sweater? Why honor those players who honored their team and their organization with their talents, perseverance and efforts throughout a career? And, indeed, why in the world should the Toronto Maple Leafs bother recognizing those players and coaches who have been selected to the Hall of Fame? After all, it can be argued that they have received the ultimate recognition and that such an effort by the team itself might be redundant.

The answer is simple. Teams like the Montreal Canadiens have learned that you don't honor the players by retiring their sweaters or placing special displays in prominent areas of the arena; you honor the generations of fans who attended the exploits of these players, and who shared in their careers with their support. You honor the *shared* commitment of player and fan, in other words. The Toronto Maple Leafs would be honoring not only themselves with these kinds of ceremonies, not just players who were decades removed from the height of the action, but the city and the tens of thousands of fans who have supported them over the years. This isn't just Darryl Sittler talking; I've heard this opinion expressed by former players, fans and the media, over and over again.

Class will always show. I played eleven-and-a-half seasons in Toronto, two-and-a-half in Philadelphia and one in Detroit. Detroit is an organization in much the same state as Toronto—inured to constant losing, and saved only occasionally by the presence of other equally lame teams in the somnolent Norris division.

However, the Philadelphia Flyers, like the Canadiens, the Flames, the Oilers and the Bruins, was a winner because the team had learned how to treat players on and off the ice. Owner Ed Snider and the Flyers sent a personal telegram, champagne, and flowers addressed to Wendy to our hotel room. From Toronto? Nothing. Neither a card, nor a telephone call, nor even the tiniest acknowledgment that one of theirs had reached a pinnacle of recognition.

That is why I was so glad that Alan and I entered the Hall on the same night, and that my best friend Lanny McDonald was my official presenter. The hockey people who really mattered were there, including the best coach I'd ever had, Roger Neilson.

It wasn't as if the Leafs were unaware of my induction that night. After all, it did take place in Toronto, a short subway ride from Maple Leaf Gardens. And, though a lot of people don't know this, I had seen Harold Ballard that same day. That morning, I had taken my son Ryan down to the Gardens to watch the Leafs practice as the team was a couple of days away from its season opener. Apart from Guy Kinnear, the trainer, no one remained from my Leaf days, although I exchanged greetings with Brad Marsh, a former teammate with Philadelphia, and a fellow ex-London Knight. He skated over and shook my hand, and another Knight alumnus, Rob Ramage, just acquired from the Stanley Cup champion Calgary Flames, also came by to say hello. Shortly afterwards, I looked up into the stands, near center ice between the reds and the greens, and noticed a familiar sight.

"Come on Ryan, let's go renew acquaintances."

There, near his usual spot, was Harold Ballard. For years he had held court in this section during practices, primarily because it was just around the corner from his office and apartment on the second floor. I wrote "near his usual spot" because something was different; Ballard was in a wheelchair, a shrunken version of the bombastic man who had terrorized two decades of Leaf players and management. He wore his usual jacket and tie and, a rarity, a hat, but the shirt collar looked to big for a man who had always filled his clothes to bursting. Another change: the hangers-on were noticeable in their absence, none of his regular courtiers was to be seen. There was also no hint of the ubiquitous Yolanda, whom I had read and heard so much about in the media.

Harold now was permanently on the defensive, assailed at every turn. The bible of the sport, *The Hockey News*, had me on the cover of its current issue, with the headline: "Hall of Fame: Darryl Sittler welcome there, but not at the scene of his finest moments." Inside, the story was more an indictment of Harold Ballard than a recap of my career. It seemed I was the living symbol of Ballard's incompetence; but even this could not disturb me or detract from the positive aspects of my selection to the Hall.

"Reflecting on his remarkable career—a storybook odyssey through 15 winters, played out in three quite separate acts—the ultimate irony was not lost on Darryl Sittler," the article read.

"Sittler conceded that he is recognized most for his contributions to a team that will no longer acknowledge him, and that his strongest allegiance remains with the same team, despite its indifference to him.

"It is an incongruity he can only in part understand, but has accepted. And it also somehow neatly captures the essence of his career, the unholy marriage of talents and tempests . . . 'Most fans still recognize me for being a Toronto Maple Leaf. I'm the same way. The best things that happened to me in my career happened while in Toronto.'"

The subject of all of this media venom was talking to a couple of out-of-town radio sports-show hosts as Ryan and I approached. Harold looked away from them and up at me, with a stern look that might have been tinged with pain because he didn't like to depend on anybody or any device to get around.

"Make sure you behave yourself when you're up in front of the microphone tonight." The old sarcasm was replaced by an almost plaintive whine.

"No problem. Are you going to be there?"

"Naw, the health's not too good."

Harold was living Leaf tradition to the end; many thought he couldn't or wouldn't acknowledge my selection to the Hall of Fame as a Leafs success story, something which might shine a positive light on the organization, even for the briefest of moments. He had been inducted into the Builders' section—what irony—in 1977, and followed seven years later by Punch Imlach. Others had acknowledged his induction into that select group, but he couldn't bring himself to acknowledge my acceptance, or the fact that I belonged. He probably worried that I might use this occasion to rail against him for the pain suffered prior to my departure from Toronto. Having led the kind of life he had, and done the things he did, he could not understand that I might want to accept this great honor with dignity and class, and not use it as a pulpit for a strident attack on him.

To this day, there has never been any formal acknowledgment of my induction by anybody in the Leafs organization. A few days after induction night, I participated in a season-opening pre-game ceremony at the Spectrum, and was greeted with a standing ovation by Philadelphia fans who had only known me for parts of three seasons.

In the years after my retirement and prior to the Hall of Fame induction, I had often wondered if my career and contributions had been a mirage. It seemed that my career had just petered out and nobody had noticed.

This lack of follow-up has been a recurring theme in my post-hockey life and most journalists preparing stories and reports about my life and career tend to focus on this situation. Like all of the Leafs of the second Imlach era, I was long on player-management strife and very short on victory celebrations. Most of the players I had shared All-Star and Team Canada experiences with knew what it was like to circle the ice at some NHL rink with the Stanley Cup proudly held high. They also knew what it was to receive post-career recognition from their former team. Unfortunately, I was a stranger to all that, and rather than retiring with recognition and dignity, I quietly slipped out of the NHL after a less than memorable experience with Detroit.

Recognition came from outside hockey first. My retirement was into its quiet third year, so you could imagine my delight when I learned that I was to receive the Vanier Award in early 1988 as one of "Five Outstanding Young Canadians for 1987." The letter that was delivered by messenger to my home was dated January 20, 1988, and informed me that I would be joined by four other recipients of note: Garth Drabinsky, Claudette MacKay-Lassonde, Premier Frank McKenna of New Brunswick, and Shaun McCormick.

"The Vanier Awards program is named in honour of the late Governor General Georges P. Vanier and was established in 1967 by the Canadian Junior Chamber/Jaycees to recognize the lifetime achievements of five outstanding young Canadians between the ages of 18 and 40," the letter read. I was being recognized for the many years of charity work I had carried out during my career as a professional hockey player, work which had immeasurably enriched my life.

Garth Drabinsky and Frank McKenna were both celebrities in their own right, the former as the young boy who had overcome polio to become a founding partner and the guiding force behind the Cineplex Odeon Corporation; the latter as the recently elected Premier of New Brunswick whose Liberal party had swept to victory the previous October, winning all fifty-eight seats in the provincial legislature.

Shaun McCormick and Claudette MacKay-Lassonde might have been less well known than the three of us, but their accomplishments spoke volumes. In retrospect, and considering the incredible and tragic happenings of December 1989, Mrs. MacKay-Lassonde's feat of pursuing engineering studies at the University of Montreal's Ecole Polytechnique and finishing at the top of her class in her first year, was an accomplishment that took second place to none. She founded and was elected as President of the Women in Science and Engineering Association (WISE) in 1977, and seven years later was acclaimed as President Elect of the Association of Professional Engineers of Ontario (APEO).

Shaun Patrick McCormick was left a paraplegic by an accident in 1969 at the age of twenty-one. Instead of letting the accident and life in a wheelchair embitter and confine him, he chose to sail full speed ahead into life, resuming his studies at St. Francis Xavier University in 1974, later becoming instrumental in the formation of the Disabled Individuals Alliance (DIAL) in Halifax. He went on to serve as Vice-Chairman of the National Coalition of Provincial Organizations of the Handicapped, and as a Nova Scotia representative to Disabled Persons International.

To include the names and short biographies of these persons in this book is as much of an honor for me now as it was to share a podium with them on March 4, 1988, in Toronto. Indeed, simply being in a position to get involved with various charities and charitable endeavors was a reward in itself for me.

A little more than three weeks after I received the Vanier Award, I was honored for my junior hockey career as a "Knight to Remember," in London. That special ceremony at the London Gardens on March 28, 1988, prior to a playoff game with the Sault Ste. Marie Greyhounds, was very special for me, but even more so for my children. Earlier that month, to celebrate the twenty-fifth anniversary of the Gardens, a special contest had been held to select the all-time London junior all-stars and MVP. I was selected MVP, beating out Dino Ciccarelli, and was picked to the all-time Knights team at center, with Dan Maloney and Ciccarelli as my wingers, Marsh and Ramage on defense and Pat Riggin in nets. The all-time second team had no slouches either, starting with Dan Bouchard in nets, Rick Green and Brad Schlegel on defense and Dave Simpson at center, flanked by Dave Lowry and Jim Sandlak on the wings.

Very few people outside London or the Ontario Hockey League know Bob Wilson, the owner of the London Knights and a man who has worked hard to make his franchise everything it can be on the ice, and in the community. Very conscious of what junior hockey means to London, Wilson decided to honor past Knights for their contributions. In doing so, of course, he honored the current class and gave them an appreciation of their accomplishments. Howard Darwin, now owner of the Ottawa 67s, was the owner in London when I played for the Knights. Actually, when I first joined the team we were called the Nationals and changed to the Knights in mid-season when Darwin bought the team.

Now, more than twenty years later, a forward named Wayne Smith had worn the No. 9 of the London Knights for the last time the previous evening. On this night, the sweater—framed and under glass—was presented to me at center ice by Wilson. From that point on, No. 9 was retired. It was only the second number retired by an OHL club; Dale Hawerchuk had his number 10 retired by the Cornwall Royals a few weeks earlier.

"Please welcome Darryl Sittler of the London Knights," said my good friend Pete James, the emcee for that evening and a sportscaster at CFPL since my day. Pete has been a fixture in London from time immemorial. Our whole family stood proudly at center ice, Wendy gently cradling the roses that had been presented to her earlier in the ceremony. My three children stood wide-eyed, not knowing quite what to make of all this. Although Ryan and Meaghan were conscious of the fact that I had been a popular player in Toronto and Philadelphia, they had been too young to really appreciate what it all meant. So it was a new experience for them to be with me out at center ice. Even Ashley was there, and the standing ovation went on for several minutes.

"We love you Darryl," one fan shouted out, and this profession of love was greeted with more applause.

Meaghan commented that she was very proud, and hadn't realized what I had meant to the people in London as a junior hockey player. My kids thought it was a real neat experience. It was also a revelation to them to see me with tears of pride in my eyes when I received my sweater during the ceremony. This showed a side of me that my kids had not previously experienced. Ryan didn't say much, he's the eldest child and he tends to keep things inside, but I had the impression that this was new to him also.

Because Ryan was older, he had taken part in our family-oriented events with the Toronto Maple Leafs and I have a lot of pictures of father and son in the blue No. 27 of the Maple Leafs on the ice at the Gardens. Ryan had also taken part alongside Wendy and myself in the on-ice ceremony at Maple Leaf Gardens when Harold Ballard honored my 10-point night in 1976. However, all of these things had taken place when he was four and five and were faint memories at best.

The tears were still fresh when I said a few words of appreciation: "This sure brings back a lot of warm memories," I began. "I feel so good that maybe I was able to leave my mark here. I always tried to lead a life that would be a positive influence on people. I was by no means perfect, but if that number 9 hanging there can help someone, then I feel good about it." And when I thought of all the great players that had worn London sweaters, my pride and sense of achievement was even greater. Last, but not least, I was very glad to see that the London franchise was still going strong when many of its counterparts had declined or disappeared since my playing days.

A little more than five months before the Hall of Fame induction, I got to "share" in my only Stanley Cup victory. I was in Orillia with Jack Valiquette, Tom Hussey, Don Stoutt and Bill Swinimer and we stopped in at a roadhouse on Thursday, May 25. The television set was tuned to the sixth game of the Stanley Cup final from the Montreal Forum, with the Calgary Flames leading the series 3-2.

My best friend, Lanny McDonald, had his heart broken two years before when the Montreal Canadiens had defeated the Flames at the Saddledome to win their umpteenth Cup. He was in tears in the dressing room that night, and many observers felt it was because he knew it was time to retire and that this had represented his last chance at the Cup. After a lot of soul-searching that summer, Lanny decided that he still had something to contribute to the Flames and came back for another try.

Now, two years later, the Flames were 60 minutes away from Lanny's dream.

The Flames led the series 3-2 going into that night's game and coach Terry Crisp, knowing that he had the seventh game back home as insurance, dressed Lanny for the Forum game because he realized that Lanny's presence would help keep the younger players calmed down and focused. Aware of all that background, I perked up when I noticed that Lanny was playing and paid more and more attention to the game as the third period wound down.

Then a very familiar sight for me—Lanny steaming down the right wing, taking the pass, dropping his shoulder and snapping one across ice by a very surprised Patrick Roy. Top shelf. It proved to be the winning goal in a 4-2 Calgary win that gave the Flames the Cup and Lanny his ring.

As the game wound down, I left my group and stood quietly by myself near the TV set, drinking in the pictures and sound of the game. I didn't want to be bothered by anybody, or asked any questions; I was caught up in the emotion of the whole thing. When the final siren went and the Montreal fans rose and showed their class with a standing ovation for the victorious Flames, I stood quietly by the television set at a roadhouse in Orillia with images dancing in my head of that September afternoon in 1976 when my goal had won the Canada Cup on the same rink. While Lanny celebrated his first Stanley Cup, I was running my own mental videotape—skating around with the Canadian flag proudly held aloft, the exchange of sweaters with the Czech players, the look on Bobby Orr's face, and the roar of the Forum crowd—all of these images flooding into my mind. I immersed myself in that winning experience for a short while, and in a way it helped me identify more closely with the feelings Lanny must have been living that very moment as he partied on the ice with his Calgary teammates.

Whatever Lanny was thinking at that moment, he probably knew that I was watching somewhere with a tear in my eye for both of us—for him, because he had finally won his Stanley Cup—and maybe even for myself, because I knew I never would.

If anybody had deserved that Stanley Cup moment because of the career he had had and what he had represented on and off the ice, it was Lanny McDonald. Leo Durocher was wrong; nice guys do sometimes finish first: honesty, perseverance and hard work do pay off. Later that fall I was able to express my gratitude personally to Lanny at his official retirement dinner and tribute in Calgary, even though that was tainted by a minor disappointment. Lanny's dinner was preceded the previous day by a special on-ice ceremony at the Saddledome that I was supposed to attend. I was in Saint John, New Brunswick, playing in an Oldtimers game and my flight was fogged in so I missed the ceremony. There was even the slightest twinge of envy that night as tribute after tribute was heaped on a man who richly deserved them. Wouldn't it be nice if all organizations would treat a player who had been loyal to the organization over a long career with the respect and honor that he had earned? I mused to myself.

Thoughts of Lanny were paramount on my Hall of Fame night. The experiences we had shared were serious, light, rich, funny, sad, heart-breaking and hilarious. They were even explosive ... or potentially so.

Late in the '70s, Lanny and I took part in a joint *Toronto Star*-Ikea promotion. It was simplicity itself; we were to appear at an Ikea outlet between seven and nine o'clock on a Friday night and sign autographs. The only hitch was that somebody eavesdropping on a conversation at the Hot Stove Lounge of all places, had apparently heard someone else say that Lanny and me were going to "get it". This was construed as a death threat.

The eavesdropper called the Peel Regional Police; the police called us, and played the tape of the phone call into their switchboard for us. All subsequent conversations that afternoon seemed to start, "It may be nothing, but ... "

"Do you still want to go? We'll understand if you decide to pull out," a store representative told us.

"We'll do it," I said. "We don't think there's anything to this."

About three hours before the autograph session, the store was evacuated and the bomb squad went in with the K-9 corps. They looked high and low, over and under. Nothing.

"Not to worry, guys. It's probably nothing," a policeman told us. I appreciated the use of the qualifier "probably"; it sure made me confident.

"We'll have plainclothesmen all over the place, and they'll escort you back to the police station afterwards, just to make sure nothing happens in transit."

Lanny and I reassured each other, and we weren't nervous at all as we began our first ever stakeout . . . er, Swedish autograph session. Half the time I was gazing over the people lined up for autographs I was wondering which ones were plainclothesmen, and which ones were potential axe murderers. But, nah, I wasn't worried. Neither was Lanny.

Things went smoothly for an hour or so when all of a sudden there was a hellish bang. Lanny jumped straight up, and I dove for shelter under the table.

It turned out to be a teenager who had dropped a massive three-ring binder full of autographs on the floor. The flat side made the resounding noise. After the dust settled and we began signing autographs again, I began to fear that a plainclothesman might shoot some twelve-year-old waving a dangerous Bic ballpoint under my nose.

There were no other incidents; we retrieved our car in the parking lot and prepared to follow a carload of police to the station. As I turned on the lights, I saw a car several rows back do the same thing. We backed out and turned right to follow the unmarked police car, and the mystery car mimicked my every move. There were two males in the car.

"Uh-oh," I thought. "Here it is."

I turned left, and the mystery car turned left. I turned right. Ditto. I gestured to our official escort and one of the policemen gave a signal to pull into a gas station at the next corner.

"Okay Lanny, hang on," I warned. I signalled for a left turn off Dixie Road, then swung *right* into the gas station. I think I saw that in a movie somewhere. It always fools the bad guys. Of course, the guy driving the mystery car stayed with me with ease, stopping right behind me at the gas island. Lanny and I piled out and ran for our lives.

Suddenly cops with drawn pistols were everywhere, in a scene right out of *Hunter*.

"Out of the car! Get out of the car! Hands on the roof and spread 'em!"

The two nineteen-year-old Maple Leaf fanatics who had planned to follow their heroes home just to see where they lived must have dined out on that story for a year.

Lanny and me; we'd been through the wars.

All of this emotional baggage was on my cart as Dick Irvin, himself a Hall of Fame inductee the previous year in the Broadcasters' category, finally spoke the words I had been anticipating for almost four months: "A tour through the Hall provides you with a unique opportunity to see the stick the Rocket used to score his 500th—the first man to get that plateau.

"Wayne Gretzky's first skates, as you saw, and the stick that our next inductee used the night he scored those ten points. Finally, Darryl Sittler and that famous stick will be reunited where they both belong, at the Hall of Fame." He called upon Lanny, as my official presenter, to say a few words.

As usual, Lanny did not disappoint.

"If you could equate life and friendships to the game of hockey, there are many similarities. There are players you need for scoring punch, to make that big play. There are those that stand out for their defensive skills. Some are a must-keep, only for their team spirit.

"There are even some," he added with a wry smile, "that you'd even like to trade away. And, if you're lucky, maybe one or two players would emerge as your team leaders, as the cornerstone of the franchise.

"The ones who can do it all. Those players are there for the tough games in life, and the games just for fun. They'll carry you through when you just can't seem to make it, and they're never too proud to lean on you, too.

"Those players are rare, just as those friends in life are rare." At this point, the TV camera panned to Wendy Sittler and Ardell McDonald sitting proudly together in the audience.

I am lucky enough to have one of those players in my team in life . . . and his name is Darryl Sittler. As we honor Darryl here tonight, we love to remember him as the proud captain of the Toronto Maple Leafs, leading his country to victory in the '76 Canada Cup, that unforgettable evening at the Gardens, scoring ten points in a game to mark the record books with his own bit of history.

But we also honor him as he leads his life. Darryl has always led by example. In the dressing room, he would show a quiet confidence, usually at the top of his lungs. He would lead us by example; he wouldn't tell you what had to be done, he'd go out and do it.

Off the ice, his work for charity was endless. He's the man the players looked up to for strength; he's the man people look up at with admiration. He's a strong family man, a dedicated husband and a man who cares about people. And truth be known, he's probably one of the best practical jokers in the game today. I should know.

Tonight we honor Darryl Sittler as a great hockey player who made history happen. I honor Darryl Sittler as a man I'm proud to call my best friend.

I almost tripped, rushing out onto the stage to give Lanny a big hug. The rest was a blur. Watching myself on videotape afterwards, I noticed I was so excited that words were running into and over each other. But it didn't matter; the feeling I had up there during my acceptance speech was great, and might only be matched by the one I'll have a couple years from now when I get the opportunity to watch Lanny take his rightful place in the Hall.

My childhood hero, Jean Béliveau, was there and at the end of the evening when all the members of the Hall of Fame in attendance went up on stage, it was a special feeling to know that I finally belonged to the same club as he. Earlier that day, during the rehearsal, he shook my hand and congratulated me. I had told him many years before at some NHL function, while I was still playing, that he had been my idol as a boy. I even got his autograph that night. Yup, a pro NHLer holding out a piece of paper for an autograph like any starstruck kid, and proud of it, too.

In 1990, when Gilbert Perreault and Bill Barber were inducted, I was back for the dinner as a "veteran" Hall of Famer. I hope to be back for more ceremonies in the future because I'm very proud of this achievement.

Today, I wear the Hall of Fame ring with a lot of pride and no less emotion.

3

A Career Beckons

RETURNING TO YOUR roots most often is the best barometer of how far you have come in your chosen career or profession. Because my roots were hockey, the return is by car. Two things I recall vividly growing up as a fledgling hockey player: my mom and dad driving me to games all over southwestern Ontario as I was growing up; and the day my mom drove me to London and left me standing in front of Turk Broda's office with the only suitcase I had ever owned clutched tightly for support. It was quite an emotional scene for her as the first of the Sittler brood flew the nest. I wasn't exactly brimming with confidence either.

On this late June weekend in 1990, I've returned to where it all started, St. Jacobs, Ontario, world headquarters of Home Hardware stores and, until about a decade ago, a sleepy little farm community just outside Kitchener.

Today, as the result of "quaintification", St. Jacobs is a weekend haven for yuppy antique collectors and sightseers. It seems that King Street would be naked without a half dozen or so buses disgorging tours that started in Toronto or Buffalo or some other big city. The attraction is Mennonite country and a lifestyle most Canadians can only dream about now. The Forge & Anvil Blacksmith's shop on King still does a lot of business from the horse-and-buggy trade of the Mennonite farmers who don't believe in electricity and the combustion engine. As practical as this shop is to the Mennonites, it is just as important as a tourist attraction for the busloads of people who visit the town every weekend from spring through to the fall.

Thirty years ago, my brother Ken and I would earn seventy-five cents an hour on Saturdays sweeping these same streets clean of horse manure. There were no city folk around who thought this was quaint or "so very real" as they snapped pictures of us. We would shovel up the manure, filling a big barrel mounted on a cart, and when it was full to overflowing we would dump the whole mess in the Conestoga River. Remember, this was the pre-ecological era.

All of us kids worked back then, and I was a champion potato picker at about ten years of age, all in an effort to help make ends meet in a family that would eventually number eight children: Linda (1947), Ken (1948), myself (1950), Gary (1952), Debora (1954), Tim (1958), Rod (1961), and Jeff (1965).

Jacob Sittler, my paternal grandfather, was born and raised in this area. His grandfather was a Mennonite but Jake, and his seven daughters and five sons, including my dad Ken, were all raised as Evangelical. Several generations of the Sittler family were confirmed, married and buried at St. James Lutheran Church. (I even sang in the choir there.) The change-over happened when Grandpa Jake lost both of his parents at a very young age and was raised from the age of seven by his maternal grandfather, Jacob Kercher. Mr. Kercher, a wonderfully generous man, stepped right in and helped raise Jake's two sisters and three brothers as well. You did those things back then in farm country; there was no question of splitting up the family or calling in social agencies.

Grandpa Jake is still as chipper as ever on this humid May day in 1990. He's outlived four of his sons (including my dad) and a daughter, and was married to my grandmother Lydia for forty-five years until a stroke carried her off. He then married Frances, the widow of Ed Hausenpflug, the town barber, more than twenty years ago. That, too, is often how it's done in farm country.

Now that he's pushing ninety Grandpa Jake doesn't move as fast as he used to, and he has to step lively if he wants to avoid the traffic jam that clogs up his front yard at 50 King Street. Last fall, he was part of a huge Sittler family contingent that came to Toronto to see one of his grandsons inducted into the National Hockey League Hall of Fame. A family portrait of that group is prominently displayed in his living room.

We walk slowly down King, and I marvel at the changes. The old Snider Flour Milling Co. is now the Mill Race Café and Country Mill. At 9 King Street there are the River Works and Children's Shops, and not far from where I went to school at St. Jacobs Public

School, the Jacobstettel Guest House Inc. on Isabella Street does great business as a top quality inn.

The signs come one on top of the other—The Meetingplace at 33 King is a center for tourist information and, ironically, the site of a multi-media presentation on Mennonites. You can visit the EBY Room, the Martin Room, and the Gift Shop. Inside, there is a print of a Mennonite farm in Russia, unframed and available at the Hunsberger Galleries for $200. You can also buy Garfield and Ziggy the Cat posters.

Growing up here was a godsend for a boy who wanted to become a professional hockey player. We were close enough to Toronto to have the televised hockey games and the influence of Ontario minor hockey on area teams. And we were far enough away from the big city to have outdoor rinks and natural outdoor ice on ponds and rivers of our very own. Not far from where we lived back then was a family of Mennonites, owners of Frey's Hatchery. Being Mennonites, they were not allowed to play organized hockey, so their dad built them their own rink—it had floodlights and everything—so Marvin, Aden and David could play. They were the envy of us all because their dad got them full equipment, a rarity in those days.

Every day after school we'd dump our books on the kitchen table, chugalug some milk, grab our skates and sticks and head off to the outdoor rink, munching on cookies or an apple to keep the hunger pangs away until supper. The shinny game lasted from December to March, or whenever the weather gave out. When it got dark, we'd flick on the floodlights and keep playing.

It was a daily ritual to play until everybody got called home to supper. After supper it was homework and bed, and few of us had trouble sleeping after that kind of physical activity. Sometimes, when it snowed, lightly enough so we didn't have to scrape it off, we'd substitute a ball for a puck and keep going. If the snow kept coming, however, the game would stop and the shovels and scrapers came out. We weren't what you could call the Zamboni generation, waiting for some rink attendant to resurface our playing area. (Under no circumstances were we the Zamboni generation; Resurface Corporation, maker of the Olympia ice resurfacing machines, had a plant in nearby Elmira from whence it supplied the lucrative southern Ontario arena market. *We* knew that Zambonis were American, not Canadian, and invented by a guy who lived near Los Angeles.)

Because St. Jacobs had no rink of its own, I played all of my minor hockey in Elmira, a few miles down the road. If you were one of the better players, you had all of the hockey you could handle. We didn't have double-letter elite teams back then, but we still managed to play a lot. For example, when I was twelve years old I played peewee house league, and on the peewee all-star team. And, since I was good enough to play bantam house league, I played there too, and made that all-star team as well. Some nights I'd play one game, go back to the dressing room and change shirts, and play in the next game right after with the older boys.

Two years later, my talents were spread across three divisions, bantam, midget and juvenile, and it wasn't unusual for me to play continuously from seven until ten. And my dad was there for all three hours, drinking arena coffee out of styrofoam cups and cheering me on. Some nights it was bedlam, as my younger brothers might be playing somewhere else and family resources were strained trying to get us to our appointed places.

My older brother Ken wasn't much for team sports, he was into scouting, but that was a time-consuming activity too. Scouts back then went all over the place on camping trips or doing social service things in the community. And big sister Linda had her own active social whirl that took some attending to; the Sittler kitchen looked like Grand Central Station on some evenings.

What really helped in my case, especially in the early years, was the attention of my uncle Tom Sittler, dad's kid brother. He was many years younger than dad, and was my second big brother. He had played junior and then senior hockey, and took me to games, or fishing in the summertime. He got me interested in the sport, and we were all heartbroken when he was killed in a car accident at age twenty-one. I was still very young when that tragedy struck, but I remember vowing to make it for Uncle Tom.

I progressed steadily up the ladder into midget, where I suffered my first setback at age fourteen. I tried out for a Junior C team as an under-age player, but lost out to a player who I thought wasn't as good as I was. This is probably the most common occurrence in hockey at any level each year. My dad and I were quite upset and I remember we talked it out for hours. We finally agreed that we would accept the decision and I would play twice as hard for the midget team and show them that they had made a poor decision. It worked, I had a great year and our midget team went all the way to the provincial finals. The Junior C team missed the playoffs.

The following year, I made Junior C easily and was one of the leading scorers in the league. Whether I knew it or not, I had stepped across an invisible threshold because that was the year I became a "prospect". My big scoring year was noticed by all of the Junior A teams and when the annual midget draft was conducted, I was selected third overall by the London Nationals. (They changed ownership and became the Knights during my first year with the team.) It was about this time that the dream of becoming a professional hockey player began to take real shape. I remember watching a Leafs game on TV with my dad one night when I was fourteen or fifteen, and he quietly turned to me and asked: "Do you think you'll ever play at Maple Leaf Gardens?" I felt tingles up and down my spine at the thought and wondered if he thought I was good enough to take a serious run at it.

During the summer after London drafted me, their coach, Turk Broda, came to my house and my mom remembered him eyeing me up and down like I was a prize racehorse. That clinched it, I was a real prospect and I was getting closer.

Turk took my parents and me out to dinner at the Breslau Hotel for ribs. That was big news in itself. Turk pointed at me halfway through the meal: "I'm going to make you into a hockey player," he said, as I sat shyly in awe of the former Maple Leaf goaltender. As it turned out, he was one-third right, lasting out my first season before he was relieved of his duties. Gene Taylor, our trainer, replaced him the following year, only to be replaced, in turn, by Bep Guidolin, another former NHLer. Such was life in the OHA.

I didn't much feel like a prize racehorse or a prospect after Labor Day, 1967, when my mother drove up to the front of London Gardens on a beautiful clear day, left me in front of Broda's office, suitcase in hand, said goodbye and drove away.

I was equal parts excitement and homesickness as I prepared to take the Big Step. I had no idea what the next twenty years of my life had in store for me. That's usually an issue for someone in their early twenties, and I was pondering it at just sixteen. All in all, it worked out quite well, right from my home away from home at 666 Elias Street with my landlady Gladys Saylor, to my relationship with Turk Broda.

I had a good season that first year. The following summer I got a job building swimming pools, right after school finished. Mixing cement and sand is really hard work—I did it to build my upper body. I was offered a job at the London Knights Hockey School for six weeks and that was my first opportunity to skate with a lot of pros. It was during that period of time that the realization really hit me that I had a chance to have a professional hockey career. I judged my own abilities by playing against these second- and third-year pros, and thought for the first time that the dream was closer to becoming reality.

The funny thing about dreams, though, is that they can turn into nightmares very quickly. In my second year I tore the ligaments in my knee and had major surgery at the end of the season. I was in a cast for six weeks and had to spend that whole summer in rehabilitation.

London was a great experience for me on all fronts. I spent three years boarding with Gladys Saylor, a widow who had been boarding players at her place for several years before my arrival. She always had two of us at a time—Glen Sherton was my roommate in my first year, John Gould my second and Kirk Sutherland my third—and spoiled us rotten with food, laundry and other services. Gladys adopted us as step-sons and made it easy for scared kids who were away from home for the first time. We kept in touch for many years after I left the Knights, exchanging letters. I lost contact with her when I was traded to Philadelphia and she also moved.

I went to school in London, taking Grade 12 at H. B. Beal Secondary School and then two years at Fanshawe College. I began with a business course in my first year, and then switched over to a construction technology course in my second year. As it turned out, my younger brother Tim took and graduated from the same construction technology course several years later at Conestoga College in Kitchener.

While I was at H.B. Beal, a friend of mine introduced me to Wendy Bibbings, an attractive blonde girl whose parents attended most of our hockey games. I like to tell friends that Wendy chased me until I caught her, but I want to live to a ripe, old age. We got engaged in the summer of 1970 and were married June 5, 1971, after my first season with the Maple Leafs.

My arrival with the Nationals could not have been better timed. Garry Unger, Walt McKechnie and Moe St. Jacques, the team's centers from the previous season, had all turned pro. London needed centermen and I got a chance to play. Turk gave me all the ice time I needed, as long as I produced.

Turk Broda was old school, as Taylor and Guidolin would prove to be after him. To him hockey was a simple game: check your man and he checks you; beat him one-on-one more often than he beat you, and you'd usually be on a winning team. Practices usually contained some shooting and skating drills followed by a scrimmage. Nobody had ever heard of "hockey systems" back then. The flashback picture I get of Turk has him chain-smoking Camels and downing a cocktail or two on the long train ride to Montreal to play the Junior Canadiens. Gene Taylor does not conjure up the same image.

When Bep Guidolin came along, little changed in the way we played, but he got a lot out of us because he was so colorful and full of energy. We had a good team that last season with the Knights and nine of us were drafted. Some of the top players along with myself included Dan Maloney, Gord Brooks, Dennis Giannini, Gary Geldart and Brian Chinnick, as well as Dan Bouchard in nets. There were other strong teams in the league, however.

Roger Neilson's Peterborough Petes had players like Ron Stackhouse, Rick MacLeish, Ron Plumb and Tony Featherstone, while the Toronto Marlies were led by Dale Tallon and resident thug Steve Durbano. Durbano was a major-league-caliber animal who got into trouble in every rink in the league. He won more fights than he lost, and had memorable battles with guys like Maloney and Bert Wilson, on our team, and Gary Connelly, André (Moose) Dupont and Allan Globensky in Montreal, to name a few. He and I once got into it. We locked arms and he couldn't get free; he got so frustrated by that turn of events that he spat right in my face.

Niagara Falls had a strong team too, and I remember such names as Phil Roberto, Don Lever, Don Tannahill, and Steve Atkinson. I also remember scoring five goals against the Flyers one night and receiving a ring from Ted Dilts Jewelers in London. St. Catharines had Marcel Dionne, Dennis O'Brien, Pierre Guité, Dick Redmond, Al McDonough and Jerry Korab; Kitchener listed Walt Tkaczuk, Bill Barber, Jack Egers and Don Luce; Oshawa had Ivan Boldirev, Bob (Hound Dog) Kelly, Bob Stewart and Terry O'Reilly, and the Junior Canadiens had an unbelievable Memorial Cup team that included Gilbert Perreault, Rick Martin, Réjean Houle, Marc Tardif, Bobby Guindon, Dupont, Norm Gratton, Bobby Lalonde, Serge Lajeunesse, Jocelyn Guevremont and Jean-Pierre Bordeleau.

The competition was first-rate and by my third year, I knew I had an excellent chance to make the NHL. Playing in the OHA was a wonderful experience for me.

Sometimes, when the best things happen to you and, as a result, you gain some notoriety, the people close to you can be hurt by it. My kid brother Tim suffered because his last name just happened to be Sittler.

Tim was a very talented player up to midget age and it was felt that he might follow me into the NHL if he got the right break and developed well. Unfortunately, he got the wrong break—he was chosen eighth in the midget draft by the Kingston Canadians. Tim wasn't first-round material; and to compound things, the Canadians were about as far away as one could get from Kitchener, and still be in the OHA, back then. Expectations were very high when he went to camp that year, but he didn't play well and there were suspicions that they kept him around to justify their high draft choice. In January, he was sent back home and played Junior B for Elmira. The following summer, Tim was traded to the Hamilton Fincups, who moved to St. Catharines before the season began. He didn't make the cut there, and began playing Junior B in Hamilton. Then the Windsor Spitfires wanted him, he made their team, but a deal couldn't be worked out with St. Catharines. He resumed workouts with St. Catharines, moved over to Peterborough and was odd man out when the Petes traded the rights to Paul Reinhart to Kitchener for five players. When they showed up, Tim was cut. He ended up playing Tier II with the Guelph Platers for two years, who won the Centennial Cup at the Canadian championship, both years.

I draw from both my experiences and Tim's now that the scouts from the OHL and NCAA schools are seriously interested in recruiting Ryan. A solid six-foot, two-inch 190-pound left wing/center of seventeen as I write this, Ryan was drafted in the second round of the AHL draft by the Detroit Ambassadors and has attracted the attention of all the major NCAA Division I schools. Wendy and I are both leaning toward the college route, recognizing the value of an education in the 1990s; but we want to expose him to both options and allow him to make the final decision.

Every time the telephone rings for Ryan, I remember watching my mom drive away from the London Gardens on that sunny September afternoon in 1967.

4

The Leaf Is Green

I GREW UP as the only Montreal Canadiens fan in a family of Toronto Maple Leafs followers. My hockey idol was the incomparable Jean Béliveau. So it only made sense that I'd be drafted by Toronto on June 11, 1970, at the Queen Elizabeth Hotel, having been passed up not once, but twice, by Montreal.

Unlike today's top fifty or sixty picks, very few of the better players eligible for selection attended the draft session that day; it hadn't yet become the agent-player talent auction it is now. Another reason was that this draft edition would be the Punch and Gilbert Show. The brand-new Buffalo Sabres and Vancouver Canucks were joining the league and the news before the NHL meetings that June centered on two things—whether Gilbert Perreault of the Montreal Junior Canadiens or Dale Tallon of the Toronto Marlies was the best player in the country, and which of the two new teams would win the "spin of the wheel" for first pick in the expansion draft on Wednesday and first pick in the amateur entry draft the day after. Punch Imlach must have worn his lucky suit that day: he won both spins, and Perreault would wear the blue-and-gold of the Sabres throughout his illustrious career.

After Perreault and Tallon went to Buffalo and Vancouver respectively, Boston had the next two picks and selected two players who would, after trades, beat the Bruins in the Stanley Cup final four short years later: Reg Leach and Rick MacLeish. Then Montreal was up for two and they opted for two westerners, goalie Ray Martiniuk from the Flin Flon Bombers and Chuck Lefley of the Canadian National Team. Another westerner, Greg Polis of the Estevan Bruins, was selected seventh by Pittsburgh.

Toronto Maple Leafs had the No. 8 pick and they selected me. I was hard at work building swimming pools in London; I'd been a Maple Leaf about five or six hours before I found out. I heard the news on the radio on the way home from my summer job that evening, and learned at the same time that teammates Dan Maloney (No. 14) and Danny Bouchard (No. 27) had been picked by Chicago and Boston respectively.

Perreault and Tallon got fussed over by their new teams, which were both desperate to build fan support and credibility, and by the media. All I got were a few congratulatory phone calls from family members and friends, happy that I'd finally seen the blue-and-white "light" and come over to the right side.

Today, some twenty-odd years after the fact, I can't remember anybody from the Leafs telephoning me or writing me that summer. They contacted my brand-new agent, R. Alan Eagleson of Toronto, and worked out my first contract. The two of us had met in Maple Leaf Gardens earlier that spring when the Knights were in for a game against Tallon and the Marlies. That had been my last visit to the Gardens, and I was not to return there until training camp began and I joined the more than forty players invited to camp.

No press conference, "meet the press" media tour, or new car to show off my status as the franchise's top pick and potential future star. No Leafs sweater-pulled-over-head photo opportunity at the Toronto draft table in Montreal.

The next day, I was back pouring concrete again, building swimming pools. I do remember thinking that being drafted by the Leafs was very convenient for the Sittler family because Kitchener was only sixty miles away and London, where Wendy would remain working for another year, was not too far away either.

In very real terms, I first began to feel like a true Maple Leaf early in training camp on the day I signed my first contract with the Toronto Maple Leafs Hockey Club. The deal had been ironed out between Alan Eagleson and Jim Gregory several weeks earlier, and I remember hustling out of Maple Leaf Gardens with the cheque for my $10,000 signing bonus burning a hole in my pocket. I got as far as the bank at the corner of Yonge and Carlton before I relieved myself of that burden.

A team's first draft choice enjoys equal parts of status and pressure in that first camp. And even though NHL teams of that era were more nonchalant with their newest potential stars, at least in terms of media hype, the player reaction was no different than it is today. If anybody was expected to make it cold onto the team as a rookie, it would be the Leafs' first draft choice, especially if he was a graduate of the OHA.

They weren't selecting eighteen-year-olds back then, there was no going back to your junior team for ripening. We were all twenty, and if we didn't make the Big Club, it was Hello Tulsa or Oklahoma City.

It was a beautiful, sunny, late-summer day when I walked into the Leafs dressing room for the first time. Trainer Joe Sgro took me over to my locker and there was a sweater with No. 27 hanging in it: this was the number assigned to me for training camp. That really threw me.

I was proud to be the Leafs' top draft pick that year; there was a sense of heightened excitement and exposure. While no one in the media or on the team had made any mention of my place in the scheme of things, there was subtle acknowledgment that I was the top rookie, you can feel that as a player. The number 27 confirmed that certain status. It was management's way of saying that there were high hopes for me in the organization. To tell the truth, I felt a bit embarrassed by it all. Back then, I was really shy and modest, I wouldn't say boo to anybody. My attitude was to keep my head down and work, work, work. The perfect rookie: seen and not heard.

I wouldn't be surprised to hear from veterans on that team that they thought I was a ghost or an apparition during my first week or two. I might not have said three whole words to anybody. One of the guys who sticks out most in my memories of the first camp is Jimmy Harrison. He went out of his way to make me feel comfortable and was the first veteran to invite me out with the guys for a beer after practice. I might have been a disappointment then, too, because I wasn't much of a beer drinker. One thing Harrison and I had in common was that he was an outdoors guy, he enjoyed hunting and fishing, and so did I. That helped us hit it off.

Beyond the first-day memories of the weigh-in, and Joe Sgro escorting me to my locker, the most vivid impression of my first training camp was my first turn on the ice. When I got out there, I couldn't believe how fast and strong these guys were. I felt out of my element, not in the same class as the veterans. I was a little apprehensive, especially up against guys like Jim Dorey whom I'd watched as a junior. He could be a bit of an orangutan at times; he'd take the shirt off and the shoulder pads and fight with anything and anybody—if the Zamboni had come too close he would probably have punched it in the snout. And now here I was going into the same corner with him, both of us after the same puck. He was the type of guy who'd smirk when he tested you. Job One was overcoming the fear. A lot of players don't like to admit it, but believe me, it's there.

Dorey must have liked me. When we did go into the same corner after the puck, we bumped vigorously and I didn't back down. However, the thought that maybe I'd have to fight this guy took up permanent residence in the back of my mind. "Maybe he's going to challenge me; I don't want it, but what am I going to do if he does?"

So what did I do? I took out another veteran defenseman. We were working a drill where the puck went into the corner, the forward went in first and the defenseman followed hard on his heels to check him and try to take the puck away. I was paired with Brian Glennie, a guy who would lay a bodycheck on you, but who was not a fighter; he didn't have that kind of temperament.

On this occasion, I got to the puck and Glennie took me out very hard. My reaction was to swing around with my arm. As I did, I caught him flush with my elbow, splattered his nose, and broke it. To make matters worse, Glennie had a bigger than average nose to begin with.

He was steaming, and I felt bad about it too as a lot of the veterans gathered round his prostrate form in sympathy. I hadn't done it to hurt him, it was a game-situation reaction, that's all. I had reacted spontaneously, but he was down with his broken nose and blood all over his face and shirt and here I was, the rookie, standing sheepishly wondering which of his friends would make me pay for it.

The next day, Glennie arrived with a monstrous cast on his nose. The veterans were merciless: "Blunt, what *is* that, a *garage*?" How many people have to wear a cast on their nose? They were giving him the gears and I was in the room praying that they'd just shut up. The less said, the better for me, I figured. Of course, they knew the rookie was squirming off in the background. I can't remember if I ever apologized but we did eventually kid about it later. Brian became one of my better friends. His nose healed (although some of our longstanding friends have their doubts on that score every time they are confronted by the famous Glennie proboscis).

I think the players realized that I hadn't done it maliciously. My personality helped. I'd quickly built the reputation of a pretty quiet guy who worked hard and kept his mouth shut. If I had been smart-assed and cocky, I might have brought something down on myself.

Other images I retain from that first camp include the quietness and gentleness of Ron Ellis; the intensity of Norm Ullman, and the speed and skills of Dave Keon. Davey was a very intense guy, very abrupt and sarcastic. Despite his acerbic personality, he was a tremendous hockey player, setting a record for short-handed goals in my rookie year. Dave Keon was all work ethic; he'd stay out after practice every day, work on that backhand, work on the forehand, shots high off the post, face-offs . . . anything. We soon became a familiar sight after practice because I also had the habit of staying out there until the Zamboni driver kicked me off the ice.

The thing that really impresses you most in your first professional camp is the huge difference in hockey between the previous April and that September. That previous spring I was a leader on my junior team, and now I was just one of a cast of thousands at a pro training camp. I couldn't believe the difference in speed and size between my junior teammates and opponents, and the pros. The inevitable reaction is to doubt yourself, of course, wondering whether you will ever overcome that obstacle, or even whether you could possibly improve to that level of competition. Everything I was trying to do on the ice was flat out, but I was always a half a step behind. And half a step is the difference between the airplanes and first-class hotels in the NHL, and bus rides and motor inns in the AHL.

It was a question of size and maturity. Larry Robinson once mentioned that he had felt the same thing in his first camp as a tall, skinny kid who weighed about 175. During the twenty years he terrorized forwards in the NHL, his best playing weight hovered between 210 and 215, or thirty-five to forty pounds more than he weighed at that first camp. It was the same with me; I weighed about 175 pounds in September 1970; my best playing weight for my career was around 195 pounds. That training camp I despaired a bit— "Geez, I'll never get that big and fast."

Another image still kept from that first camp is of Bill and Earl, the two physical education instructors from Royal Military College who ran our off-ice camp. We did circuit training, weights, running and calisthenics to military marching music. I had weight trained a little bit in the off-season, but never had done anything quite like this before. We went through this routine every day before practice. Another thing I remembered was running around Maple Leaf Gardens: getting up early and running up the steps to the top of the Gardens, and back down again. I can remember Keon always being one of the first guys to finish . . . he hated to lose, period.

I would always push myself to the limit. At the start, I might have been able to do only eight or ten repetitions while a guy like Dorey could do them all day. But over a period of time, I improved; I got stronger and quicker. It was a long process, not something that happened overnight. And there were enough mornings when I fell out of bed feeling sore all over and doubting my future as an NHL player.

That feeling was especially prevalent during my first regular season, especially since I didn't score my first goal until November 28— a long distance into the season. If I hadn't been the number one pick, I might have been down in the minors before too long. Back then it was quite common to serve an apprenticeship in the minors. Five spots ahead of me that draft year, Reggie Leach had been sent down already. I wanted to stay in Toronto, for my self-esteem. There was the monetary consideration too—my two-way contract; I would be making only $9,000 a year in the minors, and I'd make $15,000 with the Leafs.

I really couldn't gauge myself by comparisons with juniors in my graduating class who were now in the NHL alongside me. I was on the fourth line, so I didn't get a lot of ice time. Some of the junior stars like Perreault and Tallon played a lot on expansion teams, but I was in vastly different circumstances on a veteran team. My only real point of comparison had come even before I reported to the Leafs, in summer hockey back in London. I was on the ice daily with guys like Walt McKechnie, Dean Prentice, Darryl Edestrand and Bob Cook, all pros. I wasn't up to their standards that summer, but they'd made it to the NHL and I knew I wasn't far away.

During the regular season, I put in my time and apprenticeship after practice, or as first guy on the ice before the regular workout. This work ethic, I'm convinced, kept me out of the minor leagues. Jim Gregory or John McLellan noticed, they'd come by to pat me on the back and say, "You're working hard, kid, don't change your ways."

The veterans were impressed with my attitude, too. Normie Ullman will tell you, "I never saw a rookie work this hard."

The major problem was a talent glut at my normal position. The Leafs had Norm Ullman, Dave Keon, Mike Walton, George Armstrong and Jimmy Harrison in the middle though they moved Armstrong over to the left wing and I soon followed him. I had always been a centerman and leading scorer in junior but now I was learning a new position in a very tough league. Instead of going in over the blueline and taking a chance offensively, I was out looking for my winger. It was pretty much the same story in my sophomore year. I never really felt comfortable until they finally put me back at center, then things just took off.

My first professional coach was Johnny McLellan, a long-time hockey man who was a nice, easy-going guy who wouldn't hurt a fly. John wasn't a strict disciplinarian and we had our share of players who took advantage of that. But this was a team with a strong nucleus of veterans. He didn't have to do much policing.

When I joined the team, it turned out that I was the only single guy there. Later in the season, when Denis Duperé was called up, our complement of bachelors doubled. Another rookie I remember was Billy McMillan; he played with Dave Keon and Garry Monahan on a line and was quite a bit older than me. McMillan had played for Father David Bauer's Canadian national team alongside guys like Marshall Johnston and Terry O'Malley. Back then I was boarding with Wendy's aunt and uncle in Mississauga, and McMillan and his wife Marjorie lived right across the street so we commuted to the rink together.

As I have mentioned before, the Leafs were a veteran team. We had traded Tim Horton to the Rangers the previous spring, but then turned around and re-acquired Bobby Baun from Detroit that summer. Norm Ullman, Dave Keon and George Armstrong, like Baun, were holdovers from the championship teams of the 1960s, and younger guys like Mike Walton and Jimmy Harrison were solid. We also had some up-and-coming talent in Paul Henderson, Rick Ley, Brad Selwood and Bernie Parent. The whirling dervish, Brian Spencer, was up and down all year between the NHL and the AHL. He became fourth-line left winger for a while when I got hurt halfway through the season compliments of Captain Crunch, Gilles Marotte, the block of cement who masqueraded as a defenseman for the Los Angeles Kings.

When Marotte was out on the ice, the most prudent plan of attack was to stay away from his side. I forgot that rule of survival during a game at the Gardens. I saw him out of the corner of my eye and raised my arm to protect myself. Somebody crashed into me from behind and somehow my arm got caught between the two. The only "give" was inside my arm and the radius bone was devastated. They didn't have to operate, the doctor pushed it all in—got it all together. I was ten weeks in a cast, and had to wear a brace on it for two years after that.

It was the first time I wondered if my career might be over. "Give it to me straight, doc. If it's real bad, I want to know."

He wasn't sure. "I don't know how you're going to come back at all. That thing's shattered in ten pieces, it's going to take a long time."

One of my strengths had always been my shot; I'd scored a lot of goals because of my quick release. Now I couldn't shoot the puck. I remember trying to do a push-up and not being able to because I couldn't bend the arm. Twenty years later, I still don't have the normal flexibility. The fractured arm eventually became an obsession, I seemed to spend all of my waking hours in rehab, doing all sorts of wrist curls, squeezing balls, and anything else I could do to get that wrist strength back.

I returned for a couple of games in the playoffs, wearing a leather brace that was reinforced with a steel plate that wouldn't let my wrist go back farther than a couple of inches. I had been warned; if I was ever to get hit the same way again, I was done. The brace restricted the way I could shoot the puck, especially the motion for snapping off a wristshot. I wasn't right for another couple of seasons.

My first year was interesting on and off the ice. A lot of it had to do with the fact that—for a Kitchener boy who'd thought London, Ontario, was a metropolis—the size of Toronto was almost incomprehensible. Added to that was the excitement of playing in Los Angeles and all those new exotic cities, the plane travel and the first-class treatment.

Like many teams, the Leafs decided to take a mid-season break. Unlike most teams, we took it at a time when we were doing poorly, and we went to the Playboy Resort at Lake Geneva, Wisconsin. It was done on the quiet; neither the media nor anybody else knew where we were going. We were just going to get away from it all, not practice, take it easy at a quiet resort, shoot some skeet and unwind.

Remember, this was a "family team" and I was the only bachelor on the roster. A couple of the guys told their wives where we were and the excrement hit the aerofoil device. Several wives got together and got a petition going, took it to Alan Eagleson, got it drawn up all legal-like, and were going to sue the Toronto Maple Leafs and management for taking their husbands to a Playboy Club. The Toronto newspapers thought this made an interesting story, to say the least, and ran with it.

The real irony was that there was nothing much to the Playboy Resort—a few bunnies serving cocktails, but that was about it. Playboy Clubs, despite the overblown image, were pretty tame places. What was supposed to be a three-day jaunt lasted a day and a half. The pressure management got from the media and the wives caused an instant change in our itinerary.

Before we left Lake Geneva, we almost lost a trainer. The dining room overlooked a heated pool at the main resort building and a bunch of us who'd had a few drinks over lunch decided to go swimming. We were in the shallow end of the pool on our knees, water up to our chins. We called Guy Kinnear over: "C'mon in Gunner, the water's great!"

Guy wore eyeglasses with the proverbial Coke-bottle lenses. He returned to his room and was back a few minutes later with his swim trunks. He put down his glasses and prepared to dive in, thinking we were in the deep end. Were the guys going to tell him? Not a chance.

In he dove. While it lasted, it looked like a half-gainer.

Unfortunately, it lasted about seven feet shorter than Gunner had planned.

Clunk. He split his head open, and was lucky he didn't break his neck. They had to take him off to hospital for many, many stitches.

I suppose that's what sports psychologists mean by team bonding.

Another thing I remember from that first year was hearing story after story of the feats of strength of the late Tim Horton. Nowadays, I hardly start a day without a coffee and muffin from a Tim Horton's doughnut shop; I think it was all the subliminal advertising I underwent in my rookie year.

Horton had been traded to the Rangers the previous spring but that didn't prevent Keon, Baun, Armstrong and Ullman from telling endless stories about hotel doors knocked off their hinges, automobiles pushed for blocks, and the like. I took this all with a grain of salt, until we were in Madison Square Garden in the playoffs and a fight broke out on the ice. Jimmy Harrison and a couple of our guys were into it; I can't remember who was fighting for the Rangers. I happened to be standing near Tim Horton, gloves off, when I saw one of our guys in a bad position. My reaction was to go and help. Horton reached out and grabbed me, squeezing the bicep near my elbow. The kind of thing your father might do when you were about six or seven years old.

With about the same result: my arm went numb.

"You really don't want to go anywhere, kid," he said very gently. I excused myself, said sir half a dozen times, and wondered if I'd ever get the circulation back in my arm. Here was a forty-year-old guy holding off this feisty twenty-year-old rookie, with thumb-and-forefinger. Yes, but *what* a thumb-and-forefinger. If Tim Horton had an Austrian accent, he would have been Arnold Schwarzenegger.

During that same fight, Bernie Parent's mask came off and somehow ended up in the crowd. King Clancy ran around Madison Square Garden, rescued the mask and lived to tell about it.

"Who was that mask man?"

King was in his seventies at that time, so this was no mean feat in that loony bin. It was important, too, because goalies had only one mask back then.

One other thing I remember from my rookie season was my first game at the Forum in Montreal. I remember facing off against Jean Béliveau, looking up at him and the feeling that came over me. Here he was, right in front of me, the man who had been my hero. You hear so many athletes saying things like this and it can sound so corny. But I really understand when I hear another athlete say something like that because I've experienced the feeling myself.

Don Cherry told me on the *Grapevine* program we did together in 1990 that whenever he asks a young player in the league, "Who was your hero growing up?" it's amazing how many times my name comes up. I've never looked at it that way but I guess at the end of your career, you reach a stage where a lot of the new guys coming in have been watching you since they were kids.

That first face-off against Jean Béliveau meant something special to me. In later years, when I was going through some difficult times in Toronto, he sent me a letter of encouragement on his personal stationery, and that really moved me.

One thing that happens to most rookies is that, after a year or so in the pros, they discover a large number of people with clay feet; big name people who turn out to be all too human. And, in some cases, the image that those people projected was synonymous with our team's image.

My first disappointment was Stafford Smythe. As a youngster growing up in Canada following the fortunes of the Leafs and Canadiens, the Smythe family name, because of its relationship with the Leafs, had a special place. Growing up in a small town, I had probably put some of these people too high on pedestals. I had heard a lot about Conn Smythe and his son Stafford. It was with a shock that I came to know Stafford as a perennial drunk; coming into the dressing room after a game, out in the stands after practice, on a road trip—whenever I saw him he was drunk. I was a young kid in the NHL and here was a Big Name Leaf executive with his shirttail out, his tie all askew, sprawled against the wall in the dressing room after a game. It was not something I could understand.

When I write this, I'm not being judgmental. I'm just trying to describe the situation at the time, and the many influences in and around the Maple Leafs, especially the kind that were way over the head of a rookie.

Stafford Smythe and Harold Ballard represented two-thirds of the Toronto executive triumvirate in the late 1960s, having taken over from Conn Smythe with third partner John Bassett. But the transition was far from smooth, and when Revenue Canada came calling in 1969, the smell they discovered when they went through the club's financial records made rotting fish seem pleasant. Stafford Smythe was running the show right about then, and made a lot of news when he fired Punch Imlach after the Bruins swept the Leafs in the playoffs a couple of months earlier. Shortly thereafter, he was in the news again when the twenty-one-member board of directors met and voted to ask Smythe and Ballard to resign over allegations of financial impropriety, and the third kingpin, John Bassett, cast the deciding vote, a decision seen as a betrayal by Smythe and Ballard. To the consternation of the board, they refused to resign, and further embarrassed the hockey establishment several months later when they were charged with tax evasion and fraud.

That's probably why I never saw Stafford Smythe sober. Two months after Ballard and Smythe were charged, Stafford and Harold raised six million dollars and bought out Bassett. Stafford never made it to trial; a month after the Bassett deal, he died after his second operation for a hemorrhaging esophagus and stomach. He died October 5, 1971, the day of the first game of my second season with Toronto.

How did all this affect me? In my early years with Toronto, not much of this really sank in because, as a player, my focus was on playing hockey. Harold Ballard, Stafford Smythe and John Bassett were all part of the big business side of hockey and I really hadn't been exposed to that yet. I was naive. Even when Harold was sentenced to prison, it seemed to be part of a different reality. That isn't to say that the court trials and the unsavory publicity didn't reflect on the team.

Some of the players were totally mystified. How could guys who were so powerful, had so much influence and so much money, get involved in something like this? Then we turned that question around: Did they get involved *because* they had so much money and so much influence? The consensus was that it was probably a combination of both. My feeling was simply that the guys were crooks, got caught, and deservedly so. That might be very simplistic, but that's what I felt.

Now that I can look back with a little more maturity and distance, the kind of question that arises is, "What kind of role models were these guys for the rest of us?" Back then, that wasn't an issue, especially for a second-year player. Later on, when I graduated to team captain and had responsibilities that included being a role model myself, I began to realize how these negative perceptions had wormed their way into the woodwork at the Gardens. One incident with Conn Smythe brought this clearly to my attention.

I had a totally different feeling about Mr. Smythe than I had about Harold Ballard and Stafford Smythe. In my first year as captain of the Leafs I was speaking at a dinner and told the old mushroom joke about being locked in a dark, moist room and every now and then management would come in and throw shit all over you. I was using the joke as an analogy to describe the kind of turmoil that the Leafs were experiencing back then.

A few days later I received a handwritten letter from Connie Smythe. It said something like: "As Captain of the Maple Leafs, you shouldn't swear in public. In reference to the word 'shit', I would suggest that from now on you use the word 'manure'." It was polite and very correct in an old-fashioned way, and very reminiscent of the lessons my parents had tried to enforce as I was growing up. I never forgot it; after that, I never did swear or curse in my public-speaking engagements.

That kind of attention to detail and overwhelming care for the image of the team was something that had characterized the Maple

Leafs back in Conn's day. We were living in different times, however. Image was counted in numbers of rear ends in the seats and concession sales between periods.

The Toronto Maple Leafs of his day were long gone when Conn Smythe died on November 18, 1980. His passing came at a time when the Leafs were in constant turmoil and upheaval, not his legacy at all. I was a pallbearer at his funeral—the pallbearers were all captains or ex-captains of the Leafs. That day stands out in my mind. It was a real honor for me to be part of that funeral with George Armstrong, Syl Apps, Bob Pulford and guys like that. What stands out from all this was that we buried the Maple Leafs tradition with Mr. Smythe that day, though we didn't know it then.

I was given a personal reminder of that in a thank-you card from Hugh Smythe, Conn's son and Stafford's younger brother. He wrote:

> My father was often accused of being a poor loser. He denied this—as he has lost more times than almost any man. It was never easy, and he tried to make sure we all learned something about how to give a little more and do it better next time. He has lost again, and his loss like his wins, rubs off on all of us. Thank you for joining us—the team captain always had a greater share of the burden, and occasionally a special share of the wins.
>
> Hugh Smythe

Maybe I should donate that thank-you note to the Maple Leafs. Words like those belong on a plaque on prominent display down at the Gardens.

Harold Ballard was a very different kettle of fish from Conn Smythe.

In the early summer of 1973, Alan Eagleson and Jim Gregory negotiated a contract that would keep me in the NHL and out of the WHA. Throughout the negotiations, King Clancy and Gregory would have to go down to the federal penitentiary at Millhaven to discuss my deal with Harold. Ballard had taken up residence there the previous October, sentenced to "three years for fraud, and three years for theft ... both terms to be served concurrently," as the judge had said. There was word Harold would be up for parole in October 1973, or after serving one-third of the sentence.

We finally reached agreement and a press conference was scheduled at Maple Leaf Gardens on Monday, July 2, because Harold had managed to finagle a weekend pass. It was the first time I'd seen him since he'd gone to jail. Alan and I walked into his office, and if we thought we'd be greeted by a downtrodden guy with the pasty white complexion of a con, we couldn't have been more wrong. Tanned like a beach boy and wearing a bright yellow-and-black checked shirt to show off the glow, Harold was the very picture of health and happiness. And heavier than I'd ever seen him. He was very gregarious.

"C'mon in," he bellowed. "C'mon in, c'mon in!"

Like we hadn't heard him the first time.

It took a couple of seconds to sign the deal—we'd sign another copy for the photographers and cameramen later—and the three of us spent the rest of the time going through Harold's Happy Days at Millhaven Photo Album.

"This is the life, kid." He tossed a bunch of snapshots on the desk. There was Harold, clowning around in a guard's uniform, sitting with his feet up on a desk, bottle of beer in his hand and cigar in his mouth. You could see a color TV over his shoulder in the picture. Eagleson and I couldn't do much more than laugh right along with him.

"It's all steak dinners and beer, kid. Loved every minute of it, shouldda done this earlier!"

Unfortunately for the people at Correctional Service Canada, he maintained the same theme a half hour later during the press conference to announce my signing. He couldn't help himself—the reporters hadn't talked with or seen him in a while—so they gathered around with the mikes and the cameras and the notebooks and Harold started talking about steak dinners in jail—"the good life"—and that got him into a little hot water. No pun intended, but that press conference was probably Harold's "coming out." This was the precursor to the Harold Ballard the Toronto media would grow to love and hate when he came back full time a couple of months later.

I don't remember many incidents with Harold from my first three or four years with the Leafs, for reasons I've already explained. At the beginning, the players didn't see Harold around much because Jim Gregory did most of the team management, the day-to-day operations. The players, much like the fans, read more about Harold in the papers than we actually saw of him, although he did travel a lot with the team. He'd sit up in the front by himself, or with his good friend King Clancy.

I remember that he loved candy bars, or anything sweet. We

chartered a lot and when the stewardess would come by, he'd grab a handful and put them on the seat next to his. This struck me because this was a guy with diabetes defying the odds.

Ballard was always giving the world the finger, figuratively speaking. He seemed to have that attitude in life, thumbing his nose at everybody—"I'm Harold Ballard and that's all there is to it." Frank Sinatra said it more politely when he sang, "I did it my way."

One thing I'd like to establish, though, is that I've always felt that Harold really had a passion for the team; he really wanted it to be successful, really wanted it to win for himself, for the players and the fans. His lifelong curse at the helm of the Leafs was that he was not really a smart hockey man, and that he never really knew who to listen to for that wisdom. That was even true of his lifelong companion, Francis (King) Clancy. They were really good buddies, and King was renowned for longevity in his career and for having been a Maple Leaf forever, long after he stopped playing hockey. As the two of them grew older and closer together—both of their wives had passed away—they turned to each other. Instead of getting new, fresh ideas as the game and players were changing, they hung on to the old stuff. That was one of the reasons Harold reached out for people like Punch Imlach and John Brophy. Harold believed that these were the men he needed for success, when nothing could have been further from the truth.

When Stafford and he were together, Stafford was club president and had the name, which meant there was still a Smythe in the organization. Then Bassett was bought out, Stafford died and Harold went to jail; when he came out, suddenly the Leafs were all his. You had to wonder if he spent the year at Millhaven planning what kind of Boss he would be. It seemed that before that time, Harold was a bit player with little character associated with his role. Suddenly, Harold was a star.

Another question had to do with casting: was Harold his own creation, or the creation of the media in Toronto? Who built him up into the caricature he became? My impression is that the moment the Harold Ballard story started to unfold, he fell in love with his own fame. I never met his wife, but I heard that she was a real Christian lady and that he really had a lot of love and respect for her. She probably tempered his actions; he probably had this big kid inside himself which he contained during his marriage. When she died in December 1969, he lost that necessary counterbalance.

It seems that everything came to a head at the press conference that announced my new five-year deal; this press conference launched him. It was a heck of a show. "Ha! Ya sent me to jail; I come back with a tan, I put on weight, it's a country club." In other words, "Tell the world I shoved it right back at 'em." And, "Harold Ballard, Toronto media personality, is now available for interviews at any time of the day." From then on, he was unstoppable.

So while the other teams were staffing strong front offices with sports administration graduates, forward-thinking hockey experts, and legions of business people, the Leafs were lurching along behind Hal and King, like a little blue-and-white wagon being dragged down a dusty summer road by two kids in short pants.

Harold Ballard was also famous for generous gestures. Every year we had the Christmas skate with the families and kids, and each year they'd have either Johnny Bower or one of the old ushers dress up as Santa Claus. One year Santa came slowly out of the stands, all the way to ice level, and he turned out to be Harold Ballard. He was Santa Claus for our Christmas party—you didn't know it until you got up close. That was the other side of Harold . . . sitting there with little kids on his knees, giving out gifts.

If Harold was Santa, King Clancy was Chief Elf. I always enjoyed King Clancy; we'd shared several speaking engagements at banquets and sports dinners and he was always very good with the crowd as a master storyteller. King took over as coach once when Johnny McLellan got sick, and his entire contribution was to come into the room and tell a few jokes before exhorting us to "lay the hickory on 'em."

I remember one occasion with King during a mini-slump. He always watched the practices from up high in the stands and after one workout, I was shooting pucks when King called me over to the glass. He grabbed my stick and started to show me how to shoot a wristshot. He was about seventy-five at the time.

Out of respect for him, I listened quietly. I had played hockey all my life, I was a veteran NHLer by then, and spent summers teaching hockey school. How we taught kids to shoot was a little different from the technique King was trying to teach me. When I say that, I don't undervalue King's former contribution to the team, or his good intentions. He must have felt that if he could help me in any way, then he'd try to do that. But the advice I was getting wasn't very good.

As venerable as he was, King could annoy players too. When I signed the five-year deal mentioned earlier, I jumped from $15,000 a year to $29,000. I had scored 29 goals the previous season and the WHA had come calling. All of this WHA talk upset King Clancy and he bet Johnny McLellan $100 that I wouldn't score 30 goals. That got back to me. It bothered me because here was a guy upstairs putting me down, figuring that because I had signed a five-year contract, I would tail off.

I finished the 1973-74 season with 38 goals and 46 assists for 84 points, and pointedly asked McLellan if he'd ever collected on his bet.

Harold and King went everywhere together. A classic example was at the 1975 All-Star game in Montreal. It was my first All-Star game and I flew down with Gerry McNamara and Johnny Bower. Harold and King were on the same plane. When we arrived at Dorval airport, we retrieved our bags, piled into a limousine and drove to the Bonaventure Hotel. Four of us were sitting in the limo, waiting for traffic to clear, when we looked up ahead of us to where the Murray Hill airport bus was parked. Who should be sitting right at the back of the bus but Harold and King. The owner and vice-president were on the cheap "milk-run" bus that stopped at every downtown hotel, while player and scouts were taking the twenty-dollar limo. It stuck out.

I checked in at the hotel, freshened up in my room and went back to the lobby to see what was happening, when in trudged Harold and King with their bags. That was the kind of guy Harold was, he knew the value of a buck, even if it meant arriving at the hotel an hour later than everyone else. Whenever Harold and King travelled, they always carried their own bags, never had a porter carry them. Bell captains and room service waiters would have starved to death if they had depended on these two for their livelihoods. And they were always together; always out early in the morning on walks.

The togetherness of Harold and King meant that they were easy targets for our more imaginative practical jokers. In one incident, we were in St. Louis just before Christmas. I don't really know how much Harold drank, or if he did, because he never drank around the players. That trip the guys had bought a few bottles at the Duty Free to take back into Canada.

We had a lot of Gatorade, we called it Googenade, though I don't know why. In St. Louis, the visitors' dressing room is actually two rooms; the defensemen sit in one, the forwards in the other. We were beating St. Louis pretty good that night and between the second and third periods, Ian Turnbull, getting a jump on the festive season, snuck into the forwards' room where the Gatorade was kept in a huge barrel, took out a bottle of vodka and dumped it in the Googenade. The trainers filled up the bottles from the barrel and had them on the bench for the third period. A few guys were laughing and sipping this vodka and Googenade on the players' bench. Harold came into the dressingroom after the game and dipped a Dixie cup into the Googenade, which he often did, and took a sip.

He could taste the booze right away and spat it out.

"What the heck's in this stuff!"

Another King-and-Harold story. Harold had just bought his latest toy, the Hamilton Tiger Cats of the Canadian Football League, and the two old cronies loved to taunt Toronto football fans, especially when Harold had Ti-Cat decals painted on the Gardens ice. Dave Williams jumped on that; he'd go and touch the tigers each time he scored a goal. I met Harold in his office one day and he had a problem he thought I might help him with.

"They've just called us and they want us to enter a float in the Grey Cup parade. We're trying to put together some ideas on a float to represent Hamilton. What do you think of this one? We'll put a twenty-two-foot-high tiger on the float. In the mouth of the tiger, we'll put a Toronto Argonaut without a sweater on, and we're gonna hang the sweater from its behind. Whattaya think? Won't that go over big in downtown Toranna!" Harold and King spent hours cackling away upstairs at Maple Leaf Gardens, thinking up projects like that one. To them, Toronto was the world's largest playpen.

When Jim Gregory was hired, he moderated the Romper Room mentality a bit. Harold wasn't as bad as he would become later because Gregory had a real way of managing him, monitoring him. Maybe there was a lot more happening upstairs that didn't get out because Gregory kept it behind closed doors and didn't let the media get hold of it—talked it over with Harold and let him settle down before he did something. I give Jim a lot of credit for that.

Early during my tenure as team captain, the team went ice fishing. I had gotten into the habit of arranging group outings for the guys to do as a team, to get away from the pressures of the game. This often resulted in an organized trip. We'd load up a bus with chicken or sandwiches, a few cases of beer, and we'd go ice fishing on Lake

Simcoe. The camp we usually went to had Bombardiers that would take us out on the lake. On this specific occasion, some of the guys were working on a major buzz when we got out onto the lake. Turnbull promptly commandeered a Bombardier.

Two guys drove these oversized snow tractors for us—they looked like tanks and held up to twelve persons. One of the two drivers had gone inside to make a call when Turnbull jumped into the driver's seat and took off out onto Lake Simcoe with eight or ten guys laughing hysterically in the back. That set off a day of drinking and carrying on, with not much fishing. When we returned to Beaverton that night, the guys were well along. While I was inside settling up our bills, some of the guys were wandering around town.

We had neglected to bring back the little poles and lines they had supplied and the outfitter wanted to charge us for them. I told him they were right out on the ice where we had left them, and nobody was going to steal them, so I wasn't going to pay.

"When it gets light out tomorrow, go pick 'em up. They're in the fish huts." Truth be known, one or two of the fish huts might have been hard to find under the beer cans and chicken bones, but there wasn't exactly an ecological disaster. Our disagreement was straightened out without further incident, and we returned to Toronto.

Two or three weeks later, I got a call. Ballard wanted to see me in his office. He tossed a letter across his desk at me. "Read this."

It was from the outfitter. It said, more or less, that the Visigoths had invaded the Roman Empire, pillaging and looting anything and anyone in their path. There were complaints about several team members using downtown Beaverton as a carnival site, and a recitation of other horrors. The conclusion was drawn that the Toronto Maple Leafs had besmirched a fine tradition and reputation by acting like a bunch of rowdy truck drivers. I thought it was an unjust slur on truck drivers. There were a few complaints about environmental damage accruing from the presence of foreign matter (chicken bones, biodegradable; beer cans, non-biodegradable) on the lake ice and then he hit Harold E. Ballard where he lived.

"And they didn't pay the bill."

I gave him back the letter and an explanation and waited for the explosion.

Harold had a strange look on his face. "You know what I'd do about this if I were you?"

"No, what would you do?" I replied, thinking uh-oh, here it comes.

"I'd shit in a brown paper bag and send it back to the guy!"   .

The Maple Leafs Forever.

"Now get outta here!"

With a guy like Harold upstairs, you had to figure we'd have some characters in uniform too.

My favorite character among all the players in Toronto was Jim McKenny. He's pretty special today, too. Nobody who played with us in the 1970s can remember all of the "Howie" stories, but they all have their own library of yarns. My first has nothing to do with a guy known throughout the league as a flake. I was in my second year and it was during a particularly bad period for me. Early one morning, after a game, my phone rang at about 1:00 a.m. It was Jim McKenny and he just wanted to try to cheer me up, make me feel better.

It was a "don't get down, things aren't as bad as you think they are" type of phone call. If I kept up my hard work, the way I played and practiced and trained, basically things would work out, he said. That conversation stayed with me because the Jim McKenny everybody else knew was the team clown. But there was a sincere side to him, a sensitivity that he rarely showed. In this case, he was taking the time to respond to a teammate who wasn't feeling great. I valued that.

One year, Howie represented the Leafs at the All-Star game. He had gone on Players' Association business as a team representative when it turned out that our All-Star couldn't make it because of an injury. The NHL thinkers huddled, noticed that McKenny would save them airfare and asked him to play. Midway through the game, the East All-Stars were about to face off when McKenny called time, held up the game and TV broadcast, skated over to Phil Esposito and said something to him. A few days later at practice Red Kelly, who was coaching us at the time, turned to McKenny: "Jimmy, what were you talking to Espo about? Were you giving him instructions on how to line up at the face-off?"

"Nah, I was just showing him an incredible blonde in the front row reds."

That was the type of guy he was. I remember in my first years that in Chicago, the Blackhawks had the organist play a fight song at every lull in the action. So guess who comes down the ice with the puck in the middle of play, right by both benches and singing real loud while stickhandling away ... "Here come the Hawks, the mighty Black Hawks" ... whatever their team song was; guys on both benches were busting their sides laughing.

Once his hockey career was over, he became a sports reporter with CITY-TV. I was playing with Philadelphia or Detroit at the time and we were in Toronto the night before a game. I turned on the TV sports in my hotel room and there was Howie. The Leafs, as usual, were doing badly and there was the usual talk of wholesale changes, upstairs and down. The cameraman had Howie in close-up, just head-and-shoulders on screen. He reviewed the Leafs problems and concluded, "Unfortunately, things aren't going to change until ... " and as he said that, they zoomed back and he was standing in the middle of a cemetery, beside an open grave. I cracked up.

I can remember when Tiger Williams wrote his book after he retired and Howie interviewed him about it for television. I can't remember exactly how the line went, because the two of them were discussing a story involving female hockey fans: "Thanks a lot Tiger, I've always wanted to tell my kids those stories but I never had the guts to do it. Thanks for doing it for me."

Tiger came back: "Howie, when are you going to write a book?"

"I have to wait until my wife dies before I write mine."

Howie's personal problems have all been well-documented. But what a lot of people fail to realize is that Howie is a guy who really gave everything he had and wanted to do well. He did the best he could; he always battled.

But, knowing Howie as a person—I really want to say this the right way—he was as loyal, sincere and dedicated to being a Maple Leaf and a professional player as anyone could be.

He's solved his problems now, and I'm as proud as anyone can be for him. A couple of years ago, I had the opportunity to go down to the Goofy Games with him and spend some time and talk. My son Ryan got to know Howie spending time with him in Florida, and they both took a liking to each other. As far as I'm concerned, that's a great vote of confidence.

5

The Rest of the Big Six

IN 1972, AFTER Stafford Smythe died of stomach cancer, Harold E. Ballard began exercising hands-on control over the Toronto Maple Leafs franchise. It is no coincidence that the 1972-73 season was a watershed year for our hockey team, a year when the Leafs would be irrevocably sentenced to mediocrity for an entire generation. Quite simply, Harold Ballard refused to believe that the World Hockey Association was serious, and when WHA representatives came calling, they left with the heart of our team, especially our blueline corps.

The first, and greatest, loss was Bernie Parent, the man who would eventually be considered alongside Ken Dryden and Tony Esposito as the top three NHL goaltenders of the era. We had acquired Bernie in the Bruce Gamble and Mike Walton trade in February 1971, and in the season-plus he played for us he was nothing short of miraculous, posting a 2.59 goals-against average and four shutouts, even though his record was 24-25-12, or under .500.

Bernie had been making in the neighborhood of $25,000 a year on the contract that brought him to the Leafs, when Gary Davidson and Dennis Murphy, both from the San Diego area, announced that they were selling franchises in a new league that would begin play in October 1972. Harold Ballard was not alone in giving these two upstarts short shrift; after all, they were only flakes from southern California, an area that had never been a hockey hotbed. Other well-established NHL franchises also sneered when the WHA announced its intentions. The Boston Bruins, the reigning Stanley Cup champions, would see players like Derek Sanderson, Wayne Carleton and

Gerry Cheevers move to the new league and their chance for repeating as Cup champs fly right out the window. The short-sighted NHL executives were laughing on the other side of their faces when the new twelve-team league began play on schedule that fall.

The Miami Screaming Eagles never played a single game in the WHA, but they cost us the services of Bernie Parent. As the 1971-72 season wore on, and it became apparent to anyone with 20/20 vision that Parent represented our goalie of the present and future, Stafford Smythe and Jim Gregory undertook negotiations to substantially increase Parent's salary and tie him to the Leafs with a long-term pact.

This proved to be a killer one-two punch for the Leafs; Smythe's sudden death, and the announcement of the new league. Franchise rights were selling at $25,000 per city and, to give the new league a foot up in its bid to corral players, the WHA held its first player draft in February of 1972, right in the middle of our season and months ahead of the NHL draft in June. Bernie's agent backed away from the Leafs and waited for the offers to pour in. The stampede to sign existing NHL, AHL and CHL players to WHA contracts started shortly after the new league's draft. Miami selected Bernie and soon thereafter his agent was offered a five-year deal at $150,000 a year. This was outrageous money in terms of the existing salary structure and was followed by even richer offers to Derek Sanderson (Philadelphia Blazers) and Bobby Hull (Winnipeg Jets).

Many stories circulated after Bernie defected to the WHA, and it's difficult to know exactly what went on. One theory had it that Harold Ballard interfered with Jim Gregory's efforts to negotiate with the Philadelphia lawyer, Howard Casper, who was operating as Parent's agent. Another theory was that after Gregory refused to talk WHA-size numbers with Casper, the lawyer contacted the Leafs and said he'd negotiate only with Ballard and no one else.

When apprised of the kind of money that was on the table, Harold put his foot in his mouth, advising Parent's lawyer, "If he can get that kind of money, I won't stop him." The moment he uttered those words they became reality because, in effect, Ballard was giving Parent his release. There was no way that the Leafs could go to court and claim that the goaltender had broken any deal with Toronto.

Bernie Parent sent shockwaves through the National Hockey League when he flew down to Miami on a quiet Sunday in mid-season and announced that he would join the new league for the

1972-73 season. The NHL responded with legal action and lost quickly when the WHA replied with an anti-trust suit, alleging that the NHL could not interfere with the right of players to choose their own league. The NHL reserve clause—team rights to hockey players—was relevant only *within* the NHL and had no effect in a competing league, the court ruled.

Bernie brought Florida travel brochures to practice and passed them out among the players and a number of teams began courting our players, as they were doing throughout the league. Other NHL teams reacted better, however, rapidly undertaking serious negotiations with the players who formed the nucleus of their playing personnel. Everybody was resigned to losing marginal players, third- and fourth-line players who were going to receive first- and second-line salaries in the WHA. Nothing could be done about that short of blowing the entire NHL salary structure right out of the water. The Ottawa Nationals wanted Dave Keon, the Alberta Oilers were anxious to sign Jim Harrison, while the New England Whalers came after Rick Ley and Brad Selwood. The Miami Screaming Eagles never soared in the WHA, but Bernie signed a five-year deal with the Philadelphia Blazers. He lasted only one season with the team and expressed a desire to return to the NHL. However, he ruled out a return to Toronto and the Leafs traded his rights back to the Flyers for Doug Favell and a first-round draft choice.

The next mis-step in the management comedy of errors came the following summer. By not paying attention to the danger of the new league, the Leafs had quickly lost Parent, Ley, Selwood and Harrison, though they managed to sign Keon, then thirty-two. The real boner came in the expansion draft that summer when the club protected the four players they had lost and, as a result, lost Brian Spencer to the New York Islanders. Just before Rick Ley left, he told a Toronto newspaper that they could "lay the blame on management," and early the following season Paul Henderson was quoted in the same vein. (We would eventually lose Henderson, Keon and defenseman Mike Pelyk to the new league, but the biggest loss by far was that of Parent. He wouldn't be adequately replaced until the arrival of Mike Palmateer four years later.)

As many expected, the new league had its share of problems in its first year. Several clubs—the Ottawa Nationals, the Philadelphia Blazers and the Los Angeles Sharks—were moved to other cities, with the Nationals becoming the Toronto Toros. That led to more problems for Ballard, and this time they involved the son of his former partner and now avowed enemy, John W. Bassett. The younger Bassett, John F., had made a name for himself in the entertainment industry and Ballard even let him use Maple Leaf Gardens to film a Hollywood hockey movie called *Faceoff*. When John F. bought the Nationals and they became the Toros, Harold and Bill Ballard smacked their lips in anticipation of thirty-five more high-rent events on the calendar at the Gardens.

As it turned out, the Toros played the 1973-74 season at the tiny Varsity Arena and moved into the Gardens only in 1974-75, although that almost didn't happen either. In 1974, the NHL and WHA made peace, with the new league withdrawing its anti-trust suits and the NHL making arenas available to the new league in centers where there were two teams and the WHA franchise sought ice. The key phrase in the agreement was "at a fair price." Harold, who had been ready to rent Maple Leaf Gardens to the Toros the year before, bridled at the suggestion that he might have to cut his rates. That deal almost fell apart when the Toros, who had already signed Frank Mahovlich from the Canadiens, came to a five-year agreement with Paul Henderson. When Ballard heard that Henderson had switched teams without even leaving Toronto, he blew up and refused to allow Bassett into his building. But Harold had always placed principal ahead of principle, and the Toros, with Henderson and Mahovlich in the lineup, played at Maple Leaf Gardens that season.

Harold got his own back, making the Toros build their own dressing room in the Gardens, hiking up the rent an extra $3,500 per game to use the television lighting used during NHL games, rather than the dimmer illumination that was provided for Marlies games. He also took the cushions off the high-priced golds.

I wonder what he would have done if I had signed with the Toros.

It has been reported in several places that I had a verbal agreement with the Toros and that I backed out at the last minute. That is not true, although I did receive what I think was a serious offer in 1973. The Sittlers and the Eaglesons were invited to step up a notch socially one evening that spring: dinner at the Bassetts in the very ritzy Bridle Path area of Toronto.

When the original WHA draft had taken place, I had been selected by the Alberta Oilers. After the Ottawa Nationals became the Toronto Toros, my rights were traded to Toronto for Ron Climie. When Nancy and Alan Eagleson, and Wendy and Darryl Sittler rang the bell at the Bassetts' that evening, we were to meet John F. and some of his partners, including George Cohon of McDonald's Restaurants of Canada and Rudy Bratty, a major real estate developer in Toronto. I was still very much small-town Ontario and I didn't really know who these people were, or exactly what they represented. Alan and Nancy were a lot more comfortable with them than were Wendy and myself. The person I was probably most comfortable with there that night was little Carling Bassett.

Dinner was wonderful, and afterwards we retired to the salon for dessert and coffee.

John Bassett stood up. "Okay Alan, what's it going to take to sign this guy?"

We hadn't discussed the possibility of an offer before visiting the Bassetts; more than anything, this was a getting-to-know-you meeting as far as I was concerned.

To my surprise, Alan replied, "A million dollars for five years and you've got him."

The man the Toronto papers liked to call Johnny F. didn't even blink. "He's signed!" (I was making $29,000 a year at the time.)

Wendy squeezed my arm and I exchanged glances with Alan and somehow, I still don't know how, managed to convey our dismay to him. The look said pointedly, "I'm still a Maple Leaf and we'll talk this over among ourselves. I'm not leaving here signed."

Alan Eagleson did not get where he is by being slow on the uptake. Barely glancing my way, he turned to his audience and didn't skip a beat, ". . . and free hamburgers at McDonald's for the Sittler family, *and* a farm north of Toronto"—he was going to drive the grocery order up so high for each partner that they would eventually have to say "enough." Then we would have time to get back together and discuss it properly, first Wendy and myself, and then Alan and myself. I didn't want to make a decision that night, and Bassett made it quite clear that he didn't want to get into a bidding war with the Leafs.

I ended up signing with the Leafs for five years, with $145,000 for the first year and a $50,000 signing bonus. With a few add-ons and annual salary escalations it came to a $850,000 deal, money in the bank, considering the shaky nature of the WHA.

More than the money, however, was my desire to continue playing in the NHL, which was recognized as the top league. While others like Bobby Hull and J.C. Tremblay were recognized superstars when they switched leagues, I was just getting established in the National Hockey League and wanted to make it there with the Leafs. In my mind, there was no difference in offers when you factored in what it meant for me to play with the Leafs. It was "no deal" to the WHA offer.

Still, how many people can say they've been offered a million bucks for dessert?

While the Leafs were in the process of losing solid performers such as Parent, Henderson, and later Pelyk and Keon to the WHA, we were also beating the bushes for talent and striking it rich. Although 1972-73 saw a major exodus of veteran Leafs, it was also the year we picked up some good new players. The true frustration, though, was realizing that it was a revolving door at 60 Carlton; I'm sure dyed-in-the-wool Leafs fans still lose sleep wondering what kind of team we might have had if we had been able to keep all the top-notch players we had in those years: Pat Boutette and George Ferguson (1972-73); Lanny McDonald, Ian Turnbull and Bob Neely (1973-74); and Mike Palmateer, Jack Valiquette and Dave Williams (1974-75). During the winter of 1973, Gerry McNamara went on a European scouting trip and returned to Canada with Borje Salming and Inge Hammarström in tow. They'd join us for the 1973-74 season. Imagine the Toronto team that might have been had we been able to keep Ley, Selwood, Pelyk and others with Salming and Turnbull, in front of a goaltending tandem of Parent and Palmateer.

On the ice we had gone from a team with veterans on offense and a young, but rapidly developing, defense to a team that was slowing down up front *and* having trouble keeping the puck out of, and a regular goalie in, our net. In 1971-72, with Bernie Parent and Jacques Plante backstopping us and the young rearguards Ley, Selwood, Pelyk, Dorey (traded in mid-season) and Glennie anchored by veteran Bob Baun, we finished fourth in the East Division, 33-31-14 with 209 goals for, and 208 against. The following year, with two new expansion teams in our league, and 12 teams in the new league, we somehow conspired to drop to sixth, out of the playoff picture. Plante, teamed with rookies Ron Low and Gord McRae, and playing behind an inexperienced defense that included such players as Joe Lundrigan, John Grisdale, Dave Fortier and Larry McIntyre, gave up 71 more goals than in the previous year. Our increased production of 247 goals scored could not offset the problems in our own zone.

You don't have time to reflect on the journeymen who pass

through a team over the years; yet, when their names are mentioned, the faces and the memories come flooding back. Lundrigan, Grisdale, Fortier and McIntyre would all be gone by the following season but I can picture them today as if they were standing in front of me right now. Lundrigan was a Newfoundlander, a big, happy guy who was a bit amazed to find himself in the National Hockey League, and enjoying the experience as much as he could. Grisdale came from the college ranks and though he was limited in his skills, he played to the maximum within those limitations. He was an excellent team man and I really liked him. Larry McIntyre was a mild, unaggressive guy, who had come up through our farm system. And Dave Fortier was another big, strong boy who was also a good team player, not a finesse guy by any means, who went on to play a couple more years with the Islanders.

I liked all four of these guys, but as a group they couldn't come close to filling the void created by the departures of Ley, Selwood and, early in 1972-73, Jim Dorey. Bernie Parent was never adequately replaced either as Dunc Wilson, Eddie Johnston and Doug Favell took part in the Great Leaf Goalie Airlift over the next four years, but to no avail.

Half of what the sports beat reporters would later label the Big Six joined the team in the fall of 1973. I was already there, and Borje Salming, Lanny McDonald and Ian Turnbull all skated for us when we took to the ice for our first game of the season. We were also new behind the bench as Harold Ballard promoted John McLellan to assistant general manager and hired Red Kelly as coach. Kelly was just what a team with no middle needed: we were either fresh-faced rookies, like the aforementioned trio, Hammarström and Bob Neely, or grizzled veterans like Norm Ullman, Ron Ellis, Dave Keon and Eddie Shack, who had just returned to Toronto after a tour of the league. We didn't have a lot of young veterans in between, and that would cost us.

As I have mentioned earlier, Lanny McDonald is my best friend and ours is the kind of friendship that stands the test of time and distance. We didn't hook up right away, however, when he joined us in 1973. It wasn't that way at all. For one thing, Lanny's arrival in the NHL coincided with the start of the World Hockey Association, so there was the awareness among the older pros of the huge salary differentials. He and Turnbull were in a graduating class of junior players who received large signing bonuses and bigger contracts right from the outset than players who had signed even the previous year.

We didn't play together for a couple of seasons because I usually was with Ron Ellis and Paul Henderson, and Lanny had a slow start, scoring about thirty goals in his first two seasons combined. Several press row experts, especially Don Ramsay of the *Globe and Mail*, rode Lanny mercilessly in the newspapers, claiming he was yet another in a long string of draft duds and the Leafs should get rid of him while they could still get something for him. In fact, Jim Gregory had virtually traded him to Atlanta early in the 1975-76 season when Lanny turned it around and became the goal scorer we all knew he could be. We went on a seven-game road trip that started in St. Louis and swung out west, and Lanny suddenly began popping them in at almost a goal-a-game clip. When we got home, there was no more talk about him rejoining Tom Lysiak, his former center in junior. He'd found a center with Toronto who liked him just fine, and we'd both found a scooter on the left wing in Errol Thompson. It was great vindication for both of them because they had spent a lot of time together as Black Aces.

In his first seasons, Lanny lived downtown because he wasn't married. I was, and had a house in Mississauga so we didn't see a lot of each other except at the rink. As with most things, relationships take time to build. I guess the relationship developed when Lanny married Ardell in the summer of 1975, between his second and third seasons, and they moved to Mississauga. We drove to practice every day—I'd pick him up and we'd drive in together. That's usually the way it is; if you're winning or losing you share those close feelings before you are brought together by circumstance. We got to playing together, shared some successes and both got invited to the Canada Cup training camp in 1976. That's really where the relationship grabbed hold and developed. We roomed together at the Bonaventure Hotel in Montreal and cheered for each other to make the team.

We made it, though not without our ups and downs, and when I scored the winning goal in overtime in the final game, I was almost flattened by the world's largest flying mustache against the boards behind the Czechoslovakian net. But that's the stuff of the next chapter. During the Canada Cup camp we spent most of our free time together and were occasionally joined by Wendy and Ardell because the Team Canada organizers arranged some special events for the wives. After we won the series, the four of us went to a lodge in Parry Sound on Georgian Bay. Training camp had started with the Leafs, but we were given time off for a break and got to know each other even better.

I'm not a sociologist or a psychologist so I can't give you long explanations why some people hit it off or have the right chemistry. It must be like that in many walks of life; you form a bond with somebody when you've actually sweated and gone through the emotional lows and highs together. It's hard to put that into words but the feeling comes with all that. When you experience friendship at that level, it's great.

But it was something more than just playing together on the same line. I think we have an unspoken faith in each other. Lanny McDonald is a truly genuine guy, down-to-earth, sincere, a character with a big heart. The great love he has for his wife and kids has to be seen to be believed. Perhaps the most amazing thing is that he had love left over for the rest of the world, especially the thousands of people he touched directly in the Special Olympics movement. Most people who have gotten to know Lanny closely sound the same. He's not Mother Teresa and I'm not nominating him for the Nobel Peace Prize or anything. However, he's a one-of-a-kind type of guy and has the dependability and generosity inside that make him a friend for life.

What I valued most, as a hockey player and a friend, was Lanny's strength. I had been appointed captain of the Toronto Maple Leafs at the beginning of the 1974-75 season, a great honor but also a tough task. As any young captain would, I hoped I could do the job well. In order to be effective as captain, you really must have the support of your teammates. Guys like Mario Tremblay and Doug Risebrough never wore the "C" with the Montreal Canadiens but still were considered leaders. The same goes for the Watson brothers playing behind Bobby Clarke in Philadelphia, or Bob Nystrom and Clark Gillies with the Islanders.

Lanny was that type of player. There are guys who are leaders and character guys, and everybody knows it. I was fortunate in that, while I was the guy who wore the "C", these guys were as much a part of that leadership role as I was. And without that, even though they never got the recognition that I got, I wouldn't have been able to be as effective. Tiger Williams had the same leadership qualities, but I'll talk about that a little later.

Lanny was our team's backbone—tough as nails outside, and soft as mush inside. I'll never forget one occasion when we all got to see "soft as mush" turn to "tough as nails" in an eye-blink and the transition almost scared Pat Boutette to death.

Lanny and Ardell had just become the proud parents of their first daughter, Andra (named after Red Kelly's wife—Ardell and Andra Kelly had worked together with deaf children in Toronto). Lanny was three feet off the ground, he was so proud. He had permission to visit Ardell in hospital one morning and when we came off the ice after practice, Lanny was waiting for us in the dressing room with the first batch of baby pictures—those newborn shots you get at the hospital on the day of birth. Proud papa McDonald was gushing and passing round the photos when Silvertongue Boutette pushed his way into the group and said, right out of the blue: "Let me see that little sleazebag."

The look on Lanny's face was death—Booter's. Patty obviously had meant it as a joke, just to get a rise out of Lanny, but pleading sick humor wouldn't have helped if Lanny had wrapped one of those strong hands around Boutette's throat and started to squeeze. Lanny, the new family man, thought about it for microseconds, considered the source, and then graciously allowed Booter to see another sunrise. Boutette immediately retreated to the nearest dressing room mirror to count the new gray hairs he'd felt suddenly sprouting during that very brief but very dangerous moment.

Lanny's great excitement and pride in his new child could not help but spread to us all. Ardell was still in hospital and her mother, Lucille Moyer, was in from Calgary to help prepare for the new mom's homecoming the following day. Wendy and I had decided to drop in and see Lanny after a dinner with some friends. This decision seemed to make a lot of sense at about one or two in the morning, under the influence of the very fine dry white wine that had accompanied our meal. On our way out of the restaurant, I got a couple of lobsters out of the live tank, "because Lanny was so excited he had probably forgotten his dinner", and shortly thereafter we were ringing the doorbell at the McDonald residence. You have to see Lanny torn out of bed in the early morning hours to appreciate just how much that mustache can droop. It didn't last long though; his new-father adrenaline kicked in and we took the crustaceans into the kitchen where we staged lobster races on the floor. Lucille Moyer, a wonderful woman, stood there glaring at me, with one of those "you idiot!" looks in her eye. (Long after we'd left, Lanny was up scrubbing the kitchen floor, worrying about the lobster smell upsetting his wife's delicate sensitivities.) Lanny may have been groggy with lack of sleep, but he appreciated the gesture. Come to think of it, I never did find out what happened to the lobsters.

Lanny was down to earth, although on one occasion Red Kelly found him downright too earthy. We were on a road trip during his second or third season and this particular flight was jammed. Lanny always enjoyed playing cards. We had a group of regulars: Jack Valiquette and Claire Alexander were always available. On this occasion, we found ourselves sitting idly at the gate, waiting for permission to taxi to the runway, as it got hot, hotter and hottest inside the plane. To conserve fuel, or whatever, the air conditioning wasn't turned on and we started to cook.

No problem. Lanny got the idea to take off his shirt; and was sitting shirtless for our card game when Red Kelly happened to look back. He came to the rear of the plane.

"What the hang are ya doin'?" Red never sullied his lips with swear words. It was all hang and dang. "Ya think you're out on the back forty?" Lanny was totally embarrassed; he never honestly thought he could offend anybody by simply taking off his shirt.

If Lanny was all earth tones and passion, Borje Salming was just the opposite—all talent and cool. And Ian Turnbull was somewhere in between. Borje and Ian joined us together in the 1973-74 season, one from Sweden and the other from an all-star career in the OHA with the Montreal Junior Canadiens and Ottawa 67s.

Borje was probably the best and purest athlete on our team, a great hockey player who, had he played with a more successful team like Montreal or Philadelphia during his peak years, would probably have won a Norris Trophy or two as the league's best defenseman. He was always in top condition, not an ounce of body fat on him, and worked hard in practice and in games. Added to that was a level of skill rarely seen in hockey.

How good was Borje? He was up with the very best, and there wasn't a player in the Toronto dressing room who felt otherwise. I remember one year when our players were pushing for Salming to get the Norris Trophy ahead of Larry Robinson, saying things like, "Robinson has it easier because he plays for such a great team." But Robinson had to share ice time with Serge Savard and Guy Lapointe; Borje played with Ian Turnbull who was no slouch, so it was moot.

Those debates raised the question: Is it easier to star with a lesser team, or with a great one?

The obvious answer is that it would depend on the individual and the situation. But that doesn't get you any closer to deciding whether Borje should have received more votes for the Norris or not. There are those who are first-string players or stars but who play for a weak team and who might have difficulty adjusting to the status of second-string player if moved to a team that was strong overall. In my estimation, with his talent and heart, Borje would have fit right in and had a great career with Montreal or any other leading team. You could also wonder if Ian Turnbull had been alone or without Salming on the Leafs, would he have been better? When Borje went down with an eye injury early in our 1978 Stanley Cup playoff with the New York Islanders, Ian played the best hockey of his life and made a significant contribution to our winning the series.

It could also be argued that Robinson, Savard and Lapointe probably lost out in terms of Norris Trophy votes because the three played together. Early in the 1970s, the comparisons were all about Brad Park and Bobby Orr. Later it was Robinson and Denis Potvin. I always felt that the three Canadiens were ahead of Park, especially defensively. But Park and Denis Potvin got a lot of their points on the power play and often played forty-five minutes each a game; Lapointe, Savard and Robinson had to share ice time and man-advantage opportunities.

There are no definitive answers to these questions, but by asking them you situate the true talents of Borje Salming. He definitely deserved to be included in all conversations of this nature.

Away from the rink, Borje liked the good life, and that was semi-public knowledge for many years, especially on one or two occasions when he was part of a group of players in hot water over curfew violations on the road. Late in his career, this took a more public turn when he was suspended by John Ziegler for admitting to cocaine use. Simply put, he was a guy who didn't like a lot of off-ice responsibility. All he wanted to do was play hockey. When he came to the rink, he played hard without exception. Borje was a very talented, competitive guy. But if I was looking for someone for the young guys to look up to, someone who would set an example away from the rink, it certainly wouldn't be Borje.

I remember a Borje Salming incident early in Punch Imlach's reign which he later tried to use as proof to all and sundry that I wasn't a true leader. We had played a game in Winnipeg on a Friday night and flew home on a red-eye charter because we had to play our usual Saturday night game at Maple Leaf Gardens. The plane got in late, so we didn't have the usual skate that morning—we were expected to come to the rink late Saturday afternoon. Borje's wife and kids were up in Collingwood on a ski trip and, instead of going home to rest, he went up there to be with them. He walked into the dressing room that Saturday night with a skier's tan. I couldn't believe it: Borje had been skiing the day of the game, a cardinal sin if there is one in pro hockey. I could never entertain the remotest thought of skiing during the season, let alone on the day of a game. Never mind the possibility of injury; on game day you want to store up all the energy you can.

I took him aside: "Borje, you just *can't* do those things."

"Well, *you* go to your cottage," he answered in a mild protest.

"Yeah, but when I go up there, it's to relax, put my feet up. No different than what I would do at home. I'm thinking of the game, not racing down the hills. If they find out about this upstairs, they'll go nuts." Imlach would pull out the remaining few hairs on his head if he discovered that one of his stars was cavorting on the ski slopes.

That night, Salming played his usual all-star-caliber game and gave no evidence of tiring at any time in the contest. Eventually, but too late for direct action on his part, the word got to Imlach. The comment came back to the effect that "if Sittler was the leader he pretends to be, he should have grabbed Salming by the neck and threatened him. Why should I have to handle these things upstairs?"

But that was Borje. If I had an impressionable rookie straight out of the boonies to initiate into the pleasures of NHL travelling, the guy I *wouldn't* appoint as his personal Big Brother was Borje Salming. The gifted Swede was in such good shape that he could "party hearty" and not show it the following day. If the rookie was going to party, I'd want him accompanied by somebody who was going to show the ill-effects of such self-destructive behavior, because at least there would be a valuable lesson learned. Of course, given my druthers, I'd rather that he didn't partake too frequently of the late-night life, period.

Borje and I played together for a decade and shared many wonderful moments on the ice. But away from the game we were never close; we went different routes. It was nothing active, it just seemed to be an unspoken understanding. Even after I'd retired and he was one of the few players still with the team that I'd played on, I'd see him the odd time when I was down at a Leafs game and waiting around to meet somebody. We would say hello, but we didn't have anything much to say to each other.

Another thing about Borje that mystified the team was that many of us had trouble understanding Harold Ballard's deep loyalty to him. Harold knew about all of Borje's peccadilloes and turned a blind eye. It might have been because Harold had always been a high liver himself and identified more closely with this kind of behavior than with that of the typical law-abiding player. Few resented Borje's special status; they were more nonplussed than anything else.

The weird thing about group dynamics is that Ian Turnbull had many of the same traits as Borje, and was a true party animal, and yet the most serious player on our team, Tiger Williams, seemed to really like Salming and indulge him and Jim McKenny—they reciprocated—and yet refused to forgive the same behavior in Ian.

In his autobiography *Tiger, a Hockey Story*, he wrote that "in some cases, the anger I felt about the drinking didn't prevent me from liking a guy a lot. McKenny was a good example. I used to call him 'tomato-head,' because he'd drink all night and then come to practice dehydrated and without food or sleep, and he'd work so hard in practice that his face would turn bright red. But I liked the guy, because he was funny and very kind, and we got on well even though he knew how much I loathed the boozing." Tiger felt that Ian Turnbull had a whole lot more talent to waste than Jim McKenny, and that McKenny genuinely tried to make up for his excesses in hard work.

Tiger's feeling for Ian Turnbull dated from his very beginnings with the Leafs. Ian and I will never forget his entrance. We knew that he was our second choice in the 1974 draft, picked after we'd selected Jack Valiquette in the first round. And we'd heard about his background, all about the 900 penalty minutes he'd racked up in just three years in Swift Current.

It was the first day of training camp and, as usual, I was one of the first guys on the ice. I was skating around slowly, shooting the puck lazily against the boards and into the empty nets at each end of the rink when I noticed Tiger skate onto the ice. I watched him take those long strides and turn on the speed—down to the end of the rink with no indication that he was going to turn and follow the boards behind the net. He didn't turn, he just jumped up and hit the glass as hard as he could.

Down to the other end of the ice, same thing.

Bam.

"Who *is* this guy?" We were leisurely skating off our summer tans, and he was motoring around with his game-face on, a look that said "this ain't for fun, I'm here to work, boys."

About fifteen minutes later, the whole team was finally out there and we worked through several drills before we lined up to scrimmage. At the first face-off, he lined up beside Ian Turnbull. The moment they bumped waiting for the puck to drop, down went the gloves and Turnbull found himself on the wrong end of a tattoo. Tiger did a number on Turnbull in the early going but Ian was as strong as a bear and eventually wrestled Williams into submission.

Let's give a big NHL welcome to David James (Tiger) Williams.

Later in training camp, we were in Chicago when Keith Magnuson, a pretty tough guy in his own right, blind-sided Tiger near the bench. Magnuson landed a couple of punches, and that's the only time I ever saw Tiger's knees wobble. He's a tough guy. He could take a punch and go with the best of them, pound for pound.

Now how about a big CHL welcome for David James (Tiger) Williams. Right after that game, Tiger got his ticket to Oklahoma City. He came back in mid-season and stayed, making a hit on us and our opposition.

We were on a West Coast trip shortly after he rejoined us and discovered how serious he was about hockey. Tiger roomed with George Ferguson, and Fergie enjoyed the occasional cocktail. Red Kelly called an early curfew one night in Vancouver and everybody made the bed check. The plan was that Fergie and some friends would go out again after Red had finished his room inspection. Fergie was already feeling no pain when Tiger decided that "last call" had come and gone. He also hit upon a novel solution; he hid Ferguson's shoes.

Fergie looked high and low but without luck, getting madder and madder as his frustration mounted. At some point in the argument Ferguson drove his fist into the door or the wall and broke his hand. The media got hold of the story and made it look like he'd punched Tiger, but that wasn't the case. Even Tiger didn't have a jaw that hard.

Notwithstanding his on-ice reputation, Dave Williams was probably one of the most earnest and businesslike hockey players ever to play for the Leafs. There weren't any shortcuts as far as he was concerned. When Tiger broke into the league, he fought all the heavyweights, making his presence felt. Looking at him back then, I would have predicted a career of five or six years; he'd come in, serve a purpose, and then move on. Seeing him play fourteen years, and developing his talent the way he did, was quite an inspiration. Everything he did was full out; Tiger practiced as hard as he could and was always in magnificent shape. His greatest strengths were his conditioning and intensity. Teammates knew they couldn't pull anything over on him. If you were dogging it in practice or a game, you could expect to get it from Tiger. I've been told that this description also fit John Ferguson to a T during his playing days with Montreal.

Tiger might line up beside a floater in practice and stick him in the stomach or say something, just to let him know that he had received his personalized wake-up call. Ian Turnbull, it turned out, was a regular recipient of Tiger's "in your face" encouragement. And, on occasion, even Lanny and he would have a tiff in practice. Tiger would do something to agitate even a saint, Lanny would show flashes of his quick temper, and the sticks would come together real loud. It was never boring.

This kind of clockwork predictability could work against Tiger, too. One morning in 1975, he was out well ahead of practice when he noticed a strange sight, "Cowboy" Bill Flett skating out onto the ice with him. When life was proceeding normally, Flett would beat Red Kelly onto the ice by fractions of a second. Flett skated around a bit, shot the occasional puck at the net, and then sidled up to Tiger. He was a big, bearded and barrel-chested forward who had had some excellent scoring seasons with the Flyers during their Stanley Cup years. Now, however, he was on the downside of his career.

Flett maneuvered the conversation into a discussion of physical strength, and eventually he and Tiger began to wrestle on the ice. About a minute into this, Flett's face suddenly contorted in pain, he screamed and clutched his knee. Tiger went for the trainer; as it turned out, Flett had stretched knee ligaments and would be out almost two months. Flett had hurt himself skidooing the day before—right up there with skiing as a mid-season recreational taboo for pro hockey players—and knowing he wouldn't be able to hide the bad knee, had tried to make it look like a legitimate hockey injury.

Away from the rink, Tiger could be rather unpredictable. Don Giffin, the interim president of the Leafs following Harold Ballard's death and current Chairman of the Board, belonged to a private club out in Pickering. He was on the board of directors and often in the fall he would take a group of players out there for a day of pheasant hunting and socializing. On one such occasion he invited several of us back to his home in Mississauga, in a beautiful area not too far from where Lanny lived. I wasn't there, having gone home at a reasonable hour, when the guys got into Mr. Giffin's fine rum. Tiger's a gun collector—he probably has a hundred of them—and so, it turned out, was Giffin.

"Ever seen anything like this baby?" Giffin is rumored to have boasted, while extracting a big bazooka, a real elephant gun, from one of his cabinets. Everybody had gathered around to admire it when Tiger piped up, "Got any shells for this thing?"

Giffin, silly him, figured Tiger just wanted to *see* how big a shell would go into this cannon, so he went to an ammunition drawer and got one out. Tiger promptly loaded the shell into the gun, strode resolutely out onto the front porch, took aim and fired, sending an innocent streetlight to the great electrical equipment shop in the sky.

Boom! Bits of metal, glass and wiring were everywhere.

By this time it was two o'clock in the morning.

Tiger was laughing, "haw, haw, haw," while Giffin struggled to maintain consciousness. He'd never fired this gun before, and *he* was the one who lived here. A quick thinker in the group suggested that they turn off all the lights, what with the police sirens getting louder by the second, and the boys stayed real quiet until the investigating officers poked about in the shrubbery, rang a few doorbells, then shrugged their shoulders and went about their regular business. Tiger had a Jeep back then. After everything had calmed down, he drove the vehicle through backyards to get out of the neighborhood—just in case the cops were lurking about.

As I mentioned earlier, Ian Turnbull was another player with great talent, but unlike Borje, he wasn't conscientious about conditioning or practicing; he was the type of guy who'd do as little as he could to get by. I don't think Ian ever reached his full potential because of his lackadaisical attitude, but in his early years with us he had such great skills and natural ability that he contributed a lot.

He also was the type of guy who enjoyed testing his coaches and could drive Roger Neilson or Red Kelly to distraction. It might not be one single act, but a combination of things—his attitude in the room, his ineptitude in practice, or defensive lapses, or lack of concentration in a game. I sat beside Ian all the years in the dressing room; he had a different way of preparing himself, but who's to say what's the right way and what's the wrong way.

Another factor was Ian's intelligence; he was a very bright guy with a lot of interests outside hockey. He and a partner named Rick Sutcliffe had a restaurant called Grapes down the street from Maple Leaf Gardens, and Ian spent a lot of time and effort supervising his many other investments. He was often preoccupied with those business affairs. I always believed that hockey was the driving force of my career, and even if I did a lot of other things like endorsements, hockey always took priority. That was why I didn't want to invest too heavily in those days because if I had my own investment or money deal, and somebody was running it for me, I'd want to be there to know what was going on because it was my own money. And that effort would take away from my concentration on hockey. In Ian's case, his other investments were just as important as his hockey. He had two parallel careers, restaurant owner and hockey player.

Then again, he was always in the shadow of Borje. Salming was a great player; they had joined the team at the same time, and that might have had an effect on Ian. His behavior may have been his way of refusing to compete with Borje for attention. He had learned beside one of the best, playing with Denis Potvin on the Ottawa 67s in his last two years of junior.

Whatever their personalities, these four players—Lanny, Borje, Tiger and Ian—represented much of the true backbone and character of our team. Now, all we needed were some very good role players, and a goalie.

We got the goalie in the 1974 draft. By 1976, Mike Palmateer was ready.

Palmy had the reputation of being a cocky little S.O.B. and it was richly deserved. But he was one of those guys his teammates loved. I liked his cockiness, which showed up more in his demeanor than his talk. I think that part of that rep was the fact that he was very boyish looking; he wouldn't have appeared out-of-place with a bantam AA team.

Mike was very confident, he didn't have a lot to say in the dressing room, didn't do much or very obvious things to prepare himself before the game. But the Leafs were like most teams; the goalie is apart from the rest of you and has to do what he has to do to prepare. And only he knows exactly what that is.

With Palmy, too, there was a knee problem. He was a game performer, not a practice goalie. Some guys like Bunny Larocque were practice goalies, but Palmy didn't like to practice that hard. He saved his stuff for the game.

What got us believing was his attitude; he treated every goal scored against him as a fluke. He could get you pumped up, and the crowd behind him, almost effortlessly. You could shoot the puck right at him in the middle of the net and he'd make it look like the toughest save in the world. Someone else like Ken Dryden would just stand there, the puck would hit him and he'd flick it away like a mosquito. Palmy could turn the same play into a Hollywood production, make a spectacular save of a routine shot. The crowd would respond and this would probably tick off the player on the other team a little bit. And then we'd get going. Maybe the next time that player went in, he'd try to whistle one by Palmateer's ears instead of picking the corner. And Palmy would be way out of the net to challenge him, right in his face.

If he had to, he could take care of business in the crease, as Gary Dornhoefer found out one night. Dorny and Montreal's Yvon Lambert were probably the best in the league at planting their rear ends in a goalie's face and refusing to move, no matter how many times they were chopped or knocked over by defensemen. One night Dorny wiggled one too many times, and Palmateer dinged him right off the head with his stick. Dornhoefer went down like a ton of bricks.

Mike Palmateer was young and cocky. He was a showboat.

We had finally found our goalie.

6

Gold Medal Times

CANADA WAS THE center of the sports world in 1976 as Montreal was the host city for the Games of the XXI Olympiad. On the personal front, 1976 was a year which I'll never forget. Everything I touched in my own personal Spirit of '76 seemed to turn into gold.

It all began on February 7 when I set several NHL records in a 10-point outburst against the Boston Bruins at Maple Leaf Gardens. That exploit came the day after Harold Ballard had been quoted in the Toronto papers as saying: "Errol Thompson and Lanny McDonald are excellent wingers; now if we could only find them a centre."

My penchant for big games continued in the playoffs when we faced off against the Philadelphia Flyers in the semifinals. It was an ugly series, full of emotion, stickwork, fights, police arrests and Harold's usual blarney. The Broad Street Bullies were taking on the Carlton Street Chickens—Harold's own epithet—and Ballard was in his element. When we unexpectedly took a lead early in the series, Harold told some acquaintances in the higher echelons of the league "to tell the Jew (Ed Snider) we won't be back in his building." Ethnic slurs aside, by the time we got to the sixth game down 3-2, even Harold wanted us to win to force a deciding seventh game at the Spectrum, no matter what his personal feelings for the Philadelphia owner.

And by the time we'd arrived at Game Six on April 22, Ontario Attorney General Roy McMurtry was well on his way to legislating against hockey violence at all levels in the province, including the NHL. His research into hockey violence had received a major boost on April 15 when four Flyers, Joe Watson, Mel Bridgman, Bob Kelly and Don Saleski, faced a total of nine charges after a fight with fans, policemen and players near the penalty box during Game Three of our series. Watson, a veteran defenseman who usually left the fighting to Dave (Hammer) Schultz, Bob (Hound Dog) Kelly and André (Moose) Dupont, was tagged with five charges consisting of two counts of common assault, two counts of assaulting a policeman, and one of possession of a dangerous weapon (his stick). Hound Dog was charged with assault causing bodily harm when he whipped his hockey glove into the crowd and it struck an usherette; Bridgman received a single count of assault causing bodily harm for a fight with Borje Salming; and Saleski had one assault count, and one for possession of a dangerous weapon. Watson and Kelly eventually pleaded guilty to reduced charges in 1977 and paid fines, while the charges against Bridgman and Saleski were dropped.

It had been a frustrating series for me; I'd been shut out in the three games of the previous round and through the first five games of this confrontation when we skated out to battle for our playoff lives that night. We were ready, though, both on the physical side, with players like Tiger Williams and Dave Dunn holding up that end of it, and mentally as well. That night I broke out in a big way, scoring five goals in an 8-5 win, but even that feat paled when compared with the violence.

Referee Wally Harris handed out 185 minutes in penalties that game, a playoff record, and that boosted the six-game total to 516 minutes, well beyond the 390 minutes that had stood as the previous mark for a series of that length. Dave Schultz, who had received a major and misconduct in the second period, finally was tossed out with double misconducts in the third period when he came to Bobby Clarke's rescue during the latter's altercation with Tiger Williams. We eventually lost the series at the Spectrum, and the Flyers themselves lost to the Canadiens in the finals.

The next time I saw Clarke, he and I were sitting in the same dressing room and trying out for the same team—the squad that would represent Canada at the first-ever Canada Cup that September. Lanny and I were the only Toronto representatives invited to the training camp in Montreal, and every time we turned around there was another Montreal Canadien, Boston Bruin, Buffalo Sabre and . . . Philadelphia Flyer. We felt a little lonely but we recognized the sense behind it—the Canadiens, Bruins and Flyers were the top teams in the league and the only ones to have won Stanley Cups in that decade.

Team Canada management came from the same ranks, with Montreal's Sam Pollock in charge of everything, Philadelphia's Keith Allen and Montreal's Toe Blake serving as his assistants, and Montreal's Scotty Bowman as head coach with Halifax Voyageurs' Al MacNeil, Boston's Don Cherry and Bobby Kromm of the WHA's Winnipeg Jets as assistants. Syl Apps and Jean Béliveau were "special advisers" so we didn't go short of hockey talent or inspiration.

We were short of Toronto representation, but that was a perennial problem ever since the Leafs had fallen on tough times. Lanny and I were the only Leafs on Team Canada and hyperconscious of that fact. The most unfortunate of Harold Ballard's legacies would not be his steadfast refusal to have the Soviets or other international teams play on his rink; rather the fact that Toronto's decades-long lack of success meant that Toronto fans were pretty much excluded from a more personal stake in Canada Cups and other headline international hockey competitions. The blue-and-white heroes never really seemed to be good enough for Team Canada or Team NHL, even though Paul Henderson had been the hero of the 1972 Hockey Summit.

Therefore the two of us definitely had our share of the pressure, knowing that the Toronto media and fans would put our every move under the microscope. Imagine the disappointment if we didn't make it! So Lanny and I went to the Canada Cup training camp very much feeling like underdogs, thinking we could make it, but not quite sure, given that we'd be competing against such established offensive stars as Clarke, Gilbert Perreault, Pete Mahovlich, Phil Esposito and Marcel Dionne at center, and Rick Martin, Reg Leach, Bill Barber, René Robert, Bobby Hull, Guy Lafleur, Jean Pronovost, Danny Gare and Steve Shutt on the wing.

The odds did not look good, but we both were determined to do our best and let the chips fall where they may. Then Lanny made a lot of enemies in the French media during an intra-squad game when he hit Serge Savard with a solid and legal bodycheck. Savard sustained a leg injury, though he came back to play in the series. The way the Montreal media played it up you'd swear that Lanny was working for the KGB with a mission to take out as many true true-blue Canadian hockey players as he could before he was sent packing back to Toronto when the "serious twenty-five" players were named to the official roster. It was an anxious day of French-to-English translations of the sports pages for the only two Maple Leafs in camp.

The memories flood back of that series in Montreal. The 1972 and 1974 NHL and WHA showdowns had opened the door, but both of those series were one-on-one with the Soviets. This was the first series in which the best Canadian team would meet international superstars in a true test of international supremacy.

In a lot of ways, it was the series of the Bobbys, Orr and Hull. Although Hull had competed for the WHA All-Star team in 1974, this was Bobby Orr's first and last exposure to international hockey. I knew him very well from my involvement in the Orr-Walton sports camp in the summer; he was a good friend and a great competitor on the ice. Of all the hockey players I played against, including Wayne Gretzky and Gordie Howe, Bobby Orr sticks out in my mind more than anyone else. No one dominated on the ice the way he did. His sheer control of the game was amazing and, at the same time, he was the most exciting player of our generation.

That's no slander against Guy Lafleur or anybody else—they were all great players. But for the short period of time between 1968 and 1974 before his knees gave in, Bobby Orr was the best I've seen. He was the big story of 1976, especially for the Europeans who had heard so much about him. One enduring memory was of a bus trip back to Montreal from Quebec City after an exhibition game. I can see him sitting there all the way back to Montreal with huge ice packs on both knees, to get the swelling down so he could make it back out again for the next game.

He was a special hockey player, and he remains a very special person to this day. The following spring, he was at home watching the Leafs play the Penguins in a playoff series. We were ahead late in the contest, the Penguins had pulled their goalie and Lanny already had two goals in the bank when we broke away together late in the game. It was the most natural thing for me to feed Lanny for his hat trick.

The puck had hardly settled in the empty net when our telephone rang in Mississauga and Wendy answered. It was Bobby Orr.

"I was just watching the game on television," he said, "and I thought I'd tell you what a nice gesture that was by Darryl—setting up Lanny for that third goal." Needless to say, both Sittlers were thrilled with that accolade.

Bobby Orr was the quietest, shyest hero. He had won everything there was to win, and twice led the NHL in scoring, as a defenseman, an unheard-of feat. But you'd never know it from skating with him in practice or warm up, or seeing him with adoring kids at his sports camp. It was almost as if God had said: "I'm going to make the perfect hockey player," and then had to build a wee structural weakness in the knees just to make him human.

Bobby Hull, on the other hand, was the picture of health in 1976. I remember that because I was there in Montreal for nearly all of August and September; running up and down Mount Royal, training, doing stress tests and exercises, on and off the ice. We'd learned from the surprise of 1972, when the Soviets had shown Team Canada that two or three weeks of scrimmaging was no substitute for serious preparation for an international tournament. Now in 1976, here was Bobby Hull leading the way, one of the oldest players on the team but his body a finely-tuned machine that left many much younger athletes far behind. The lessons he taught during that preparation period stayed with me for a long time—maximum effort included off-ice preparation and led to enhanced on-ice performance. Late in my career, when I was as much as fifteen years older than some of my teammates, I still placed in the top three on my team in the conditioning tests year after year. Bobby Hull's example had proved to me that it was possible.

That whole experience for me, as I look back and analyze it, was comparable to my first training camp with the Leafs as a rookie. Here I was sitting in the same dressing room as Orr and Hull, and even though I'd played in the league for six years, I still felt like a kid as I looked around at my new teammates ... Bobby Clarke, Phil Esposito, Serge Savard, Rogie Vachon. I *was* a rookie again. There was also Denis Potvin and Larry Robinson who were a year younger than I was, and already famous. One thing about such a gathering is that while you don't know if you're going to make the team or not, you're grateful just for the opportunity. Your attitude is so thoroughly positive, you'll do whatever they ask you to do. You won't miss a curfew. And you'll do what it takes to keep yourself keen all the way through.

The toughest problem in such an event is organizational; players from eighteen or twenty teams have been brought together, and not just any players; these are the stars and the power-play specialists on their own teams, and suddenly they are being asked to play different roles. Players handle that differently; some can accept it, others have trouble dealing with it. Just as thorny is the problem of heavy representation from three or four very successful teams—all with distinctive and very different playing styles. Which style will be best suited to beating the Russians? And will the players of the other two or three top teams be willing to adapt to that style? Will their coach be disappointed that a top coaching rival is calling the shots?

We had players from the Flyers, with Clarke, Barber and Leach, who were good offensively but also great defensively. Then there were Gainey, Shutt, Lafleur and Mahovlich of the Canadiens, much the same as the Flyers with more speed, and the wide-open, purely offensive French Connection line of Buffalo that represented other styles and temperaments. And you knew that place would be found for individuals like Esposito, Hull and Dionne.

It was my first experience with Scotty Bowman and I enjoyed it immensely. What I liked most about him was his up-tempo practices, everything was bang, bang, bang at high speed. His abilities behind the bench were superb too, he seemed to be able to get everybody into the game quickly. He was a good bench jockey; he'd play you at center or left wing, but he got you in there. Most importantly for Lanny and myself, Scotty was scrupulously fair about ice time given to all players and no one came away feeling he hadn't been given a full opportunity to make the final roster.

Many of the players at the Team Canada training camp practiced and played with one eye on the calendar, each of us having mentally drawn a big, red circle around the date September 1. That was the day the final lineup would be announced, and Team Canada would open the first Canada Cup series the next evening in Ottawa against Finland. The four European teams came to North America with their tournament lineups, having made their cuts back home. Team USA also had some moves to make, but their top twenty-five in a talent-thin camp was a foregone conclusion.

That left us, and we knew it every time we suited up for an exhibition game. The problem we had was that everybody was doing so well. Our first two exhibition games were back-to-back contests against the Americans in Quebec City. It was 7-3 for us in the first and 10-3 in the second, with lots of changes in each lineup. Back in Montreal, we dumped the Czechs 7-4 and looked good again, although there was some suspicion that they might be playing possum.

This was no ordinary team from Czechoslovakia; after the Soviets had won the Olympic gold medal at Innsbruck, Austria, that February, the Czechs came back to win the World Championship at

Katowice, Poland, and looked very strong doing it. The team that came to North America that summer included three Stastny brothers, Peter, Marian and—no, not Anton—big brother Bohuslav; Milan Novy, Milan Chalupa, Jiri Bubla, Miroslav Dvorak, Frantisek Cernik, Ivan Hlinka, Frantisek Pospisil, Bohuslav Ebermann, and two tough goalies in Jiri Holecek and Vladimir Dzurilla.

They were quickly established as our main competition because the Soviets, inexplicably, passed up on their chance to win the Canada Cup by leaving many of their best veterans at home: Aleksandr Yakushev, Boris Mikhailov, Vladimir Petrov, Yuri Liapkin, Gennadi Tsygankov, and their second-best goalie, Aleksandr Sidelnikov. Valeri Kharlamov, who had impressed so many Canadian hockey fans just four years before, had been eagerly awaited but was in Moscow hospital recovering from injuries suffered in an automobile accident. What came to North America was a very young team, and even the great Anatoli Tarasov was quoted in the newspapers as saying Soviet fans were upset because so much talent had been left at home.

Of the three remaining teams, the Swedes remained the biggest mystery, not because we didn't recognize some of their players, but because we couldn't gauge their relative strength as a team. With Borje Salming, Inge Hammarström, Thommie Bergman, Anders Hedberg, Ulf Nilsson, Juha Widing, Per-Olav Brasar, Willy Lindstrom, Dan Labraaten, Lar-Erik Sjoberg and the Abrahamsson brothers, we knew that the nucleus would be strong.

The Finns and Americans were both a couple of years away. On Team Finland, we recognized Matti Hagman, Pekka Rautakallio, Tapio Levo, Heikki Rilhiranta and goalie Markus Mattson, but that was all. And Team USA that year had many familiar names: Mike Milbury, Lee Fogolin, Rick Chartraw, Bill Nyrop, Robbie Ftorek, the Bennett brothers Harvey and Curt, Craig Patrick, Gary Sargent, Lou Nanne, Mike Curran and Pete LoPresti. But they had no firepower, and General Manager Bob Pulford and Coach Harry Neale knew that their team would have to play tight-checking hockey to have any chance of winning. But tight-checking hockey rarely wins international tournaments, even on the smaller North American rinks, so, in essence, this was going to be a four-team competition.

The only question left was, would Lanny and I make the team? Wednesday, September 1 dawned as a beautiful late-summer day but it was excruciatingly quiet at the Bonaventure Hotel as thirty-five athletes anxiously awaited the word. Mercifully, it wasn't long in coming: René Robert, Jean Pronovost, Paul Shmyr, Dave Burrows and two of my former London junior teammates, Dan Maloney and Dan Bouchard, were told that they wouldn't be playing. Lanny and I had made it and we permitted ourselves brief congratulatory smiles and high fives. That was all, though, because we opened against Finland the following night in Ottawa. Also, making the top twenty-five did not necessarily mean making the starting lineup. That was the next step up the ladder.

On Thursday night, September 2, I was in the lineup but Lanny wasn't as we steamrolled the unfortunate Finns 11-2. Goalie Antti Leppanen didn't know what hit him as Orr, Esposito, Clarke, Martin, Perreault, Dionne, Mahovlich, Lafleur, Shutt and Hull stormed the barricades. The Finns barely escaped on our first three shifts, and then it began in earnest. Matti Hagman took a hooking penalty at 3:15 and half a minute later, Rick Martin opened the floodgates, scoring on a pass from Lafleur and Lapointe. Another two-and-a-half minutes later, Bobby Hull took a pass from Orr and it was 2-0. Then Hull and Orr combined to feed Esposito thirty-three seconds later and Leppanen was sitting on the Finnish bench, with youngster Markus Mattsson replacing him.

Bobby Hull scored another and Finland got one from Lasse Oksanen and it was 4-1 after twenty minutes. Carl Brewer, an assistant coach for Finland, said after the game that it was men playing against boys, and it didn't help that the Finns were starstruck by all the NHL names facing them.

We added a pair of goals in the second and five in the third; I closed out the scoring with a shorthanded breakaway while Jim Watson was off serving a penalty. Like Paul Henderson before me in 1972, I was another Maple Leaf who would get into the habit of scoring late in hockey games. The next night, Sweden handled the U.S. 5-2 and the Czechs downed the Soviets 5-3. This was going to be a very interesting tournament.

One of the advantages of staging your own tournament, as Alan Eagleson and his international counterparts will tell you, is that you generally get to set your own schedule. And, if you're very smart, you'll generally plan it so that your toughest opponents have a tough row to hoe.

That proved the case for the Soviets. They had started against the

Czechs at the Forum on Friday night, September 3, and came back against the Swedes on Sunday afternoon in the same building. The Swedes took a 2-0 lead in the first period, with Borje Salming scoring the second goal with the Soviets down two men; but by the midway point of the third, the Forum scoreboard read CCCP 3, Sweden 2, and it looked like both teams would have 1-1 records after their first two games. However, with just under three minutes remaining, Anders Hedberg got a clean breakaway and beat Vladislav Tretiak high to the blocker side. That tie basically eliminated the Soviets after only two games. In Toronto, the Czechs walked over the Finns as expected, 8-0, and we came back that night in the second half of the Forum doubleheader to edge a stubborn and totally unimpressed Team USA 4-2. We jumped out to a 3-0 first-period lead and then needed my empty-net goal with thirteen seconds left to put the game away. We outshot them 36-16 but Pete LoPresti shut us down for two whole periods and singlehandedly permitted his team to get back into the game.

There was bad news mixed in with the good; Bobby Clarke missed the game with a strained Achilles tendon, and we lost his regular-season teammate, Jim Watson, for the tournament in the first period when he was struck above his right eye by a Gary Sargent slapshot.

Two days later, the Soviets, still in Montreal, finally got a rest in an 11-3 shellacking of the hapless Finns, while we travelled to Toronto to meet the puzzling Swedes. Scotty Bowman read the warning signs from the American game and sat out two big scorers, Reggie Leach and Danny Gare, and inserted two better defensive players, Bob Gainey and Lanny McDonald. Lanny and I had big smiles on our faces in the pre-game player introductions when Maple Leaf Gardens fans arose in a tumultuous standing ovation for one of their own . . . Borje Salming. Some of the Canadian players were a bit put out by this fan reaction, but we understood it, we played with Borje all year long and knew what he meant to our team and to Toronto hockey fans. It was quite something to see the amazement on the faces of some of Salming's Swedish teammates; this never happened in other countries in their experience, and the players who weren't in the WHA and NHL began to understand how well North American fans had accepted foreign players. By the way, Lanny and I were rewarded with standing ovations of our own.

Another reason we smiled during Borje's introduction is that we knew our regular-season teammate was in for special treatment that

night. Our scouts had told us that he was the key to the Swedish
attack and that we were going to have to forecheck him aggressively
all night. Scotty Bowman went over his instructions in the pre-game
meeting: "The left wings have to play in his face. Don't let him get
started; get on him in his own end and stay on him."

Bobby Hull sounded the charge in the first period when he delivered several crunching checks on Salming. Well-built and powerful,
Hull was quite capable of playing physically but he rarely initiated
contact. Tonight, however, was what Scotty had called extraordinary
circumstances and Hull crunched Borje at every opportunity with
checks that someone said "would stop a Clydesdale."

We had also learned something when Anders Hedberg broke away
and tied the score late in the Soviet game; Hedberg was poison with
the puck, his Winnipeg teammate Hull reminded us over and over.
Tonight, however, he was up against the best defensive winger in the
game, maybe in hockey history, in Bob Gainey—a man who could
hit him cleanly and consistently all night long, and still outskate the
Swede by several strides whenever he had to.

How well did Gainey and Hull do their jobs? We won 4-0; Hull
scored our first goal and Gainey the checker scored a pair, playing on
a line with Lanny and me. Canada was 3-0 and leading the tournament because Bob Pulford and Harry Neale must have had a defensive plan of their own that same night; Team USA and
Czechoslovakia tied 4-4 at the Spectrum in Philadelphia. Then
again, maybe the Soviet Red Army had told the Czechs about the
building and an exhibition game with the Flyers early in the New
Year nine months before. Truth be known, the final result flattered
the Czechs who needed a quick whistle by Bruce Hood nullifying a
Robbie Ftorek goal late in the third to escape with the tie.

The surprises continued two nights later. First, the Finns found
the Winnipeg Arena to their liking, even though it was the regular-
season home of Anders Hedberg, Ulf Nilsson and Lars-Erik Sjoberg, and outlasted their fierce Scandinavian rivals 8-6. The Swedes
were guilty of looking ahead to their next game against Czechoslovakia, and found themselves with a 2-2 record. That same night, the
Soviets returned to the Spectrum with a vengeance, erasing the bad
memories of January with a 5-0 whitewash of the game against the
overmatched Americans.

But nobody was talking about those two games. All conversations
in Canada started with: "Did you see that game? Ever seen anything

like it?" The tournament's only two undefeated teams had met at the Forum and when it was over, the score read The Fat Man 1, Team Canada 0.

Vladimir Dzurilla was a thirty-five-year-old veteran who looked more like a jovial performing bear with the Moscow Circus than a goalie with the Czechoslovakian national team. But he hadn't been a goalie with the team for a long time; in fact, he had come out of a four-year retirement to play in the Canada Cup. (Move over Guy Lafleur.) Dzurilla must have decided that we weren't going to score that day. And we didn't, even though Bobby Hull, myself, Reg Leach twice, Phil Esposito and Lanny all had gilt-edged chances.

In our end, Rogie Vachon was almost as good in the wide-open, up-and-down contest, finally succumbing at 15:41 of the third period to a goal by Milan Novy. I wasn't too happy, he was my check and I had let him knock me off the puck at our blueline seconds before he took a return pass from Vladimir Martinec to beat Vachon.

The upshot was we were in second place, half a game behind the Czechs and half a game ahead of the Soviets who, reports had it, were peaking. Had we won against the Czechs, we would have automatically been in the best-of-three final. Now we had to tie or beat the Soviets to make it that far.

A lot of surprises awaited hockey fans on Saturday, September 11. The Americans, the only winless team in the tournament, doubled the Finns 6-3 at the Forum and the Swedes rebounded with a 2-1 win against the Czechs in Quebec City. It didn't change anything in the standings, however, because the Swedes' earlier loss to the Finns had virtually eliminated them, and the Czechs' victory against us had guaranteed them a place in the final. We would play the Czechs, unless we lost to the Soviets. Then it would be a CCCP-CSSR final and tournament organizers would tear out their hair in clumps.

When we lined up for the pre-game introductions at Maple Leaf Gardens, nobody on our side was thinking about the veterans the Soviets had left at home, although across the ice, Viktor Tikhonov might have been regretting that decision now that his team had a chance to go all the way.

My most outstanding memory of that game was that this was Scotty Bowman at his best. He simply overwhelmed Tikhonov with his line changes and his line shuffles. Lanny and I stayed together most of the night, but we were out with different centers on almost every shift. Early in the game, Gil Perreault played with us, and then he moved over to pivot Hull and Lafleur while we played several shifts with Phil Esposito. Then Perreault played with Hull and Dionne.

It was only fitting that the Sabres' star scored our opening goal on a power play at 7:08 of the first, and after Vikulov tied it, Gil came back to set up Hull at 17:02. Bill Barber added an insurance goal twenty minutes later when he tipped in Guy Lapointe's point shot, and our defense of Orr, Potvin, Robinson, Lapointe and Savard shut down the Russians for the last two periods, to give us a 3-1 win.

We were in the final against the Czechs, which was not how the script had been written. Because of the 1972 series, everybody in Canada was aching for a Soviet-Canada final, but the Soviet coaching staff chickened out by leaving Kharlamov, Petrov, Mikhailov, Yakushev and Shadrin at home.

Another revision of the script took place on Monday night, September 13. After losing 1-0 in a classic to the Czechs earlier in the tournament, we turned this one into a rout at Maple Leaf Gardens, dumping them 6-0 in a game that was never in doubt after Gilbert Perreault's opening score just sixty-five seconds into the game. Gil had been cutting toward the net and looked like he was going to circle it when he caught Dzurilla by surprise with an off-balance shot. It went right through the pads, and we all sensed that the air had gone out of the Czechoslovakian balloon.

That's not a putdown of the Czech team. But they were thousands of miles away from home, the defending world champions and playing the strongest Canadian team that had ever been assembled (remember, Team Canada '72 was without Bobby Hull, Bobby Orr, and J.C. Tremblay) on North American-sized rinks. They were bound to have a letdown, even though the line of Milan Novy at center with wingers Vladimir Martinec and Josef Augusta was as tough as any you'd see in the NHL, and other players like Hlinka, Chalupa and the Stastnys were NHL sure-bets if they were ever allowed to cross the ocean. We respected the Czechs, the Soviets and the Swedes for their accomplishments in the Canada Cup and there was no question of taking anybody lightly. But, on this day, we sensed that they were ripe for the taking.

I assisted on Denis Potvin's goal at 7:56 of the first as we blew out to a 4-0 lead after twenty minutes, and Dzurilla was replaced by Holocek in nets. I later scored my third goal of the competition (I also had a pair in exhibition), all three late in the third period and all three the last goal of the game. You couldn't get later than this "cherry on top"—19:59 of the third in a game we already led 5-0.

Two nights later, we were back in Montreal and it was an entirely different kettle of fish. The 18,040 delirious fans were rocking with anticipation in the pre-game warm-ups, and when Roger Doucet sang both national anthems before the hockey game, I felt chills up and down my spine.

After the Canada Cup was over, two things stayed with me for the longest time. The first was travelling across Canada with the Maple Leafs, and having every local reporter focused on Lanny and me and our Team Canada roles. Many fans would come up, and not say something banal like "Congratulations," but "Thank you for scoring that goal." It was intensely personal, as if we had won it for them.

Even stronger, though, was the memory of Roger Doucet singing the Canadian and foreign national anthems before every game. It blew people away, the way he mastered all of those languages. And every time we went back to the Forum, his anthems would rekindle those memories.

The last strains of his own special version of the anthem ". . . for rights and liberty . . . ," which even made Prime Minister Pierre Elliott Trudeau smile, had barely faded when we went right at the Czechs and Jiri Holocek in nets. We were puzzled to see him there, even though Vladimir Dzurilla had been bombed for four first-period goals in the previous game and replaced. We figured that Dzurilla would be rested and back for Game Two.

He was, but it took two quick goals by Perreault and Esposito in the first three minutes and nine seconds to relegate Holocek to the bench. Out rumbled Dzurilla and our quick burst was over. The game settled down to a real struggle and, for the longest time, Rogie Vachon held the Czechs from getting closer to us, while Dzurilla prevented us from getting the all-important third goal that would put it away. Rogie blinked first, at 9:44 of the second when Novy scored, and again at 2:14 of the third when Marian Stastny tied the game. Bobby Clarke came back with a power-play goal at 7:48 to restore our lead and we settled down for the next dozen shifts to a seesaw defensive struggle.

Then it was the Czechs turn to pop two quick goals and silence the premature party at the Forum—Augusta at 15:01 and Marian

Stastny again at 16:00. Now there was the very real danger of a third and deciding game. Two minutes before, all we had to do was hold on to win the tournament; now, the Czechs were four minutes away from drawing even.

Time and time again in situations like this, Bobby Clarke and the Philadelphia Flyers had excelled. Any NHL team could tell you that the Flyers were at their most dangerous when they were down a goal or tied late in the third period; they always seemed able to reach down for that little extra and find that goal. I had had personal experience with this phenomenon earlier that spring when Philadelphia had eliminated us 4-3. And, although Scotty Bowman's Canadiens had eliminated Philadelphia four straight and stopped their Stanley Cup string at two, he had confidence in the tenacity of Flyer players on the Team Canada roster and sent out Clarke with Reg Leach and Bill Barber with a little more than two minutes left in the game.

It paid off. Clark and Leach worked the puck up the ice, Bill Barber took several whacks at it in the Czech crease and it was 4-4 at 17:48.

Don Cherry still tells the story of what happened next to anyone who will listen.

We played out the last two minutes of regulation time and returned to our dressing rooms for the first overtime intermission. Cherry had spent the game in the press box, scouting the opposition, and he came downstairs to find Bowman anxiously conferring with Kromm and MacNeil. He told them he had discovered something and explained it to them.

"Go in *there* and tell 'em," Bowman replied, and Cherry came into the room and got our attention.

"I've been upstairs watching this guy, Dzurilla, for three games," he began.

"He likes to come out real fast to cut down the angle on any rush. After you go in over the blueline, fake a slapper. If you see him come out of his net, draw it back in and go wide and deeper. He'll leave you with most of the net empty."

If any of the 18,040 fans in the building, and millions watching on television, thought that either team would lie back in overtime, they were wrong. The action was end-to-end and both goalies had to make four saves each by the midway point in the period. Countless other shots had been blocked or deflected away from danger as wave after wave of white shirts (us) and red shirts (them) ebbed and flowed.

Scotty was changing lines and combinations like a magician with ten arms and just after the eleven-minute mark, threw Lanny and me out with Marcel Dionne. We hadn't been on the ice for ten seconds when Lanny picked up the puck in our zone, flipped it up to Marcel and Dionne hit me in full flight just as I crossed the Czech blueline on the left side. I had the defenseman beat, but he had enough of an angle to stop me from cutting in to the net so I took a peek at Dzurilla and wound up.

Darned if Grapes wasn't a genius. Out came Dzurilla, just like clockwork. I drew the puck back, went about ten feet deeper, and wristed it into the open net.

The rest, as they say, is history.

That goal earned me a place on the tournament all-star team at left wing. Milan Novy was center and Aleksandr Maltsev of the Soviet Union was right winger. Bobby Orr and Borje Salming were the all-star defensemen and Rogie Vachon was the goalie.

Bobby Orr was the tournament MVP. Earlier in the series, Denis Potvin had made the mistake of blurting out his frustration one night when Orr was selected Player of the Game and awarded an Eskimo carving. An argument could be made for Denis as best on our team because he had played great throughout, finishing the series as our top scorer with 2 goals and 11 assists for 13 points and a plus-15 in the nine games. (Orr was 4-8—12 and plus-9 and led all players with 36 shots on net.)

But Bobby Orr's first international appearance, and the history of his battered knees, had reached the status of Canadian hockey folklore and Denis would have to wait his turn. In all honesty, I believe he had immediately regretted the comment, but felt even worse about it a couple of days later when Serge Savard presented him with a stuffed walrus in an impromptu on-ice ceremony during one of our practices.

"Denis, you haven't won an Eskimo carving; but we think you should have one and here it is." That cracked up everybody.

The series was finally over and we had won, and the emotion swept over everybody in the building. Somebody told me that Bobby Hull hugged Dzurilla and gave him a big smack on the cheek. A bunch of Czechs surrounded Bobby Orr, patting him on his back and making pulling motions with their sweaters. And then both teams came together with players trading sweaters; I got Bohuslav Ebermann's No. 25 and somewhere in Czechoslovakia he has my No. 27 today. I was wearing the CSSR sweater when Rocket Richard presented me with the Player of the Game Eskimo carving.

When Pierre Trudeau finally presented the Canada Cup to captain Bobby Clarke, the spectators were greeted by a victory lap of "Czech" players with the trophy. I can't remember ever feeling as I did then after a hockey game; I still get chills fifteen years later thinking about that scene and the great hockey players out there with me. The emotion was beyond words.

Other memories stand out in my mind.

After I scored the goal, the whole team surrounded me out on the ice and we went into a group hug with Lanny leading the world in oxygen-threatening squeezes, and hollering. Right in the middle of the scrum I heard a very familiar voice, but not one that belonged on skates in full uniform. It was the Eagle, and he was one of the first guys out, having jumped over the glass.

"Darryl, let me grab your stick," he said. "You'll want to hold onto it; one of these guys will get it and you'll never get it back." (There were several fans on the ice who had eluded security, a rarity at the Forum.) So I gave it to Al for safekeeping.

We got back to Toronto, and the season started. Every now and then, I'd mention casually: "Alan, you got that stick?"

"Yeah, it's in a safe place."

I didn't want to push him, after all, the Canada Cup was his baby. I knew that stick was special to him, but I hadn't given it to him; Alan had taken it with a "let me hold your stick for you" story.

I let it go for a while. Now, Alan and I were close but we did have our differences along the way. Anyway, I asked Alan about the stick on several more occasions but I didn't get it. I'd mention it at a Christmas party or a meeting and he would slough it off; I'd make a snide remark or a joke about it and then drop the subject.

I discussed the matter a couple of times with Wendy and she knew how this was starting to bother me. So on my thirtieth birthday—a full four years later because I'd scored the winning goal against the Czechs three days before my twenty-sixth—Wendy was trying to think of a very special gift she could get for me. The lightbulb went on and she called Alan Eagleson.

She was sweet as sugar pie and acted all innocent. "Alan, you know that stick you took from Darryl on the ice after they'd won the

Canada Cup? You know what I'd like to do for his thirtieth birth-day? I'd like to give that to him as a very special present."

Dead silence at the end of the line. Then, "Uh, okay, but I won't be able to get up to you, I'm real busy and I'm catching an overseas flight tonight." This was the day before my birthday.

"That's okay! I'll come down and get it." Nobody can sound more positive or enthusiastic than Wendy.

The next day I got my stick for my birthday, with a little poem:

> To Someone Very Special, who is also very dear
> A present that is part of your Super Career,
> I know it's not costly, but the sentiment is there
> I called Al and told him, I thought it only fair.
> I've got just the place to hang it up
> You guessed it! It's your stick from the Canada Cup!
> I'll always remember that Wonderful Goal
> It couldn't have been scored, by a more Worthy Soul!
>
> Happy 30th!
> From those who love you the most
> Wendy, Ryan & Meaghan.

Al hasn't said a word about the stick since.

Another story involved the Prime Minister and his wife, Margaret Trudeau. About six weeks after the tournament ended, there was a special reception for Team Canada in Ottawa on November 29 and the whole team was invited, but NHL schedules being what they are, only a few of us could make it—Lanny, myself, Larry Robinson, a few others and our wives. We first went to 24 Sussex Drive to meet the Trudeau family, and then took a bus from there over to the hall where the banquet was going to be. They were expecting about 1,000 people.

When we arrived at the hall, we mingled during a pre-dinner reception when Alan Eagleson came up to me: "Bobby Clarke didn't make it. We'd like you to speak on behalf of the team." So there I would be, giving a speech to some of the top politicians in Canada, and sitting at the PM's head table.

Alan turned to Wendy. "You're sitting beside the Prime Minister." She was horrified; she has never felt comfortable with public atten-tion under normal circumstances, and she was extremely nervous. How do you talk with the Prime Minister on his own level?

I sat beside Margaret Trudeau and we talked about kids and other related family subjects. The whole time we were conversing, I was trying to think about what I was going to say to the crowd when the time came to speak. But what with dinner and an endless flow of people coming by for autographs, I didn't have the opportunity to prepare anything.

A little later, Senator Keith Davey, an avid hockey fan, stopped by. Canada was going through a difficult period for unity—René Lévesque and the Parti Québécois had just been elected—and he said to me: "I don't know what you're going to talk about tonight; but if you could mention team unity in your speech, you'll bring the place down."

I scribbled a few basic notes and talked about how players had come together from many different teams and backgrounds, French and English, joining in training camp and working together with a single, common goal: to win the Canada Cup. Going into the Canada Cup that year, a Quebec City lawyer named Guy Bertrand had even suggested the formation of a Team Quebec.

It was a unity speech: French and English working together and winning. It brought the place down.

"What about Darryl for Prime Minister?" somebody quipped.

Ironically, a few weeks later, Margaret Trudeau was involved in that episode with the Rolling Stones at the El Mocambo club in Toronto. I figured we must have been talking about the wrong topics at the dinner table: kids, the cottage . . . family life.

With the number of Cups that have been played since 1976, and the fifteen or so World Championships held since then, it's strange how '72 and '76 stick out in the minds of most Canadian hockey fans. It is true that 1981 was a total wipeout because of the disappointing loss to the Soviets in the final. But 1984 and 1987 were no slouches, with Paul Coffey's play that set up the overtime winner against the Soviets in the '84 semi-final in Calgary, and the Gretzky-to-Lemieux goal that won in Hamilton in 1987. But those first two series had an intensity and national interest that haven't been matched.

The 1976 Canada Cup was the peak of my international career; I would play in the ill-fated Challenge Cup of 1979 and two World Championships in Sweden and Germany, but it would never quite be the same.

In 1981 I was invited to the Canada Cup training camp, held again in Montreal. I was five years older and Lanny was en route to Calgary after two years with Colorado. The tournament was being played a year late because the 1980 Cup had been postponed to protest the Soviet invasion of Afghanistan. Thirty-five players were invited and I trained very hard that summer with the intention to give it my best shot to make the team. This was a new generation; Clarke, Esposito, Hull and Orr had been replaced by the Bossy, Trottier, Sutter, and a guy named Gretzky. Rogie Vachon was gone, too, replaced by the likes of Mike Liut and Pete Peeters.

A lot of water had passed under my personal bridge since the excitement and satisfaction of the 1976 Canada Cup. The Leafs and I were close to parting company, as well. I played all right in a few exhibition games.

We stayed at the Château Champlain during that training camp and the Flames' Cliff Fletcher was in charge of personnel. We had just returned to the hotel after an exhibition game that night—and there was a message at the desk to see him up in his room. There were messages for a couple of other guys, Minnesota's Steve Payne among them.

A player can sense when he might not make it, and that the axe may come down on him. In these situations it's as hard on the GM and the coach doing the cutting as it is on the player accepting it because of the stature he has in the league. I can remember going up the elevator knowing what was coming. And when Fletcher opened the door to my knock, I could tell by the look on his face that this was something that he didn't really want to do. He was going to try to make it as gentle as he could.

"Darryl, it's a numbers game; you had a good camp but we had a meeting of the minds and decided that we're going to go with some other guys." He paused. "I want to thank you for your contribution. We feel with your experience and your past involvement with the Canada Cup, that if you'd like to stay on, we'd like to have you in a scouting-type capacity."

It was a way to salvage my public image and pride, and I had mixed feelings for a few seconds. However, it was best to make a clean break.

"It's nice of you to offer me that, but I was here to try to make the team; I didn't, and now I've got to get my mind focused on the coming season. This gives me a couple more weeks to spend with my family and get ready for training camp."

"Take some time to think about it. If you want at any point to change your mind, let us know," Fletcher replied. When team management had initially announced the Team Canada training camp roster, I hadn't been included. I was picked a day later when they added a couple of players, and there was talk about the Alan Eagleson influence in player selection. The other story was that Eagleson hadn't insisted on the presence of his clients, but pointed out to the selection committee that it might be a good marketing idea to have a Maple Leaf or two in camp.

Many hockey experts believe that if Paul Henderson and I hadn't scored the series-winning goals in '72 and '76, Toronto would have no history at all in international hockey. If you look at all of the teams—'72, '76, '79, '81, '84, '87—you'll see that Canadiens didn't go in ones and twos to training camp, they went in fives, sixes, and sevens. Likewise the Flyers, Bruins, and later, the Islanders and Oilers. Any discussion with higher-ups in the NHL that turns to the Toronto situation tends to become very animated. The Toronto Maple Leafs franchise is critical for the league's global success and that is why none of the league executives ever laughed publicly at Harold's antics. Ballard, in their eyes, ruined one of the league's proudest franchises for two decades—an entire generation—and, in the process, maligned the entire league.

Another consideration for team management when I was released was the Toronto media's reaction to the news. I did my best to ensure that there would be no negativity; the tone was: "I gave it my best shot—the guys still there are better than me and I pushed them to extremes to beat me out. Good Luck Team Canada. I hope you win, I'm behind you. I'm a fan."

Maybe we need to revise the terminology used to describe such situations. It might have been the first time I'd been "cut" in my life. When we use that word the way the public uses it, it sounds as if someone is being brutally discarded or "amputated" from the team. But, with an all-star contingent like Team Canada, in effect, you weren't cut. You were given an opportunity to try with thirty-six other guys to earn one of twenty-five places. It was an honor even to be invited to try out. How could I put this in perspective? Simply by saying that if I'm the thirty-seventh guy sitting at home and I haven't been invited to camp, I wouldn't worry about the indignity of being cut. I just wouldn't have been part of it. But people tend not to look at the situation in the same way as they do for a player who was invited, but didn't make the final twenty-five-man roster.

I could have refused to go to training camp and said something like: "I've had my shot at the Canada Cup, I've enjoyed it, let the younger guys have a chance at it."

The other side of the coin was sitting there with other players who'd been left off the team, such as Steve Payne, and listening to his cursing and disappointment: "I'll never try out for Team Canada ever again. I wasted my summer, I wasted my time." This was a player aged twenty-two or twenty-three at the time, a major contributor on his own team, who had a tough time adjusting to the disappointment. I sat there, trying to work it out with him: "Steve, let's try to turn this thing around," but he wouldn't buy the argument. In his eyes, I'd been through it once in 1976, had all the glory and won the thing in overtime. So I'd experienced both ends of it while he'd never had the chance.

I played on a 1979 Challenge Cup team that came to a very unpopular end, and a couple of World Championship Team Canadas that were pretty well ignored back home because Canadians were all concentrating on Stanley Cup play.

Add all the highs and lows together, and I wouldn't have missed any of these experiences for the world.

7

A Night to Remember

THE ENTRY FOR Dave Reece in the Retired Goaltender Index of *The National Hockey League Official Guide & Record Book* is as succinct as it gets:

Seasons:	1
NHL teams:	Boston
First season:	1975-76
Last season:	1975-76
Playoffs:	None
Games played:	14
Wins:	7
Losses:	5
Ties:	2
Minutes played:	777
Goals allowed:	43
Shutouts:	2
Goals against avg.:	3.32

All I can tell you about are the last 11 of the 43 goals Dave Reece allowed, and the last 60 of the 773 minutes of hockey he played in the National Hockey League.

February 7, 1976, a Saturday night, was my finest and most productive hour in the NHL, and Dave's last. These two points are related.

The 1975-76 season was a growing year for the Maple Leafs. All of our young talent, especially the Big Six, was coming together under the benevolent tutelage of Red Kelly and we were showing flashes of future greatness. We were good and young, and getting better and more experienced in every game; we felt we were about a step, or two impact players, away from challenging the Canadiens, Bruins, Islanders and Flyers at the top of the league.

The previous season's arrival of Washington and Kansas City in the NHL had resulted in new conference and divisional alignments. Instead of East and West divisions of eight teams each, there now were four divisions—Norris, Adams, Patrick and Smythe—aligned in the Prince of Wales and Clarence Campbell conferences. I would caution today's hockey fan not to take that alignment for granted; in those days the Norris (Montreal, Detroit, Los Angeles, Pittsburgh and Washington) and Adams (Boston, Buffalo, Toronto, California) divisions were in the Wales Conference and the Patrick (Philadelphia, Rangers, Islanders, Atlanta) and Smythe (Vancouver, St. Louis, Chicago, Minnesota, Kansas City) were in the Campbell Conference, an arrangement that would be altered again in 1979 when the four ex-WHA teams joined the NHL.

So, when we skated onto the Gardens ice that Saturday night against the Boston Bruins, we were playing a division rival in a four-point game. As Adams divisional rivals went, the Bruins were the best; they would go on to win the division ahead of Buffalo and ourselves, and the team in travelling black that night was on a seven-game winning streak. Bobby Orr was injured and out of the lineup, but the veteran defense of Darryl Edestrand, Dallas Smith, Al Sims, Gary Doak, and Brad Park was still a formidable one.

There was a problem, however. Gilles Gilbert, the goalie who had carried most of the workload that season, was out with an injury and Boston was very weak in nets in the minor leagues. In fact, after the fine Eddie Johnston-Gerry Cheevers tandem had been broken up in the early 1970s when Cheevers moved to the Cleveland Crusaders of the WHA, the Bruins had been a team in search of solid netminding. All sorts of has-beens and never-weres drifted in and out of the Boston nets—Jacques Plante, Ross Brooks, Ken Broderick—but Gilles Gilbert, a Quebec City native, was definitely the number-one man. His backup for most of the 1975-76 season was Dave Reece.

The Bruins knew that Reece would not be the answer during a long injury layoff for Gilbert, so they swung a deal that saw Cheevers return to Boston. The game at Maple Leaf Gardens was his first in a Boston sweater since the Bruins' 1971-72 Stanley Cup clinching victory. However, Cheese hadn't played in several weeks, and wasn't going to play that night.

The call would go to Reece, but everyone knew that Don Cherry and Harry Sinden would do everything possible to get Cheevers into game shape for the stretch drive and the playoffs.

Psychologists say that memories of major events in our lives are sharper than those of lesser events. That stands to reason, because we want to remember significant things, that's just being human. I remember quite a bit about the events of February 7, 1976, but not everything. In reconstructing that game in this chapter, I have enjoyed the benefits of NHL official statistics and videotapes of all of the goals to help me.

I also have the benefits of a hockey player's usual superstitions to guide me. If you believe in superstition or fate or destiny, it was all alive and cooking that night. The "numbers" in that game were amazing.

I went through my normal pre-game routine that Saturday: morning skate, return home for a meal between one and two o'clock in the afternoon, and then a two-hour nap. The exception was my pre-game meal; instead of the usual pasta, I bought some Swiss Chalet barbecued chicken, still a favorite of mine. I left home at about 5:15 and was at the rink at six o'clock or so. I distinctly remember what I wore that night, for the simple reason that the outfit became my "lucky" clothes of 1976—a tan suit and tie combination. Tan may not be anyone's first pick for a lucky color, but on this night I would score a National Hockey League–record ten points. I would also wear the same suit two months later, on the night I scored five goals against the Flyers in a playoff game.

If you like superstition or numerology (things always happen in threes, right?), you'll be interested in this piece of news: I wore that tie on one other special occasion in 1976. During the Canada Cup competition, all of the players were given official team sports jackets and ties. On the night of the final game against Czechoslovakia at the Forum in Montreal, I cast aside my Team Canada tie and wore my tan one. It clashed with the outfit, but I scored the goal that clinched the Canada Cup in overtime. Don't tell me about the laws of probability—I go with what works.

All the numbers were positive for me that night in February; we were playing on the seventh day of the second month, the Bruins were on a seven-game winning streak, and we were in second place. The game started at 8:07 and officially ended at 10:27 p.m. I scored my first hat trick at the 10:27 mark of the second period, and my ninth point at 9:27 of the third. Just coincidence, right?

You'll never convince me.

Perhaps the strangest thing about the numbers game that night was the fact that the numbers were all supposed to belong to other players. Bruins' captain Johnny Bucyk came into the game looking for the point that would move him into second place among all-time NHL scorers that night. And classy Jean Ratelle, the closest thing the league had seen to my childhood idol, Jean Béliveau, since his retirement in 1971, was after his 350th NHL goal.

On the game sheet, this was game #479 of the season; in NHL history it was #13,529. It stands today as the only league game in which a player has scored in double digits.

With all of those numbers staring you in the face, you'd figure that this was either an end-to-end offensive blowout, or a very tense, physical game full of fights and emotion. It was neither.

It started out very tentatively and very defensively. The Bruins, or as Don Cherry liked to call them, the Boston Lunch Pail Athletic Club, weren't banging as hard as they usually did; they seemed content to protect their rookie goalie and wait for the openings. This was no longer the overwhelming offensive machine of the halcyon Orr-Esposito days. Big Phil and defenseman Carol Vadnais had moved over to Broadway in exchange for Ratelle and Brad Park. Still, Boston would boast the league's fifth-best offense that year, trailing Philadelphia, Pittsburgh, Montreal and Buffalo. The firepower provided by Ratelle, Bucyk and their linemate Bobby Schmautz, as well as by Ken Hodge, André Savard, Wayne Cashman and Terry O'Reilly, was more than adequate.

We opened the scoring and I got my first point in the seventh minute of the first period. We broke quickly out of our zone three-on-three and as I crossed my own blueline up the middle, I spotted Lanny McDonald steaming up the right wing. I fired it up to him and he chugged down the wing, scoring on a wristshot from the face-off circle to Reece's left. You really couldn't fault the rookie; Lanny beat a lot of veteran goaltenders with that heavy wristshot of his.

1.   Toronto, McDonald (Sittler)   6:19

Less than a minute later, still on the same shift, I broke out of my zone towards the left-wing boards. I had my head down to take control of the puck, and when I looked up to see the play I spotted a streak of black heading right for me. It was Brad Park, owner of the most feared hip check in the league and a guy who could really hurt you if he caught you right.

I jammed on the brakes, jumped up to avoid him and pushed the puck up to Ian Turnbull who was streaking up the boards to my left. Without breaking stride, Ian took it in over the Boston line and cranked a fifty-footer that blew by Reece into the far corner. This shot, too, would have beaten any goaltender. Ian was one of the best offensive defensemen to ever play the game, as he would prove the following year with an NHL-record five goals in one game in a 9-1 win over Detroit. (That date was 2-2-77, but we don't believe any of this numerology stuff, do we?)

2.   Toronto, Turnbull (Sittler, Thompson)   7:01

Boston had made it 2-1 (on Jean Ratelle's landmark 350th) late in the first period so it was a close game when the teams returned from the first intermission. The two most incredible periods of hockey in my career were about to begin.

Just before the three-minute mark of the middle period, Borje Salming—who had wings that night—flew into the Bruins' zone. He went deep into the face-off circle to the left of the goalie, leaning in on Darryl Edestrand and fending him off with his left arm. Just as he completed his semi-circle on the defenseman, Salming flipped the puck one-handed with his right hand. It seemed to catch Reece by surprise, hitting him on the pads and popping straight up into the air, about five feet out from the front of the net. I was standing right there and bunted it waist-high past him.

4.   Toronto, Sittler (Salming, McDonald)   2:56

Seconds after we scored, Brad Park took a boarding penalty and I faced off against Gregg Sheppard, the Bruins' top penalty-killing center, deep in Boston territory to the right of Reece. Ray Scapinello dropped the puck, I won the draw cleanly back to Borje at the left point, and he drove it through Reece's legs. We were up 4-1.

5.   Toronto, Salming (Sittler) pp   3:33

Boston came right back, and this time Johnny Bucyk got his milestone point as he and Ratelle set up Bobby Schmautz at 5:19 to make it 4-2. But we weren't going to be denied on this Saturday night. Just after eight minutes of play, I cruised into the Bruins' zone all by myself; it was near the end of the shift and I just wanted to put the puck in deep, and get back to the bench. I wound up and slapped it: it knuckled and floated through the goalie's legs.

7.   Toronto, Sittler   8:12

A scant two minutes later we were on the power play, this time with Sheppard off for slashing. Jack Valiquette put the puck behind the Boston net and George Ferguson went in and got it. He came out with the puck and put it on my stick as I came in late into the slot. I one-timed it from fifteen feet and I had my hat trick.

8.   Toronto, Sittler (Valiquette, Ferguson) pp   10:27

Somewhere about this point in the game, Grapes looked down the Bruins bench at the newly arrived Gerry Cheevers.

"It was his first game dressed, and considering his last one with us had been a Stanley Cup clincher three years before, he was probably wondering what the heck had happened in the NHL since he left. I looked him right in the eye, like a coach will do to his backup goalie when things aren't going right in a game. Sometimes the guy will nod, then you point to him and he starts getting his equipment together.

Not on this night. He figured if he could avoid eye contact, he was safe. I looked down at him, he caught the look out of the corner of his eye, and turned away. Goalies always sit on the bench with a towel around their neck, figure that one out. Anyway, Cheese took that towel and put it over his head and leaned over. He was like a little kid playing peek-a-boo with an adult. The kid figures if he hides his eyes and can't see the adult, then the adult can't see him. Gerry knew two things that night; if he didn't look at me, I couldn't see him; and he wasn't volunteering to play that game." (The next night, the Bruins shut out Detroit at home with Cheevers in the net.)

The scoring fest continued as Bucyk and Ferguson traded goals at 11:06 and 11:40 to make it 7-3, but we still weren't finished in the second period. Just before the fourteen-minute mark, I had the puck at the left wing boards near our blueline when I again spotted Lanny blasting up the right wing. I flipped it up to him and he went over their blueline and just eased it toward the net. Out of nowhere came Borje, diving full-length between two very surprised Boston defensemen. He was lying on his stomach on the ice when the puck hit his stick and deflected up and over Reece's shoulder into the net.

11.   Toronto, Salming (McDonald, Sittler)   13:57

Boston got one back before the end of the period—again Ratelle from Schmautz and Bucyk—but the only guy on our team who seemed to care was our goalie Wayne Thomas. At the second intermission it was 8-4 for us, an unheard-of score against an opponent like Boston after sixty minutes, let alone forty. I sat in the dressing room in a bit of a daze, with my best-ever night of three goals and four assists, and still a period to play! Pinch me, we're back in peewee! Nobody gets seven points in two periods. That had to be a record!

The NHL doesn't keep records for the two-thirds mark of a hockey game. Conversely, it does keep records for offensive output in a single period, but I was unaware that I was in the record book for my five points during the second period, joining Les Cunningham (Black Hawks, 1940), Max Bentley (Black Hawks, 1943) and Leo Labine (Bruins, 1954) in that category. Three other players, Dale Hawerchuk of Winnipeg, Jari Kurri of Edmonton and Pat Elynuik of Winnipeg have since matched that feat, and one has bettered it. On December 23, 1978, Bryan Trottier of the Islanders had three goals and three assists in the second period of a 9-4 win over the Rangers.

I congratulate Bryan, a durable and tremendous performer during his career. I can do that lightly because I still kept two records from that game, two records that I was about to set in the third period on February 7, 1976.

Back in the Leafs room between periods, we all sat there in awe of the feat: seven points in two periods, this thing had a life of its own. I was as awestruck as my teammates; this was much bigger than a player simply having a great night. Especially if you can fully grasp the notion that this had never, ever happened before in this league, not to Maurice Richard, not to Gordie Howe, Howie Morenz, Charlie Conacher, Eddie Shore, Phil Esposito, Bobby Orr, not to any of them. This was history in the making, and Borje (with two goals and two assists), Lanny (with a goal and two assists), and all the others were along for the amazing ride.

Was there a chance of tying the individual points record of eight for a single game? To date, only two players had ever tallied eight in a game—Maurice Richard in 1944, and his teammate Bert Olmstead, ten years later against Chicago. The bubble had to burst sometime but we still had twenty minutes remaining. As we came out onto the ice for the start of the third, I looked over at the Bruins net fully expecting to see Cheevers between the pipes. The ill-fated Reece was still there.

The answer to the question that had made the rounds of Maple Leaf Gardens during intermission was not long in coming. Boston forward Dave Forbes had taken an interference penalty at 19:44 of the second period and there hadn't been enough time remaining to get our power play in action. When we lined up to start the third period, Red Kelly was well aware of what was at stake and he sent out Lanny, Errol Thompson and myself, along with Ian Turnbull and Borje Salming on the points.

The fact that the Bruins were one player short was instrumental in my next goal. Thompson had the puck in the neutral zone and fed it wide left to Borje. I was moving up the right-wing boards and Borje threw it across the rink and hit me in full stride. Darryl Edestrand was playing my side but, like his teammates, he'd first moved left with Errol, then right with Borje, and couldn't get back to me on his far left when I took the pass. Normally, a winger would be there to shut off the wide side, but the Bruins were short-handed. I went around Edestrand, cut right toward the net at the face-off circle and, having the whole net to shoot at on my forehand, put it into the far corner past Reece. Goalies will tell you that the hardest play to stop is that where a forward is coming across laterally, on either the forehand or the backhand. The goalie has to stick to the near post as long as possible to cut off the angle: if he moves too fast, the forward can shoot behind him at the post he has just vacated; if he moves too slow, the forward has the far post. As well, the goalie is at a disadvantage no matter what side the shooter is on: the backhand is a hard shot to pick up because the motion and follow-through are disguised, and the forehand gives the shooter a look at the whole net.

13. Toronto, Sittler (Salming, Thompson) pp   0:44

I had tied the Rocket and Olmstead and I had nineteen minutes left to get a record-setting ninth point. And everyone in the building knew it. When the announcement of my fourth goal and eighth point was made, the fans went crazy. Every time I touched the puck from that moment on, the decibels went way up. And every time a teammate touched it and I was on the ice, people were hollering "Pass it to Sittler" or "Get it to Darryl!"

The record-setting point came midway through the third on a play that started innocently enough. It was near the end of a shift and Thompson had passed the puck to me and headed for the bench. It was my intention to take it into the Boston zone and flip the puck in deep, and head for the bench myself, with a "We'll get 'em next shift."

The funny thing was, though, as I carried the puck into the zone, and I began to fade to the left, trying to get as good an angle on net as I could, the two defensemen played me very soft. These weren't rookies, they were Dallas Smith and Gary Doak, two veterans. Dallas was playing left defense and for some reason he seemed to get tangled up in his skates on a cross-over. At the same instant, Doak cut way over to his right. It was like the parting of the Red Sea; suddenly they just separated in front of me. Rather than bursting through for a break-in on net, I shot back to the near post while moving to the left. Reece was moving out too quickly, no doubt panicked by the sight of two veteran defenders disappearing before his eyes, and the puck dipped inside the far corner.

14.   Toronto, Sittler (Thompson)   9:27

Maple Leaf Gardens went nuts. The team was off the bench and mobbing me and the standing ovation seemed to go on forever. The fans gave the impression that they would rather we stopped the game right there and begin some sort of special ceremony. Crazily enough, I remember thinking, "I've just set the all-time points record for a single game and there's still half a period to play!"

At this point, I think I should say that while this was the highest scoring game I (or anybody else, for that matter) had ever enjoyed in the National Hockey League, I couldn't say that it was the best I'd ever played. Borje Salming, who ended up with five points, was all over the ice that night and, with a break or two, could have come close to the eight-point record himself. Lanny and Errol were flying and their speed on the wings forced the Bruins defense deep into their zone.

I had a lot of luck too. I had floated a knuckler that did unpredictable things en route to the Boston goal and Reece didn't have a butterfly net. Borje had dived full length to deflect one. I had scored another on a bunt single.

And then came the final goal . . .

After the record-setting ninth point, the crowd went wild every time I stepped onto the ice, hoping to see the first NHL player ever to score in double figures. By then, however, I was pretty sure that I'd used up all the luck available to a good-sized country, let alone just one team of players. Nine points was a pretty good month for most players. You weren't supposed to get that many points in one NHL game.

But my luck still held. Late in the period, Lanny McDonald threw the puck around the boards and I caught up with it just behind the Bruins' net. I looked up and spotted Thompson cruising into the slot and tried to fish the puck out to him. Brad Park was a veteran and he'd been watching my eyes. He stepped out to cut off the pass, but misjudged by a bit. The puck struck him on the skate and dribbled into the net between Reece's legs.

15. Toronto, Sittler (McDonald)   16:35

Bedlam. You couldn't hear yourself think in the arena for the last three minutes of play. When the final siren went, I discovered that I had set a third record, one which has yet to be broken and one which may last for a long time. While I was the eighth player in NHL history to score six goals in a game (Joe Malone of Quebec had once scored seven), I was the first ever to score hat tricks in consecutive periods of the same game. That one will be hard to match, even with the obvious offensive skills displayed by Wayne Gretzky, Mario Lemieux, Steve Yzerman and friends. I think the ten points might be surpassed or tied before someone ever scores three goals in back-to-back periods.

In the aftermath of that game, several things happened. Dave Reece returned to Boston and was sent down to the AHL. Not long afterwards, he was out of professional hockey. I feel bad about that because a game that meant a lot to me and my development as a hockey player simultaneously meant the end of another player's career. However, the very fact that Gerry Cheevers had joined Gilles Gilbert in the Bruins goaltending department, something which happened before our game, probably had a lot more to do with the demotion of Reece than that single game.

I also think that this single effort contributed greatly to my early admission into the NHL Hall of Fame. Harold Ballard thought so; he was so carried away by my ten-point night that he held a special presentation shortly thereafter to mark the event. Wendy and Ryan stood proudly with me at center ice before a subsequent home game as Harold and NHL President Clarence Campbell presented a silver tea service to me in recognition of the feat.

A little later that year, well-known artist William Biddle presented me with a special copy of his painting commemorating that feat. It was the twenty-sixth entry in the Great Moments in Canadian Sports series, sponsored by an insurance company.

That painting is still around, and Harold's silver tea service is proudly displayed in our home to this day.

8

The Artful Roger

ON A TEAM that has developed a penchant for shooting itself in the foot, one can excuse the principals for believing that good, solid moves are mistakes.

That, in part, was the reaction of a lot of people in the Maple Leafs entourage to the news that Roger Neilson would succeed Red Kelly as coach. It made sense; Neilson had proved to be an innovator and original thinker in the coach's factory up in Peterborough. He was a bachelor and an indefatigable worker. He had a keen analytical mind and could break down the game of hockey into all of its component parts, add a distinctive new touch here and there, and put it all back together much better than brand new.

He was the best coach I ever had in professional hockey. So, what was he doing with the Toronto Maple Leafs?

As I have mentioned elsewhere, we had been bounced by the Flyers in three straight playoff donnybrooks, 1975 through 1977. Red Kelly had tried everything, including his vaunted Pyramid Power, a scheme where pyramids were placed under our players' bench or passed over our sticks so we could tap into the inherent psychic energy resident in that geometrical form. Or, as they say, something like that. Shortly after the 1977 defeat, Red Kelly was let go. In his inimitable style, Ballard didn't fire Kelly; he refused to sign him to another contract, fearing that Kelly would "aggravate a back injury he had suffered earlier in his career and which had flared up during the latest season."

There was a gap of several weeks between Kelly's demise and the hiring of Roger Neilson by Ballard, which led a lot of us to believe that Harold was looking at other candidates, even though the

Neilson rumors had gone on for almost a year, or ever since he was hired to coach the Dallas Black Hawks of the Central Hockey League. The *Toronto Star* made a big thing of an application for the coaching position that Ballard received from Susan Ferguson, sixteen, of Alvinston, Ontario.

She wrote:

Dear Mr. Ballard:

I just heard a few days ago that Mr. Kelly's position as coach of the Toronto Maple Leafs is open. Since you are owner of the club, I respect your decision that it will probably be for the good of the team.

After much pondering, I have decided that I would be perfect for the job. Please read on:

First of all, I have a collection of Darryl Sittler pictures (53) on my bedroom wall, which I have saved over the past two years. I know how much you think of the talented Leaf captain, so I think you and I would get along fine.

Secondly, I have 99 per cent in mathematics in my first year of high school, and this year my final report shows that I have achieved 100 per cent in that particular subject. Therefore, it is very unlikely that I would ever mix up any of the players and their numbers.

Another point to consider is that my grandmother, at 82 years of age, knows all the Leafs and their numbers off by heart. I am sure that she would be able to fill in for me if I ever got sick.

One of the strongest arguments that I have about my worthiness of being the next Leaf coach is that I am a 16-year-old female. This gives me 49 full years as coach before I would be forced to retire. Women also live longer than men.

Think it over. I'll be waiting for your reply.

Yours truly,
Susan C. Ferguson

Harold's return letter thanked Susan for her interest in the team, and said that he had already settled on a coach. He added: "Needless to say, we shall keep you in mind the next time the position is open." He must have forgotten his promise, for I have it on good authority that only Scotty Bowman, Don Cherry and Punch Imlach were in the running when Neilson was fired two years later.

So even sixteen-year-old fans were beginning to worry about the competence of the people upstairs and behind the bench for the Leafs. Before that situation hit rock bottom, however, it would get immeasurably better, even if only for the short term.

As much as I liked Red Kelly, because he was a gentleman and a square shooter, I have to concur that bringing in Neilson was the right move at that point for the organization. Roger was a New Wave coach, different from all of his predecessors in my experience. Most of today's players have grown up with this kind of coach. But in 1977, Roger was ahead of his time.

Harold the Showman made an event of Neilson's hiring. The new coach was introduced to the Toronto media at a Maple Leaf Gardens press conference on July 26, 1977. He had been hired a month before by Ballard, and was probably the last guy to hear about it, officially. After his stint with the CHL Black Hawks, Neilson packed for a month-long trip to northern Africa and Europe. Before he left, he and Ballard agreed verbally that he would be coach of the Leafs for the next two seasons, but that the deal would not be signed or announced before his return in late July. Neilson had hardly strapped on his seat belt for his overseas flight when Harold was on the telephone to the local papers. Neilson picked up an old edition of The *Globe and Mail* (June 29) at the Canadian embassy in Vienna, and discovered a headline which read: "Roger Neilson Takes on Leafs Coaching Task." The rest of the story was pure fiction à la Ballard, recounting how Ballard had tracked down Neilson in Johannesburg, South Africa, and convinced him to take the job. The trouble was, Neilson was 2,000 miles away in Nigeria at the time, and never took a telephone call from Ballard while he was out of the country.

The Stanley-Livingstone oddity was forgotten when Roger met the press in the Leafs' board room. It was my job to welcome him, and I said a few things about what it had been like to play against him, and what I had heard from a generation of Neilson's Peterborough graduates. I was glad to see him as my new coach, and said so.

I believe the feeling was mutual. "For a coach to come to a team where the captain really is a team captain is quite an advantage," he said. "One of the fine things about the Maple Leafs is that all the stars are team men. With some teams, the stars are prima donnas."

Roger noted that we had a fine offense in place, and he was going to concentrate on the team's defense. "The Leafs can score goals, there's no doubt about that, so I wouldn't propose any system that would take away any goal scoring."

"Defensively, there's room for improvements. Two major qualities in a successful team are penalty killing and the ability to defend leads. These are prime requisites. But if a team can't score goals, there's not much you can do. Any team can check."

He promised something new, on ice and off. "I'll be using video systems, lectures, and I intend to have one-on-one sessions with players to get my ideas across," he said.

Our practices would change, as well. "Most coaches would walk a mile for a new drill; most North American athletes are highly competitive so you have to try and work that into the drills. Usually, hockey is a very monotonous sport to practice."

Part of the change, he announced, would be to incorporate some elements of European hockey into the Leafs' game. "There's lots of room for improvement in hockey, especially NHL hockey. Personally, I don't think National Hockey League teams make enough use of the center ice zone."

Roger Neilson delivered on every promise he made that day.

How would I describe Roger Neilson? Innovative. Intellectual. Reasonable. Educational. Fair. Sensitive. Knew his stuff backwards and forwards and was able to convey this information to his players. Putting all of this together, he led the Toronto Maple Leafs to their best season in a generation.

I had played against Roger's Peterborough Petes in junior hockey and one thing I remembered was that his teams never were surprised by anything we did. The trademark of the Petes was "always prepared, always in the game," whether that edition of the team was a powerhouse or not. No Peterborough team ever finished lower than third in his nine seasons there.

He brought in new ideas, and several rule changes came about because of him. In one instance, he took out his goaltender on a penalty shot and replaced him with Ron Stackhouse, a big defenseman, and told him to rush the guy as soon as he hit the blueline. Another Neilson trick was revealed in the last minute of a game; when he'd pull the goalie for an extra attacker, the goalie left his stick lying in the crease. That saved more than one goal on long shots. And when they ruled against that, he'd get a defenseman to break his stick and "accidentally" deposit it in the same area. The referee would be all the way up the ice and wouldn't or couldn't see that it was intentional.

Maybe the best way to convey my impression of Roger is to go right to the end of his tenure, and work my way back to the beginning. I received a letter from him shortly after we'd been eliminated by the Montreal Canadiens in the Stanley Cup quarter finals in 1979. Three weeks before the season ended, Ballard had fired Neilson in one of his patented piques, and then rehired him when the players intervened. When Roger wrote me this letter, there was an excellent chance that he wouldn't return as head coach of the Leafs. Still, until further notice he was coach, and he was going to do his job thoroughly.

At the beginning of each season, he'd sit down with players and we'd fill out forms on goals, weaknesses, strengths, what we as players expected to contribute to the team. He would never use the results of this interview in a negative way, to say "I told you so," or "You couldn't do what you said you could." Roger would use it occasionally as a reference point, an opportunity for both of us to try and analyze things. "Did you improve in this area? Why did you? Why didn't you?"

I believe firmly that writing something down means you'll give it more thought than if you had just said it. Writing means you have to take more time to think about it and when you hand it to somebody as a file, you'll tend to be more realistic about what you're saying because the topic will come up for discussion at a later date. During the season, and at the end of each year, Neilson would sit down with individuals and go over the interview forms. I really liked this as a player; you knew where you stood, whereas a lot of coaches preferred to keep you guessing all the time: "Does he like me? Does he hate me?" Those questions are important to a player's peace-of-mind and, hence, to his performance.

That end-of-season letter from Neilson showed how thorough and observant he was:

Dear Darryl:

It was a rather difficult season in many ways. Your support in times of trouble was certainly appreciated. No coach could expect any more. Next season I would like to see you take on even more responsibility. This would include the following:

1. Sensing when curfews are needed.
2. Advising the coach on the mood of the team re: practices, optionals, meetings, etc., and on the mood of individual players.

3. A brief weekly meeting to identify any potential problems.
4. Discussing practice methods with the coach.
5. Organize team meetings when needed. The purpose would usually be to re-establish positive thinking and constructive suggestions. (In other words, get the team up.)
6. Always be concerned with presenting a positive attitude in front of the team.
   As captain, this is probably your most important function.

Here are some suggestions for you to consider:

1. Try to effect more movement in the offensive zone. Perhaps spend more time in front of the net or in the slot.
2. Be concerned with positioning in our defensive zone on 4 on 4s.
3. Try to be less sensitive about ice time. Next year we intend to use you penalty killing. However, it is disastrous to our team when sensitivity towards ice time affects your play. It is much better to discuss the matter with me.
4. As mentioned in our earlier discussion, you are at your best when you are forcing yourself at all times. This is also the pattern of many of our players.
5. Try to be more persistent forechecking. This is when you control the play the best.
6. Once again, be sure to report in top shape. Your example is vital to the team's success.
7. Use every possible measure to build up the muscles around your knee. Perhaps you should contact Dr. Hastings.

Qualities of a good captain include insight, tolerance, and sacrifice. You have demonstrated all of these during the past two years. Particularly on this team, your example in every area is of the utmost importance. As you go, the entire team goes. It is a tremendous responsibility.

You are on display at all times. Everything you do is noted—your intensity at practice, your attitude toward a rookie, your interest at a meeting, your handling of a crisis, your comments to the media, your reaction to success or failure, your ability to lift the team, your competence as a team spokesman, your insight into player problems, your own dedication, your willingness to put the team ahead of personal involvement—and I'm sure you could list a few more. On no team in the NHL does the responsibility lie with one player. Your ability to meet this unprecedented challenge is the determining factor in the success of the team.

Roger Neilson

I use that letter in a lot of my talks today. Even when Roger came to the end of the season, not knowing whether he'd be back with the Leafs because he'd been fired once already, he would sit down and discuss things with you, and was personally, genuinely interested in helping you. He was a thoroughly professional coach.

How many NHL coaches have ever sent such a letter to their team captain? The letter noted issues on which we had disagreed, such as my frustrations over too little ice time, but these things could be, and were, discussed. The Toronto media mistakenly assumed that my frustrations over less ice time pitted me against Neilson and that, after his second season, I was one of the people who wanted him out. Nothing could be further from the truth. I liked and respected Roger from the beginning, and really enjoyed the fact that here was a man with a game plan. As far as his preparation and conditioning went it was all new stuff. It was exciting to learn it and to be a part of it.

Roger excelled at taking a group of men, and focusing on each individual in turn so that everyone felt he was an important part of the team, whatever his role was. Whether you were the power play specialist or third line checking center, you felt you belonged.

The other side of that was making you personally accountable for your play on the ice. The game happens so fast out there that if a coach doesn't take the time to analyze the game film or look back, he can be fooled by the players. They might come back to the bench and lay the blame on somebody else, "Gee, I had my man and this guy didn't have his." Players could cop an excuse, knowing that their chances of getting away with it were high if the coach wasn't into the habit of checking the game films. With Roger, there was no room for bluffing. He checked all game films play by play and there was no place to hide.

From my standpoint, I liked that. I knew we were going to get better as a group if we would all take our responsibility seriously. Roger was great at isolating any aspect of the game, like scoring chances, or specific match-ups, and then analyzing it. He knew a quarter of the way through the season how strong Darryl Sittler was on face-offs, and against whom. If I consistently lost the draw to some opponent, then he wouldn't put me out there; somebody else was a better bet. That took some getting used to, hence his reference in the letter to ice-time complaints.

Line changes were another big thing with Roger. He'd use Jimmy Jones, Jerry Butler and Pat Boutette, agitators and hard checkers, against Guy Lafleur and other scoring stars on the opposing team. That was our strategy; we had a plan and we'd go by that. His innovations also included line change procedures. Rather than having someone yelling for the line to come off and alerting the other team, he'd have the spare goalie give a special signal. That had a positive effect on the spare goalie, involving him in the game rather than having him just sitting there waiting for the starter to get hurt. Now he had a job to do. He'd hang his blocker over the boards; if you looked over and saw it before you squared up for the face-off, that meant "change on the fly."

He would originate plays, and then we'd practice them as drills until we had them down perfectly. One such invention was the power play doors drill. The play was simplicity itself, but it took a man with Roger Neilson's mind to conjure it up. We'd be on the power play, and start out behind our net where someone like Borje Salming or Ian Turnbull would set up. A guy who could pass the puck well would be stationed on the left side, near the blueline. Another forward would be standing on the right side at the blueline. The key to this play, which we used as often as we could at home, was the fact that the near door to our bench was right on the blueline. More often than not, an opposing defenseman would see the winger standing there and pinch in on him.

Meanwhile, someone like Lanny McDonald would be standing at our bench right at the far door, which was near the redline, with the door open. Salming would throw the puck to me or another center on the left side and I'd skate a couple of feet. Simultaneously, the guy standing near the blueline on the right would step off the ice onto our bench while Lanny came onto the ice out the other door, behind the defenseman. I'd hit him on the fly and there'd be a breakaway. I don't have to tell you how many times that worked.

With Roger, we practiced those things. He got us thinking on the ice. And when you see those things work in practice, you gain confidence. Compare this to Floyd Smith's 3 on 0s in practice, the kind of play that never comes up in a hockey game. Think about it; when was the last time you saw a 3 on 0 in an NHL game?

Neilson also emphasized conditioning. Sometimes a coach can't control the talent he has, even though he'll try to improve their skills in practice. One thing he can control is physical conditioning; his team can be in better shape than the next one. That comes through a program of hard work and discipline. Roger realized that with any group of twenty players, he'd have a top third, a middle, and a bottom third. If he could close that gap between top and bottom, he'd beat a lot of other teams. The best gap-closer was conditioning. His whole philosophy was that a chain was only as strong as its weakest link. So we ran, worked out on Universal Gym and Nautilus machines and lifted free weights. We all had individual training programs for the off-season as well.

The other thing was that Roger measured everything towards preparation for the seventh game of the Stanley Cup final. He left no stones unturned. He practiced all situations. He had drills that incorporated special situations for the goaltenders; 3 on 3s; 4 on 3s; other coaches never went into that depth. Before Neilson, I'd never had a coach who paid that much attention to detail. Red Kelly was like a buddy who ran simple practices and scrimmaged us a lot. There was nothing wrong with him; he was a creature of his times and the game of the 1950s and early '60s. But he didn't have Neilson's detailed approach.

One thing that really impressed me was Roger's work ethic. He'd go to bed at two in the morning and be up at six and in to work. He brought people who were equally dedicated with him, like Ron Smith, his only assistant coach, and Al Dunford, his statistician.

Roger sought to bring his players to their full potential. To me, that's a sign of whether a coach is successful. People might say, "Well, you didn't win any Stanley Cups." That's not always a sign of *coaching* success. If each NHL team began the season dead-even in talent and potential, each team's chance of winning the Stanley Cup would be about four-and-a-half per cent, with (as of this season) twenty-two teams in the league. That doesn't leave much room to rate the work of a coach if victory in the Stanley Cup playoffs is the only criterion. How well a coach utilizes or improves the talent he has to work with is the real test of coaching success.

Roger also had an off-ice philosophy, or plan. He would treat you as a human being, with feelings, family or girlfriend, whatever it was. He brought in a complete game plan at the beginning of the year, adapted to the season schedule, and worked it to a T—right down to what days he wanted off and what days would be extra work days. And he stuck by it. We discussed that on several occasions, especially with reference to curfews and the like. Roger was open to discussion.

Other guys would coach and motivate by the most recent results. "Lost both on the weekend? Okay, two-a-day on Monday." That would mess everybody up, of course. You were supposed to have Monday off and you might have had something planned with your wife and kids. You were always on tenterhooks in that system, with the quality of your play or the result of the last game dictating your practice schedule. Roger wasn't like that. With him, you knew your days off were sacred and respected. So when you did come to practice, you'd work extra hard, because the guy was fair and honest with you.

There was some criticism that because Roger was a bachelor he didn't understand family life and demanded too much of his players as a consequence. That wasn't my experience with him.

Roger was new in terms of coaching style and ideas. That, and the fact that he wasn't always forthcoming with the media, led to a lot of speculation. I think he saw them as a nuisance. We never discussed the topic, but I felt that he thought that most of the guys in the press box didn't know what they were watching. And rather than clutter their heads with a lot of complicated inside hockey facts, he fed them simplistic quotes.

As a player or coach, you might think that the journalists usually miss the point, but you can't escape the reporters forever, so you should keep things in perspective. You have to be very diplomatic sometimes, and feign a serious response to some of the most inane questions. A coach is much more vulnerable in this area than a player, because he's almost an automatic interview after each game, good game or bad.

Roger had his own transitions to make, especially after spending so much time in junior hockey where he could work on kids for three years before they moved along. As well, the players didn't make much money, partying wasn't such a problem, and there was no complacency. Those kids would listen because they were hungry and wanted to get somewhere. In junior, a coach has more "hands-on" influence than he has in pro hockey, where he might come up against

Darryl with his Grandpa Jake and father, Ken. (*Sintler*)

Darryl, age 4, in front of the family Ford. *(Sittler)*

Darryl (second from right, back row) and his confirmation class at St. James Lutheran Church, where he was also in the choir. *(Sittler)*

Darryl, age 17, as a member of the London Nationals (later Knights) junior club. *(Sittler)*

Darryl with his brothers in 1970, the year he turned pro. From left: Tim (12), Rod (9) and Jeff (5). *(Sittler)*

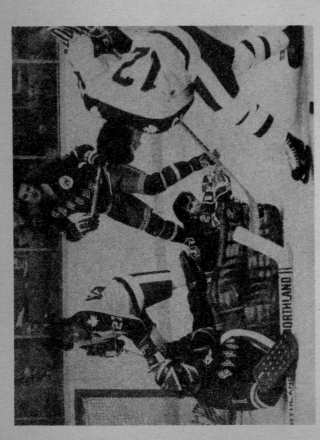

Darryl waits for a rebound that never comes. From left: Rangers Dunc Wilson, Nick Beverley and Doug Jarrett, and Leaf Errol Thompson. (*Canapress Photo Service, 1975*)

The ten-point night, 1976: Darryl and Errol Thompson celebrate after Sittler's sixth goal against the Boston Bruins. (*The Globe and Mail*)

NHL President Clarence Campbell and Harold Ballard presented Darryl with a silver tea set to commemorate the ten-point game. Wendy and Ryan look on. *(Canada Wide)*

Darryl signs his "no-trade" contract in 1973, in the presence of Harold Ballard, who was on a pass from Millhaven Pen. Jim Gregory points to the dotted line. *(Canada Wide/Sandy Solomon)*

The overtime goal against Czechoslovakian goalie Vladimir Dzurilla in the 1976 Canada Cup, September 13, 1976. *(Canapress Photo Service/Stoody)*

Darryl and his agent, Alan Eagleson, relax the day after the overtime game. *(Sittler)*

Ian Turnbull scores his fifth goal on his fifth shot of the game against the Detroit Red Wings, 1977, setting a record for defencemen. (*Toronto Star*)

Two more of the Leafs' "Big Six": Borje Salming and goalie Mike Palmateer. *(Canapress Photo Service/Bill Becker)*

Darryl, with Alan Eagleson in the background, responds to the announcement of the construction of the Ronald McDonald House in Toronto. He was the spokesperson for the campaign, which raised one million dollars. *(Canada Wide/Joe Holland)*

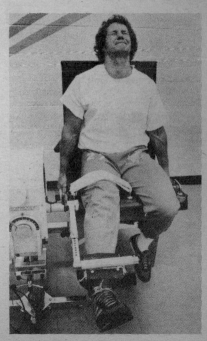

Staying in top physical shape was central to Darryl's game and Roger Neilson's coaching. But when Imlach returned in 1979, he wanted to discard the weight machines. *(Canada Wide/Barry Gray)*

Buddies off the ice, Darryl Edestrand and Darryl Sittler were into this scrum before they knew it. *(Canada Wide)*

What a fan! Florence Robertson presented this hooked rug to Darryl in 1979. Darryl, touched by the gesture, gave her tickets to a Leafs game in Montreal – she'd never been to a game. *(Canada Wide/Ottmar Bierwagen)*

Darryl and Harold frown as they study the photographer's seating plan for the team photo session in 1980. *(Canada Wide/Mike Slaughter)*

When Terry Fox passed through Toronto during his 1980 Marathon of Hope, he said he wanted to meet his childhood hero, Darryl Sittler. Darryl, just as eager to meet Terry, presented him with his All-Star sweater at the City Hall ceremony. *(Canada Wide)*

Darryl and Soviet star goalie Vladislav Tretiak exchange souvenir sticks for their sons after the 1981 Canada Cup. *(Sittler)*

Darryl arrived at this rodeo thinking he would merely be cow-milking. But he soon found out he would be doing something much more exciting. *(Sittler)*

Dynamic Duo. Darryl and Frank Mahovlich sport their number 27s at an oldtimers charity hockey game. The Leafs gave Darryl the Big M's old number when he signed as their number-one draft pick in 1970. *(Jordan)*

"A Knight to Remember." Darryl returned to the London arena in March 1988, where the London Knights framed his sweater and retired his number 9. *(©London Free Press/Photo by Bill Ironside)*

Darryl and Jim "Howie" McKenny, former Leaf and CITY-TV sportscaster, at the Goofy Games at Walt Disney Resort in 1988 to help raise money for the Toronto Special Olympics. *(Walt Disney)*

All in the family. Before signing with the Phila- delphia Flyers, Ryan Sittler was a sought-after player himself, pursued by every team in the OHL and scouted by American universities. *(Sittler)*

Meaghan Sittler played AAA elite hockey in Buffalo. Her goal is to play on the 1998 Olympic women's hockey team. *(Sittler)*

Not hockey this time, but baseball. Ashley, the young- est Sittler, in her uniform. *(Sittler)*

Darryl, Wendy, Meaghan, Ryan and Ashley Sittler and Lanny and Ardell McDonald at Darryl's 1989 induction into the Hockey Hall of Fame. Lanny, Darryl's best friend and official presenter that night, referred to Darryl as a "great hockey player who made history happen." *(Sittler)*

The tradition continues: Darryl and Ryan Sittler at the 1992 NHL amateur draft, where Ryan was chosen in the first round by the Philadelphia Flyers. *(Marc Campanelli/ Bruce Bennett Studios)*

players in his dressing room who've been in the league ten or twelve years and might question every decision of his.

A prime example. We played in Minnesota on a Wednesday night and won the game. Roger had it fixed in his head that we were going to have a one o'clock curfew after the game because we were playing two or three nights later in another city.

I went to see him. "Roger, the guys are old enough to behave in this case. And, even if you have a curfew, don't bother checking the players' rooms. If it was the night before the game, hopefully all the guys are going to be in and behaved. But two nights before, after we've won a game in Minnesota, they'll go against you if you push this too hard."

Roger went into his Columbo the detective personality. "Yeah, but what are they doing up after one o'clock in the morning?"

"Maybe they just want to go get a bite to eat after the game. Wind down a bit." Quite often, you weren't out of the building until past 11:00 p.m. and sitting down in a restaurant much before 11:45 or so. So 1:00 a.m. in a restaurant wasn't beyond the realm of believability.

One issue in Roger's overall strategy that sometimes frustrated me as a player—and I think Lanny felt somewhat the same—was that many times our game plan was so focused on our checking line being out against the opponent's top line, that we lost sight of our own offense. We should have had more situations where we would force the other team to worry about us. But these were minor disputes with Roger, items to be discussed. And we did discuss them in fair exchanges of opinion.

What did the other players think of Roger? Tiger Williams played out his option in 1978, and then signed with the Leafs even though he had received better offers elsewhere, including one from New York and Detroit where John Ferguson and Ted Lindsay were ready to start a bidding war for him. He wrote in his autobiography:

It was Neilson who got me to sign a new contract with the Leafs at a time when I could make a financial killing in New York or maybe Detroit . . . I had a good coach, and I played on what I thought was one of the best lines in the game. I had Sittler and McDonald and Neilson . . . Who needed more? So I signed up for another six years with the Leafs.

There were times, especially at the start, when we didn't understand Roger's coaching techniques. But it didn't take us

long to realize one thing. He was two or three steps ahead of
the opposing coaches. Whenever we played Montreal, the
games became cat-and-mouse matches, not only over which
team would win but over which coach would win. Scotty
Bowman was coaching the Canadiens then, and Roger considered playing them the ultimate test. We had some great
games.

Lanny had been very close to Red Kelly; Ardell McDonald and
Andra Kelly did a lot of volunteer work with deaf children, and the
McDonalds named their first daughter Andra, in honor of Mrs.
Kelly. But even Lanny was won over by Roger, and the results he
brought.

More impressive, though, was what Roger did for the team and the
city of Toronto. In our first year under Neilson we sported a 41-29-10
record, good for 92 points and sixth overall in the NHL. The 41 wins
marked only the second time in team history that the Leafs had won
more than 40 games; the previous occasion was 1950-51 when the
team had a 41-16-13 record for 95 points. All of our numbers were
great that season—271 goals for and only 237 against, eighth and
seventh overall, respectively. I had my best year ever, 45 goals and 72
assists for 117 points and third place behind Guy Lafleur (132 points)
and Bryan Trottier (123) in the league scoring race. Lanny was tenth,
with 47 goals and 40 assists.

Numbers aside, we had come together as a team in all the intan-
gibles, team feeling, two-way commitment in both offensive zones,
belief in the coach's systems, and all the rest. When the playoffs
came, we were ready to prove exactly how far we had come.

As I mentioned before, Tiger loved Roger because his role
expanded under Neilson. Roger was never beyond using tough guys;
he realized they had a role to play if your skilled players were going to
get the room that they needed. Tiger became a front-line player
under those circumstances, and in a positive way. Before Roger's
arrival, Tiger had played it physical and had the penalty record to
prove it. Roger got him to focus his toughness; continue to play
tough but take fewer penalties. Or take somebody with him went he
was sent off.

Tiger was kept very busy that season for the simple reason that he
was on a line with two guys who would end up with 92 goals between
them. That meant that Lanny and I were taking a fearful pounding

as opposing coaches reserved extra physical action for us, game in, game out. On defense, Borje Salming and Ian Turnbull were subjected to similar treatment. We tried to keep our cool, knowing we were more helpful on the ice than in the box, but we occasionally had to retaliate. I ended up with 100 minutes in penalties that year, Salming had 70 and Lanny added 54 more minutes. In November, we picked up tough winger Jerry Butler in exchange for Inge Hammarström, and Pat Boutette chipped in whenever he could. But the three of them were almost worn out by the end of February. Neilson went to Gregory and laid it on the line: "We aren't going anywhere in post-season unless we can get one more big guy to take the pressure off the skill players."

Roger had a big smile on his face on March 13. Gregory had called him up and announced: "I just got your tough guy."

"Who?"

"Dan Maloney."

"God bless you, Jim."

When I played in London, and Roger was coaching in Peterborough, he once sent Tony Featherstone out after me, after one of our tough guys had taken out their best player. I ended up that particular brawl with two black eyes and a broken hand. As a player, you want to have tough guys on your team. The day after the Maloney trade was announced, our guys practically sang and danced their way through practice. Maloney's arrival meant we could do a lot of things in the playoffs, given the right circumstances.

Of course, the moment Maloney arrived we went into a late-season slide, playing atrociously for about two weeks before we righted things. We "righted things" by blowing out the Los Angeles Kings 7-3 and 4-0 in our best-of-three eighth final of the playoffs.

Next up were the Islanders, acknowledged as the second-best team in the league after the Canadiens. While we had finished with 92 points, a 30-year highwater mark for us, the Islanders were almost 20 points better with 111, good for third overall, two behind the Boston Bruins. The Canadiens were in another league, with 129 points, believe it or not a three-point slide from the previous season.

The Islanders were supposed to take us out in five games, six if we put up unusually stiff opposition. The pundits looked good after the first two games on the Island because we returned home down 2-0. Late in the second game, Jerry Butler slammed into Clark Gillies and flattened the huge Islander. We lost it in overtime, but Butler's hit picked us all up. Two nights later, Mike Palmateer shut out the Isles and we were one game behind.

Game Four was a "good news, bad news" story. The good news was that we won 3-1 to tie the series; the bad was that Lorne Henning's stick came up accidentally and caught Salming in the eye. He was gone for the series.

We missed Borje in Game Five and lost, again in overtime, but something encouraging happened. Ian Turnbull was logging extra time, filling in for Salming, and playing great; strong defensively in our zone, and leading wave after wave on offense in their zone. We returned home down 3-2 but we knew we'd be back on Long Island in three days. Just before Bob Nystrom had scored the winning goal for the Isles, Lanny McDonald was in all alone and hit the post. We could have been going home with the lead.

Butler delivered that message midway through the sixth game with his second big hit of the series. This one sent Mike Bossy off on a stretcher, and suddenly we could see the unbelievable happening— the Islanders had their heads hanging in defeat. Nobody went after Butler to avenge the Bossy check and it seemed the 6-2 score in our favor was almost an afterthought.

Two nights later, we found ourselves in our third straight Nassau Coliseum overtime matchup. And this time, the roles were reversed. A minute into the fourth period, Brian Glennie got tripped up at our blueline and Billy Harris went in alone on Palmateer. Palmy held the fort. Three minutes later, Lanny took a beautiful waist-high pass from Ian Turnbull, knocked it down and stepped around Denis Potvin. As he made his move, he let a wrist shot go that Chico Resch still hasn't seen. Maple Leafs, 2-1.

It was deathly silent at Nassau Coliseum, except down in the Islanders zone where twenty guys in blue-and-white were jumping up and down and screaming at the top of their lungs.

We didn't have enough for Montreal in the semi-final, dropping the series four straight, but we'd given our fans a season they hadn't had in the entire decade of the 1970s. The way we felt that summer was that there was another year left in the '70s, and we could only get better.

Everybody's expectations were higher in 1979, the players', the coaches', the fans' and the owner's. We spent the season right around .500, which in previous years would have been a cause for rejoicing. But this time, Harold got antsy with it. We weren't simply mediocre, everyone might have lived with that. We were either great, or we were terrible, and that frustrated the world. There were periods during that year when we hit flat spots, and the speculation machine would go into high gear. Was it Salming, McDonald, Sittler or Neilson? Why wasn't this team doing better? We finished the season at 34-33-13 for 81 points.

Harold spent most of the New Year putting down Roger. One incident I specifically remember occurred at Madison Square Garden when Scotty Bowman was putting the NHL All-Star team through its paces before our three-game Challenge Cup series.

After the practice, Harold came puffing into the team dressing room: "Sitt, Mac! Those are the kinds of practices we should have, not this video crap."

"You get us players like these, and we'll have this kind of practice," I retorted.

Just before the trade deadline in early March, we went into the Forum for a game against the Canadiens. The players didn't realize it, but Harold Ballard had told Roger that if we lost the game, he would lose his job. Palmateer was out with a knee injury suffered against Atlanta two days earlier, but Paul Harrison stepped in and played his heart out. We led 1-0 late in the game, but they pulled it out on goals by Jacques Lemaire and Guy Lapointe.

As the final siren sounded, Ballard turned to his neighbor in the press box, Dick Beddoes, and said Neilson was through. Beddoes literally ran to the TV studio where his CHCH *Overtime* show was being staged, and breathlessly announced to southern Ontario that Neilson had coached his last. It was a very long flight home.

Harold had decided he was going to fire Roger and bring up Eddie Johnston from New Brunswick in the AHL to replace him. He forgot, as usual, to cover all the bases—Johnston said no way, he was owned by Chicago. Ballard then went to John McLellan and asked him to bail out the Leafs until season's end. McLellan liked Neilson and thought he had been treated shabbily so he, too, refused. Ballard never forgave him. What probably prevented McLellan from feeling the full blast of Ballard's wrath was his own demise, of a heart attack, less than six months later. So, from Wednesday night to Saturday morning, Ballard had no coach.

Tiger phoned me on Thursday night: "Darryl, you have to do something. There's no way that Roger should have got fired. How do you feel about it?"

"Terrible. The whole thing stinks." Neilson's firing was bad enough, but there we were, a coachless team two weeks away from the playoffs.

"Look, I had lunch with Roger today and he said he'd come back if Ballard asked him to. We have to convince Ballard to ask him."

We agreed to get the players together before practice the next morning, Friday, and we voted. Neilson got a ninety per cent support rating—Ian Turnbull was one of the few to vote against him. Ian was one of the least disciplined players on the team and that didn't sit well with Neilson. In the NHL, when something doesn't sit well with a coach, the player sits.

I went to see Jim Gregory first and he was sympathetic. He had hired Neilson and promoted him as the best of the new wave of coaches. Neilson had immediately paid dividends, only to have the whole thing turn strange in Year Two. Jim might have heard the jungle drums beating for him, too.

"Jim, this firing is crap on a lot of levels. First, Ballard fires one of the best coaches around. Second, with the playoffs around the corner, there is no way that another coach could adapt to Neilson's system in two weeks. And most of all, this is the guy who took us to the semifinal last year and coached us over the Islanders. We're throwing all this right out the window. The players feel we've let him down. Keep him and we'll do whatever we can to get this turned around."

Gregory was unsure of Ballard's opinion, but said it was worth a try to take the same argument to the top. I went over to Ballard's office.

"The players just had a vote. We want Neilson back. We don't think you've given him a fair shot, and to a man we'll tell you that it's our fault for not executing his game plan, not his. He's one of the best in the game, and the best coach I've ever had."

We returned to the dressing room, and I replayed the same message, this time in front of the players. Ballard seemed miffed; it was equal parts the players supporting Neilson, and his failure to find a quick replacement. Had he been able to put someone behind the bench on Thursday, or at least deliver someone for Friday morning, this reversal could not have happened.

"Okay, you got your coach back," he growled. He was stuck and he knew it, and it didn't improve his disposition. In future years, he'd get to know this feeling over and over again.

Ballard turned to leave the room, paused, and faced us again. "You bastards better make sure you start to do something."

He slammed the door behind him on the way out.

In the playoffs that April, we ousted Atlanta 2-0 in a mini-series, outscoring them 9-5. Then we lost 4-0 to the Canadiens, outscored 19-10 along the way.

When we lost to the Canadiens in the quarter-finals, Harold had his excuse to make changes. The way I see it is that we had lost twice in a row to the eventual Stanley Cup winner; there was no disgrace in that and no reason to panic.

We didn't have as much depth or defense as they had. But, up until late April, we all believed that we had matched them behind the bench.

Also, we knew—as a team—that somebody else was going to take the opportunity of making Roger Neilson what he was: a top-flight NHL coach.

9

Back to the Future, Round One

JULY 4 IS Independence Day in the United States. Ironically, on that date in 1979 the independence of the Toronto Maple Leafs diminished greatly. On that day, Harold Ballard made a gigantic mistake, one which was going to condemn his team to another decade of frustration, poor performance and lack of success.

On July 4, 1979, Harold Ballard hired George (Punch) Imlach as general manager of the Toronto Maple Leafs hockey club. With the 1980s only five months away, Harold turned the franchise around and pointed us straight back toward the 1960s. In his own words, our future was our past.

Had we been paying close attention late in the previous season, we might have had an inkling of what might happen should we falter. There was the infamous firing and rehiring of Roger Neilson which confirmed Harold Ballard's status as the most insensitive owner/ executive in the league. It may have made great television, what with Roger's dramatic return on the Saturday night before the *Hockey Night in Canada* cameras, but it did nothing to help the team.

The rumors first began circulating in mid-March, just around St. Patrick's Day: Harold was thinking of bringing back Punch Imlach! Ironically, the man who put these rumors to rest would be the guy who became Punch's staunchest media ally and biographer, Scott Young of the *Globe and Mail*. He wrote on March 17: "The rumors a few days ago that Punch Imlach's hiring by Leafs was imminent might have been great fun for the fans and media people who blew this completely baseless report into Topic A for a day or two, but might have been one reason why Leafs skated out Wednesday looking flat and baffled. Right now it wouldn't be a bad thing if majority owner Harold Ballard came out with an assurance that for the rest of the season Leafs can concentrate on hockey; leaving it strictly up to them." (I can't remember Harold giving us a vote of confidence after that article appeared, but I did get a hat trick the following night in a 6-3 Gardens win over Minnesota.)

Harold just might have taken Scott Young's advice to heart because little else was heard on the Imlach issue for the rest of the season. However, after our second straight 4-0 whitewash by Montreal in the playoffs, Harold was convinced that his team needed a change of direction. His mind had long been made up by the time the summer came around; Gregory and Neilson had to go, and he was looking at three candidates: Scotty Bowman, the coach who had eliminated us twice in a row; Don Cherry, who lost his job when the Canadiens eliminated the Bruins in seven games in the last conference final; and Punch Imlach, the last man to guide Toronto to a Stanley Cup.

I hated to see Roger go, despite what some Toronto newspapers were saying at the time. But Roger was gone, never to return; in fact, Scotty Bowman, a fellow alumnus of the Peterborough Petes Coaching Legion, would embarrass Harold Ballard immensely when he appointed Roger to coach the Sabres, moments after taking over that club.

Hiring Bowman or Cherry would have been a positive move, I feel. Scotty had proven his worth with the expansion St. Louis Blues and then with the Canadiens, while Cherry had been the coach who got a very diverse Boston Bruins team thinking Stanley Cup, even after Phil Esposito had been traded to the Rangers and Bobby Orr had been lost to injury.

But there were a couple of things wrong with both men, in Harold's eyes, at least. Scotty Bowman was going after a general manager's job and he definitely did not want to coach. Harold was more interested in seeing Scotty chewing ice cubes and fretting behind our bench for eighty regular season games and another twenty or so in the playoffs. In the end, Scotty relented and was signed as both coach and general manager—of the Buffalo Sabres.

Don Cherry was still available after the word came back that Bowman had gone across Lake Ontario for his NHL paycheques. I've always liked Grapes, and his players will tell you that he's a players' coach, like Roger had been. We'd been together during the 1976 Canada Cup and I had liked and respected him then. And, of course, as he's mentioned maybe five million times to anybody who will listen, he really did come in to our dressing room before the overtime period in the final and tell us to take it deep into the zone along the boards, fake a slapshot, and slide it along the ice into the net.

Actually, he didn't say that. What Grapes said was, "Droozilla always comes way out." Don Cherry still hasn't found the eastern European name he can pronounce correctly.

The real question was, however, would this town be big enough for both Harold and Grapes? Forever the showman and the headline junkie, Harold had jumped into the media circus with both feet, thoroughly enjoying the limelight. Don Cherry had proved in Boston that a coach could be popular and colorful, and still do the job, even with a perfectionist like Harry Sinden peeking over his shoulder at every turn. Grapes, his multicolored suits and loud ties, and his dog, Blue (actually a she), had become a familiar story in the NHL and generated headlines of his own.

Another drawback, of course, was that Grapes and I shared an agent, and everybody knew that Ballard would get apoplectic when the names Alan and Eagleson appeared in the same phrase. Ballard hated agents as a rule; and a superagent with the other powers R. Alan Eagleson enjoyed, especially with the NHLPA and negotiations with international hockey powers, was Ballard's worst nightmare come true.

"I almost became your coach," Grapes mentioned several years after I'd retired, "but Ballard was a day late." Harold had procrastinated so long, even more after Scotty Bowman had gone to Buffalo, that the Colorado Rockies whisked Cherry out from under his very nose. "Colorado G.M. Ray Miron—now there's a real beauty—was ordered to sign me by team owners Arthur Imperatore and his son-in-law Armand Pohan. The day after I was fired by the Bruins, they were on the telephone to Bill Watters in Alan Eagleson's office and he was on the phone to me. I had been making about $60,000 a year with the Bruins and Miron was offering me something in the $135,000-$140,000 range. So naturally, I told him to wait and I'd think about it."

One thing you can say about Grapes is that he has always possessed keen intuition—street smarts. His two decades in the American Hockey League, a lot of that time spent under the tutelage of the incomparable Eddie Shore at Springfield, had taught him that things are never what they seem in pro hockey. While Miron was flashing all that money at him, Grapes had the gut feeling that this was an owners' decision, and that Miron was not too pleased with this development. Cherry made good use of his minor league grapevine, sounding out many friends and former associates who had had dealings with Miron. The survey results were unanimous: stay away.

Miron, they said, liked to have junior people as subordinates so that it would be difficult to replace him. His coaches were seen, and rarely heard, hardly the portrait of A Man and His Dog in Boston. Cherry thought about it, and took the plunge, meeting with Miron and agreeing verbally to the deal. The way around worries about his boss was to tell Miron that all he wanted to do was coach, and that he would never actively seek, or even accept, a general manager's position. There also was the ego-boosting challenge of taking one of the league's worst franchises and building it into a contender in his own image. He agreed to a three-year contract at $135,000 per, with the usual incentives and bonuses.

The night before the Rockies officially announced his signing, Grapes flew into Denver. He was quietly watching television in his hotel room when the telephone rang; it was Alan Eagleson calling from Toronto. "The Leafs want you to coach; Ballard will give you three years at $150,000 a year." Grapes later said he was almost in tears, a Kingston boy getting a chance to coach with the blue-and-white.

"I can't do it," he told Eagleson. Even though he had not yet signed on the dotted line, which he had promised to do the next day, he had given the Rockies his word. Eagleson tried, but failed in his attempt to change Cherry's mind. The following afternoon, Grapes was coach of the Rockies. His "three years" lasted one—apparently everything he had heard about Ray Miron was true.

With Bowman and Cherry out of the picture, it was Back to the Future: the call went out for Punch Imlach.

I've always felt that the true catalyst for the move was King Clancy. I had always respected what King had meant to the Leafs, the years of service to the team, a direct link with the more glorious days of the franchise, and the kind of true blue loyalty of those people who wear their hearts on their sleeve. But, like Harold, King was firmly rooted in the past, while the ways of Captain Video had represented the true wave (discredited in Harold's mind) of the future.

Ironically, while Imlach also revelled in past glories, one of the few communications he had with Clancy during the Neilson era was to dump all over the Leafs for trading Errol Thompson, along with two first-round and one second-round draft choices to Detroit for Dan Maloney and a second-round pick. Clancy, forever famous for his religious devotion to Conn Smythe's "beat 'em in the alley" philosophy, strenuously defended the deal which was engineered by Jim Gregory after Harold Ballard had disgustedly dismissed his unaggressive Maple Leafs as the "Carlton Street chickens." Imlach, quite rightly, argued that the real threats to Toronto's playoff success were the Montreal Canadiens and the New York Islanders, two teams that could really skate and that would be intimidated by nobody. (Imlach considered Maloney part of my "London mafia," a string of players including Walt McKechnie, Pat Boutette and Dave Hutchison, who had all played with the London Knights.) He expressed regret over the fact that the Leafs, a team notoriously slow of foot, had traded away the good wheels possessed by Errol Thompson.

The sequence was clear. Clancy had put a flea in Ballard's ear and Harold, in one of his more garrulous moments, had let it be known to all and sundry that "someone like Dan Maloney is what this club needs." Gregory could read the jungle drums as well as anybody and Maloney was soon on his way to Toronto. Red Wings management must have seen the Leafs GM coming, because they exacted a stiff price.

Whether Imlach's criticism of the Maloney trade ever got back to Harold, I'll never know.

At the time of the Imlach-Clancy conversation, Punch was on his last legs with the Sabres. To give the man credit, he had built a contender in Buffalo within a short time and had taken his club to the Stanley Cup final in 1975, only to lose to Bernie Parent, the Philadelphia Flyers, fog and a bat—the flying kind. With a strong nucleus of players like Gilbert Perreault, Rick Martin, Craig Ramsey, Don Luce, Jim Schoenfeld, René Robert, Fred Stanfield, Jerry Korab and Danny Gare, the Sabres had stayed in the top four for several years, battling Montreal, Boston and Philadelphia in the upper echelons of the league.

By November 1978, however, this same nucleus of players had soured on Imlach and the players were in almost open revolt. They warred against Imlach on all fronts, but especially on the question of the National Hockey League Players' Association and union-management contacts in the NHL. Other teams in the league had long ago accepted the fact that the players' union and management could co-exist peacefully, and that player agents were a fact of life in the late 1970s and would continue to be in the future. Not Punch. He fought the union fiercely on every issue, labelling it and agents as challenges to his right to manage. It was clear that he had not moved with the times, and had no inclination to do so. Ironically, one of the events that precipitated his dismissal in Buffalo was the same type of thing Harold Ballard had become famous for: refusing to play an exhibition game against the Soviets. The league governors had met in mid-1978 and discussed another Christmas period Soviet exhibition tour with Eagleson, the devil with three horns according to Imlach (one each for being the power in international hockey relations, the president of the NHLPA, and a superagent representing many name players, including yours truly). Also grating to Imlach's anti-union sensibilities was the fact that the NHLPA pension fund would be the greatest beneficiary of such a visit. Imlach was not aware that his owners, Seymour and Northrup (Norty) Knox, had agreed to have the Sabres play one of the touring teams during this visit, and when he heard, he was furious.

"There's no way my team is playing the Russians!" he stormed.

"But we've already agreed," the owners said. Imlach grumbled and said nothing else, and his bosses assumed that all was okay. After all those years, they still didn't know their man. Imlach returned to his office and immediately began scanning the arena events schedule for the upcoming season. The only available openings for an exhibition game with the Soviets would be the evenings of January 2 and 3.

The Auditorium in Buffalo is a public facility, owned and operated by the city. As a public facility, it is available to all area residents who are willing to rent its services at the right price. Punch went to see the person in charge of arena rentals and booked both of those nights. More than a month later, Seymour Knox telephoned Imlach to ask about the progress of the Soviet game, only to be told that the game was off because the Aud was booked.

"Who booked it?" the owner asked innocently.

"I did!" Punch retorted, with his best in-your-face cockiness.

Imlach went to war with the Knox brothers over that issue, insisting that this was a hockey decision and his department, and that the Sabres had already clobbered the Russians (12-6 over the Soviet

Wings in 1976) and he didn't want to risk any more injuries to his players in meaningless exhibition games. Punch was still mad that all-star Danny Gare had aggravated what would become a chronic back injury during the 1976 Canada Cup and missed half a season. He was steadfast in his opposition to exhibition games and such on-ice affairs as the television program *Showdown*. He did not want his stars competing on the ice in anything but regularly scheduled league games and playoffs. The fact that the NHLPA and Eagleson were intricately involved in both served only to strengthen his resolve.

I was familiar with all of these stories because I used to sit in the player association meetings as a vice-president. It seemed that eighty per cent of our NHLPA time was taken up with Punch Imlach anti-union horror stories; all about how he would test the union on this and that and drive guys like Craig Ramsay nuts. Craig was the Sabres' player rep at the time and almost constantly at war with Imlach, not over his playing, because after Bob Gainey, Rammer was the best defensive forward in the league. But Imlach was perpet-ually on his case, on the ice and off, because Ramsay had had the bad judgment to accept the position of player representative to the NHLPA. So I had inside knowledge of what Imlach was like in Buffalo behind the scenes. Forget the championships and the draft picks and all that other stuff; I knew what his mind-set was.

The players had finally had enough too. While many still respected Punch's coach, Marcel Pronovost, they felt that Imlach was constantly undermining his authority by sniping at them pub-licly and running down the team. Only Gilbert Perreault and Rick Martin remained on the sidelines; every other leader or impact player on the team was aligned against Imlach at this point.

A players' revolt doesn't happen overnight. It takes a long time to get going; in Buffalo's case, about two years. The Sabres had been a few feet short of the top of the mountain in 1975-76 and, instead of climbing those extra few steps, they began to slide perceptibly back-wards. When Punch started to lose it, the process of alienating his players began, but it still took a long time. His well-publicized attacks on Jim Schoenfeld startled the team at first and they didn't know how to react. The problem was that a lot of the veterans loved the old goat. They remembered the good times, how Punch Imlach had brought the team together and how he was as much part of that blue-and-gold Sabres fabric as they were.

It was tearing them up inside, knowing that something had to be done and that Punch had to go. They had pangs of conscience; Perreault and Martin took it especially hard, but the decision had to be taken. Another example of the closeness of this team—even though Imlach had charged that the Sabres' team unity had broken down—was the fact that the other players did not begrudge Perreault and Martin their dissent. The Sabres were a team that was hurting, not a lynch mob.

By the end of November 1978, the chasm between the general manager and his team was too great to be bridged. The players met at Danny Gare's house to orchestrate Imlach's demise and a delegation was dispatched to meet with the Knoxes. After the team was swept 8-1 and 4-1 in a home-and-home weekend series with Montreal, Punch was fired on Monday morning, December 4.

The Imlachs had always maintained a residence in Scarborough and had planned to drive home after practice on that Monday morning. So when Punch heard his days in Buffalo were over, he was already on the way to Scarborough. It wasn't too long afterward that Harold Ballard began to contemplate bringing him all the way home, all the way to downtown Toronto.

Imlach stayed away from hockey for the most part in the ensuing months, occasionally dropping in to Maple Leaf Gardens to catch a game, but doing little else with any team. He still had a year and a half on his Buffalo contract and spent part of the spring of 1979 in Europe, visiting France and the U.K. While we ousted Atlanta and then fell 4-0 to Montreal, Punch and Dodo Imlach were rediscovering their family roots in Scotland. They had barely unpacked their bags when King Clancy called Punch on June 8 and offered him Jim Gregory's job. Ballard, with his usual lack of class, had not bothered to inform Gregory first. Gregory discovered he had been fired when Brian O'Neil of the NHL league office in Montreal telephoned to offer him the position of head of the Central Scouting Bureau. "But I've already got a job," Jim protested. "That's not what Harold just told me," O'Neil replied.

Harold and Punch were front and center on July 4, 1979 at the introductory press conference for the "new" GM. Imlach did not mince words. The Leafs were a country club. The reason they hadn't gone anywhere in the past several seasons was due to "lack of talent." Having only five or six players wasn't sufficient to win the Stanley Cup. The quickest route to improvement was to buy players, he added, because drafts and trading represented the slow road to respectability. It would take three to five years to produce a decent team that way.

And then he laid it on the line: "I run the hockey club. I take suggestions from anyone but that doesn't mean that I go along with them. If I get into trouble, which I certainly expect to do, I expect Harold to back me."

About the only thing missing at the press conference was a picture of Punch, his '50s-era fedora perched high on his head, standing at attention with a broom held in the "present arms" position, getting ready to sweep Maple Leaf Gardens clean. And all of this flying in the face of our players; we felt we were just a couple of players away from jumping up a level in the NHL, especially considering the fact that we had beaten the Islanders in 1978 and lost only to the eventual Cup winners, Montreal, in both 1978 and 1979. Now we had a new boss, a manager who had spent his last two seasons at war with his players in Buffalo, openly declaring war on us.

In a way it was fitting; here it was July 4, and Punch had staged his own fireworks display.

And then, strangely, nothing. Punch disappeared into the bowels of the second floor at Maple Leaf Gardens, methodically working his way through the files and having very little contact with any of the players. Technically, he was supposed to start work August 1, but he was at his desk all through July getting ready for September training camp and the coming season. About the only person he saw all summer was Ian Turnbull.

Ian's restaurant was a couple of blocks down the street from the Gardens and he'd often go up to the offices and spend some time with Imlach after the luncheon crowd had cleared out. There was method to his madness, his contract was up for renewal and he was just taking care of business. He and Punch seemed to hit it off quite well; it helped that Turnbull was one of the Leafs Imlach was counting on to lead the team, and it resulted in a long-term deal that gave him about $200,000 a year. Coincidentally, the afternoon visits stopped once all parties had signed on the dotted line.

There was little contact with the other players. As team captain, I had expected a letter or a phone call inviting me to lunch or down to the office to discuss the team. Nothing. The silence from Maple Leaf Gardens was deafening. Instead, I had dinner with Floyd Smith, who had been hired by Imlach as his new coach, one day in late July. I can remember that meeting with Smitty because his whole pitch was, "You're not going to have a problem with Punch, Punch is fine, don't worry about a thing." Floyd was a veteran who had been with Punch in Buffalo and Toronto, a card-carrying member of the Imlach inner circle. There were a few grains of salt swallowed during that meal.

The next contact came in late August. It was time for a showdown about *Showdown*, and I had been expecting the call since Imlach's hiring.

Many of today's readers may be too young to remember, so I'll explain what this was all about. Back in the mid-1970s, a company called Sports Dimensions Limited, in conjunction with *Hockey Night In Canada* (MacLaren Advertising owned the broadcast rights to all NHL games at that time), the NHLPA and the NHL, put together an intermission feature for the hockey broadcasts during the season. A group of players, usually the league's top stars, including two top goalies, would be invited to Toronto in late summer, just prior to training camp's reopening, to film a special skills competition. This included special obstacle races, penalty shot competitions, three-on-three hockey games and the like, and was a popular intermission fixture for several years. For most of that period, the program was sponsored by Canadian Pacific, so you knew it was a major league effort.

Punch wanted nothing to do with *Showdown* and had prevented stars like Perreault and Martin from participating when he was head man in Buffalo. He was incensed that Sports Dimensions Limited picked the players it wanted to appear on the program, claiming this process restricted his right to manage his "hockey resources," a.k.a. his players. But he was banging his head against a brick wall; the NHL was behind this project all the way and would not tolerate his obstruction.

I was getting ready to head off to the Markham Centennial Centre arena on a Friday in early September when I got a call at about nine o'clock in the morning from the Leaf's secretary down at the Gardens. Punch wanted to see me; could I be in his office by about eleven? I knew what the meeting was going to be about—to keep Mike Palmateer and me from going to *Showdown*. Punch had waited until the very last second, figuring he could ambush me, catch me off guard and keep me that way. The hidden agenda was to show me unmistakably who was boss, and hope that the lessons of this demonstration would carry over into the season.

I got to the Gardens office downtown at eleven o'clock; Paul Gardner was sitting quietly in the anteroom to the team offices. It clicked right away. Imlach was going to tell me *I* couldn't go, but since he couldn't defy the league and the players' association absolutely, his prohibition would be expressed by *his* naming of the Leafs who would participate. Paul was the fourth-string center, Imlach would send him in my place.

As I sat there patiently waiting to be called in, the secretary turned to me and said, "I think he's going to be a while."

Sure, Punch, the old delay game; keep me here until I'm very late for the *Showdown* session scheduled that afternoon. No dice.

"I'm supposed to be somewhere at a certain time. Can you tell him I'm here and I'd like to meet him now because I've got to get going. If he can't see me now, I'll come back another time." She went in and reported my comments.

A short while later, Imlach came out and brought me into his office. This was the first time I'd ever met him in person. I might have said hello to him in passing at some rink or league meeting over the years, but this was the first time we had had a conversation. I can't even remember if we shook hands.

"Siddown."

I sat.

"Who do you think you are?"

The strategy was full-frontal assault. I hesitated a moment, then looked him in the eye, all innocence. "What do you mean?"

"It says in the paper that you're going to *Showdown*."

"Yeah, I intend to go. I'm a member of the National Hockey League Players' Association and have been for the last three years. I was asked to go and I'm looking forward to it."

"Well I'm the GM. You don't decide to go to *Showdown*, I decide. And I don't want you to go."

"Why not?"

"We voted against that stuff, we don't believe in it. You're going to get the better players in there, and you might even get hurt. Plus, I wanna tell them who goes to *Showdown*." He tried to stare me down, but he knew that I'd been a member of the NHLPA and knew exactly who had voted on what. Better than that, I knew that Harold Ballard's No vote meant zip, the board of governors had approved the program and the league had endorsed it. This was all hot air, and it was time to call his bluff.

"The owners have voted on it, and it went through. And I'm a member of the players' association and I have an obligation to live up to my end of the deal. The sponsors have paid their money."

Players' association. Owners. Sponsors. These were all little red flags being waved right in the nose of an enraged bull. My superficial innocence in recounting the details he already knew was calculated to upset him. He was boiling inside, knew that I knew it, and that in turn goosed the thermostat even higher.

"Well, I don't want you to go, but if you do decide to go, that's your choice and you're going to have to suffer the consequences."

In my mental rehearsals for a conversation which I had anticipated all summer long, I had played this scenario over and over in my mind.

"If that means you're going to take the 'C' away from me, then that's your choice. I'll have to live with that. But if they ask me to be the captain again, if the players vote me in, I'd really have to reconsider if I wanted to do it."

Another red flag.

"The players don't vote on my team. I appoint the captain of the Maple Leafs. My captains have always been management in the past and I expect them to be management now. As far as I'm concerned, you have a conflict of interest as vice-president of the players' association and captain of the hockey club. How can you sit across the table on the players' side when you're supposed to be management?" I knew all about Punch and his captains, how he had stripped the "C" from Schoenfeld. And Leafs trainer Bobby Haggert had recounted how Bob Pulford went to put on his sweater one day and found it light one initial, because of his involvement in the early days of the players' association.

I voiced the opinion that I didn't believe that the captain was management and that, ideally, he should operate as a go-between. We could sit down and work together on things but I didn't think there was a conflict of interest.

George Imlach showed some selective memory when he discussed the encounter in his own book. He quotes me as saying, "What are the players on my team going to think if I don't go to *Showdown*?"

When I said that, it was in response to what he had said. "What are the players on my team going to think of me as general manager if I allow you to go to *Showdown*?"

That explains my "What are they going to think of me if I don't go?" reply. I left that meeting and headed for the Markham arena.

Another issue was that Harold had refused permission to use the Maple Leaf jersey because he wanted to be paid—he had that right, I guess, and nothing could prevent him from doing this. So Mike and I wore *Showdown* sweaters, instead. About an hour later, I was taking a leisurely warm-up skate before the traditional group picture. The guys from the other teams were kidding me and deep down I suspected that the Toronto media were going to make a big issue of this once they got wind of it: the opening salvo in a Sittler-Imlach war. We had just finished taking the pictures when I was called away to the telephone. It was Alan Eagleson.

"Darryl, we've got a real problem. I've just been issued a writ. I have to go to court on your behalf and Mike Palmateer's. The Leafs are going to sue you guys if you're in *Showdown*."

"Do what you have to do."

When the Leafs' lawyers showed up in court to present their arguments that Friday afternoon, the judge threw out their injunction petition. It didn't last twenty minutes. He asked Imlach a pertinent question: "If you really felt this way, why did you wait until the day of the taping to tell your people?" In other words, don't waste my time.

It was an embarrassing episode that made the Toronto Maple Leafs the laughing-stock of the NHL, not that we needed any more such incidents. Punch, stung by the reaction of the media, even tried to explain it away as offering me a way out.

> I discussed it with Ballard. I mentioned that Sittler's insistence had something to do with not wanting to look as if he were backing down to us. But I didn't think he was totally happy with his position. If my impression was right, there was one way out worth considering. "We might be able to get a court injunction against them," I said. "If we win, he's off the hook. Nobody can say that he backed down to management if he's backing down to a court order. If we lose the case, the guy's off the hook, too, because then he's got the right to go."
>
> So we went for the injunction, and lost. The media twisted the situation to make Ballard and me look bad because we took it to court for a ruling. The only reason for taking this action was to get Sittler off the hook.

And if you believe that, there's a lot of "reclaimed" swampland going for a song in Florida.

That's when the whole thing mushroomed and hit the headlines. Typical Toronto Maple Leafs storyline: training camp opens in a couple of days and the GM and team captain are at war.

Remember the ancient Chinese curse: "May you live in interesting times!"

On July 4, 1979, interesting times walked into Maple Leaf Gardens in George Imlach's back pocket.

10

Punch Drunk

WE STARTED THE 1979-80 season under the new regime with class. Infuriated with Scotty Bowman's bravado, first for turning down his job offer—most serious hockey people suspected that Bowman had just used Ballard and the Leafs to bump up the Sabres' ante—and then for the insult of hiring Roger Neilson as his right-hand man in Buffalo, Ballard persuaded Imlach to ban Neilson from the Toronto press box during a pre-season game.

Upon arrival at Buffalo, Bowman had instituted the skybox spotter system, now used by all NHL coaching staffs. Under this system, Bowman would run the team from behind the bench and Neilson would sit in the press box, reporting to the head coach between periods. Later, of course, this system was expanded to involve a second assistant behind the bench connected by closed-circuit telephone to the spotter upstairs. Every team functions that way now, but back then, it was uncharted territory. Each team was able to control access as it pleased, for the simple reason that there were no rules that governed this situation.

Only too happy to take a jab at the Sabres, Imlach complied with Ballard's edict. "If he [Neilson] wants to coach, let him coach," he reasoned. "But this is the press box, isn't it? Coaches are supposed to be at the bench." Of course, the NHL had no such rule and the Sabres used the system in every other rink in the league. Soon thereafter, their NHL counterparts joined in, with the notable exception of one team, Team Dinosaur in blue-and-white.

How can I adequately describe what the transition from Jim Gregory and Roger Neilson to Punch Imlach and Floyd Smith was like? As a Leaf, I had known only one general manager, Gregory, and three coaches, John McLellan, Red Kelly and Roger Neilson, all men I trusted and respected. Normal human beings, they all had their strong and weak points, their individual character traits, and I liked them and worked with them amicably.

And then came Punch and Friends. Life, as we had known it with the Toronto Maple Leafs, came to an end. The first indication had come during my meeting that summer with Floyd Smith. Floyd had mentioned that we should get rid of the Universal Gym equipment we had in the room.

"You don't need that stuff; we didn't have it when we won the Cup in '67."

This came from way out in left field; it was pretty much taken for granted that the modern hockey player worked on his conditioning year-round, during the season and between seasons. Part of this work was dry-land training which usually involved some sort of running program (aerobics) and work with weights or weight machines (anaerobics). Roger Neilson had been a stickler for conditioning and all of us had a program. In Floyd's and Punch's day, veterans would routinely "fatten up" during the off-season and use training camp to get back into playing shape, a phenomenon then shared with the other major sports in North America.

"A lot of things have changed since then, Smitty," I replied. "The guys today depend on these programs, and they work hard at staying in shape. It's also been proven that we come back quicker off injuries because of the extra stuff we do off the ice. Why don't you and Punch ask the trainers about this? They can tell you."

"Nah, Punch doesn't agree with it." He didn't sound convinced either way. The upshot was that when we arrived at training camp, they had a dry-land training program under the direction of Fred Atkins, a former professional wrestler. After the camp experience, some players came to me looking for a circuit training program. I believed in it and knew it had helped me improve my game and given me the strength to get through the long haul of the season. To be fair, there were some players who didn't believe in it.

When I was approached, my response was to turn this into a positive, team-oriented activity. "If anybody wants to do it, let's do it together." Of course, Punch Imlach saw this as expressing my desire to continue to run the club and defy the new management team.

Actually, "new management team" is something of a misnomer. Punch Imlach *was* the new management team, all by himself. I remember Floyd Smith being appointed coach of the Maple Leafs, but it is my recollection that Punch, who was hired as general manager, was still calling the shots behind the bench and that Smitty and Dick Duff were doing what he said. Another "Imlach oldie," Joe Crozier, was coaching the American Hockey League farm team in New Brunswick.

Despite his State of the Maple Leaf union address on July 4, Imlach had not tinkered with the Leafs lineup as we moved through pre-season. The Big Six remained in place. Paul Harrison was slotted for back-up duty again in nets, even though the team had signed a Czech defector, Jiri Crha, and drafted Vincent Tremblay out of the Quebec junior league. On defense, veterans Dave Hutchison and Dave Burrows, and sophomore Joel Quenneville played behind Salming and Turnbull, and rookie Greg Hotham was trying to get the sixth spot.

Up front, we were a grinding team with Tiger Williams, Pat Boutette and Dan Maloney on the left side, and Ronnie Ellis, Jerry Butler and Rocky Saganiuk playing behind Lanny on the right. Center was different, with a lot of question marks. Mark Kirton and Jimmy Jones, defensive specialists, had played behind me the previous year, as had Walt McKechnie, who'd missed a substantial part of the season with injuries. Still, Walt had come up with sixty points in a shortened season and was a valuable contributor. Paul Gardner, Dave's younger brother, had a shot at picking up a spot because of his offensive ability, but he was hindered by lack of speed. A dark-horse candidate was Laurie Boschman, a first-round draft choice who had notched 149 points with Brandon Wheat Kings of the Western junior league. We also had John Anderson, a third-year player who had yet to blossom into the offensive threat we knew he could be, and defensive winger Ron Wilson.

This was the team that Punch Imlach had accused of being a country club, and not good enough to do anything in the long run. Yet, no deals had been made and there was no indication of impending transactions as we moved through the pre-season schedule.

Unable or unwilling to make lineup changes at this time, Imlach contented himself with regulating everything else that had to do with hockey. We now had to wear a jacket and tie everywhere we went on the road, even if we were travelling between hotel rooms or down to the lobby newsstand for a paper or gum. This upset our original cowboy, Tiger Williams, who was fined $150 for not wearing a jacket and tie when he went up to see Harold Ballard in his office and bumped into Punch on the way out.

We had been pampered, charter members of the Toronto Maple Leafs Country Club, but Punch was going to get us on the straight and narrow if it killed us. Next to go was the ping-pong table in the dressing room, and that was quickly followed by the beer ban: no suds in the room or on the bus.

And then, because we were pampered athletes who did not understand the value of a dollar, or the sacrifices made by the "working population who commuted to and from work in the Toronto area every day," Punch ordered us to spend "the working day" at Maple Leaf Gardens. Practices meant everyone on the ice at 10:30, which meant most of us in the building between 9:00 and 9:30. After the on-ice session, we'd break for lunch and be back for 2:30 or 3:00 to go over game films and work on other things. The idea was to have us drive in with John Q. Public at nine in the morning, and drive home with him at five at night. Then we'd appreciate our good fortune a lot more. That would be fine, if we didn't spend fifty per cent of the season travelling and away from home.

One such session illustrates the reform-school atmosphere that was being built up with the team. Usually we'd practice in the morning, and then the coaching staff would invite everybody back to watch a film of the previous night's game as punishment. Guy Kinnear would put the film on, and when it was over, the players could go home. Nobody thought of hitting the fast forward switch because we knew that we couldn't get out of there before five o'clock. Duff would squeal if somebody left early. A few guys would sip quietly on a beer or two they had smuggled in, or sleep through the proceedings, sprawled all over the room.

On this particular afternoon, we were just getting started and who comes through the doors but Punch. The door opened with a bang, the lights went on, and guys were jumping up like a cannon had gone off. He scared the wits out of everybody—accidentally, of course.

That incident took place after Floyd Smith had been involved in a car accident near St. Catharines, in which two people died. We'd been without an on-ice coach for several days because of Floyd's accident.

"I, George Imlach, am the General Manager of the Toronto Maple Leafs. You now can call me George Imlach, Coach of the Toronto Maple Leafs. Now you guys better bust your ass!

"Now, let's watch some film."

A young guy was handling the machine, and Punch was treating him like a piece of dirt.

"Okay, turn the thing on. Let's go. Get going."

You could see the kid was petrified and Punch was oblivious, hounding him at every turn.

"Come on, kid, stop it there! Play it back! Let's see that! Burrows, whattya doin' on that play?"

"All right, roll it again. Okay, stop it. Who's on that play?"

This went on for about an hour. Then we had a break for ten minutes. A couple of the guys had had a few beers at lunch and brought some back to the room to drink while they watched the films. Imlach's edict was clear: no beer in the Gardens. So when the break came, they dumped the beer in the toilet and tried to hide the empties in the garbage cans in the back corner of the washroom. We went back into the meeting room, finished the team meeting and went home.

I was one of the first guys at the rink the next morning and I ran into Guy Kinnear. "You guys are in trouble now!"

"What's happening?"

"Look over there!" It was like the old camp song "99 Bottles of Beer on the Wall." All the empties were lined up. Inanimate objects or not, they *looked* guilty.

"When you guys left, Duff went into the washroom, found all the beer cans, took them all out and showed them to Punch. You guys are in trouble."

So in the post-practice meeting, they wanted the guys to own up to the beer cans in the dressing room. Nobody said anything. The battle lines had been drawn and the players didn't trust the petty, penny-ante mentality of Punch or his minions.

Imlach made a big deal of the fact that the rules he was instituting were essentially those that he had implemented with great success over the years in Buffalo, being careful, of course, not to dwell on the comparison lest anyone remember the circumstances that precipitated his departure. Floyd Smith had the rules typed out and posted in the dressing room.

The last rule was a catchall which, depending on your interpretation, protected us or threatened us. It said something to the effect that "anyone who does anything that is contrary to good hockey discipline may be fined or suspended." Punch asked us all to read the rules, acknowledge them, and then sign to acknowledge our acknowledgment. We didn't; unlike the 1960s, NHL players now had the right to arbitration in such matters and we chose to see the last rule as one which gave the team a free hand to discipline individuals at the drop of a hat for perceived misconduct, proved or unproved. Imlach saw it as the revolt of the country club, and this made him more determined than ever to root out the malcontents.

A good analogy that highlights the differences between Roger's team and Punch's team—and at this point in time, we're discussing the same players—comes from the movie *Dead Poets' Society*. This was a story about a private boys' school and a class of young men who were challenged to think by a young literature teacher, played by Robin Williams. He brought them out of their shells, helped them develop their individual skills, and this led to their developing a group identity as well. They learned to like him and trust him. Unfortunately, in the end, the hierarchy took over, and went back to teaching the old way, "by the numbers," with teachers the students feared, but neither liked nor respected.

That may seem overly simplistic to some people, but the comparison is a fair one. We liked and trusted Roger because we knew that everything he did had a reason behind it. He lived and breathed hockey and worked hard at building the team from the middle out: first develop the individual to peak performance levels, then introduce team concepts, and develop the team as a whole to peak performance levels. For Roger, it was important to eliminate all distractions from the management side.

With Punch, Smith and Duff, everything from the management side seemed to be a distraction. All decisions came from above and it was our duty to absorb and obey.

Just prior to the start of the season, Punch had a long interview with Frank Orr, the veteran writer with the *Toronto Star*. He didn't come right out and repeat the accusations of his appointment press conference, but it was easy to read between the lines:

> "From what I've seen, we seem to have a fair amount of raw ability in this club. Technically, we've got a lot of work to do because there's considerable room for improvement." Much publicity has been granted to the Imlach-Smith tandem's talk of switching Leafs from a basic defensive approach to wide-open attacking hockey.
>
> "Leafs were a good defensive team and they were well-

coached in that area by Roger Neilson," Imlach said. "We certainly don't plan to have the team abandon that side of the game. We just want the emphasis to switch to offense. We want this club to have the puck a little more than it has in the last couple of seasons."

Wasn't that nice of Punch to give Roger Neilson credit for the team's defensive play? Of course, the opposite and unspoken side of that coin was that Roger did not know what he was doing on offense. The other implication was that we didn't have the kind of team to play Punch's new offensive style of game. Ours was basically a grinding team built for wearing out others with aggressive play along the boards and in the corners, and capitalizing on the mistakes of the opposition. If Punch Imlach wanted a new team, he'd have to trade for one. But he wasn't quite ready to tell Frank Orr that he was going to make wholesale changes. I suspected that his plan was to try to force a team built for corners play to play the fast-skating, wide-open kind of game for a while, and then orchestrate trades when it became obvious that we couldn't do the job.

Many Leaf fans seemed to think that Imlach would make assorted deals and Leafs would be an instant contender. Although he did swing some excellent trades to bolster his clubs over the years, the core of the two successful clubs with which he's been associated was home grown.

"Making deals is more complicated now than it was in the days of the old six-team NHL," he noted. "Back then, there were some pretty fair hockey players who were in the minor leagues and not really needed by the NHL club. Well, another club could make a deal for those players who could help that club.

"When you're talking trades these days, you're looking at players who are part of that club's starting rotation or they're looking for someone in the same role on your team."

Floyd Smith could always be counted on to back up the Boss's analysis.

One area where this club must improve is in sustaining the tempo of their play. In some of our pre-season games, we've skated really well for half the game or even two periods, then started to hang back because we lost the tempo in our play.

We'll have to learn to keep up the tempo, to keep on skating
well, for the entire 60 minutes.

You also had to wonder if Smith and Imlach were anticipating
trouble from their inherited stars. Floyd addressed the issue in his
usual off-hand way.

Smith plans to give a heavy workload to the Leafs' top players.
    "The good players on any team have to have plenty of ice
time," he said. "They're the guys who can handle it, the ones
who thrive on it."

Thus, in their own words, the attitudes and thoughts of the men
who were going to lead us kicking and screaming into the 1980s. It
was time to get down to business: our (the players') business was
winning hockey games; their (management's) business was rebuilding the team in their own image, as quickly as possible. Of course,
that meant Punch was free to dedicate his time to freeing Maple Leaf
Gardens of the insidious presence of R. Alan Eagleson.

Three of the Big Six were Eagleson clients—Mike Palmateer,
Lanny McDonald and myself, and, sadly, for team unity at least, it
was Palmateer who was the first target. Palmy was up for renegotia-
tion and Imlach gave no sign that he would accommodate him. As
the season began, it became quite obvious that Imlach was going to
let one of the top four or five goalies in the league play out his option.
This was 1972 all over again, a replay of the Bernie Parent–WHA
raid. It had taken us four whole seasons to find a first-string goalie
after Bernie went to the Philadelphia Blazers via the Miami Screaming Eagles, and a couple more to see him blossom into the outstanding goaltender that he now was. Now all that was going to be lost.

Imlach later wrote that he talked Harold Ballard out of signing
Palmateer because Palmy had a bad knee and he didn't want to put
Ballard on the hook for one million dollars for a gimp. This was the
kind of language Ballard understood and Palmateer was playing for
the Washington Capitals the next season. Bad knee or not, that
October and November, Punch Imlach's signals to us were all negative ones.

Then Lanny and I were up for special treatment. Every time the
club lost, there were little comments to the media like, "We've got to
get the performance from the big guys," or "Our leaders have to
lead." The "big guys" meant, primarily, Sittler and McDonald. Or

the coaches and general manager would heap praise on the kids (Laurie Boschman, Rocky Saganiuk and John Anderson were playing extremely well together) in a way that downgraded my line.

The self-fulfilling prophecy soon came true. By mid-November our line was struggling and Lanny was benched for an entire third period in a home game against Edmonton. An Alberta boy being benched in a game against the team from Edmonton—purely coincidental? "I considered benching the whole line," Smith said after the game, a 4-4 tie. "Lanny was just the victim of the numbers game. I know Lanny has a great deal of pride and he'll come back to play well for us. He's a fine player, a guy you love to have on your side, but I had to do something to shake things up."

He then went on to tell everyone how our line was minus-6 or minus-7 in the last six games—we were only scoring on power plays—and how the Kid Line was going great. We were getting burnt defensively, and we would have to improve this real quick. "That line just has to play better both ways or I'll have to think about not playing them," he concluded.

His point was underlined by instituting a two-a-day practice regimen immediately thereafter. It was an interesting practice experience; Punch Imlach had Smitty convince Gardens staff to paint some lines, actually lanes, on the ice parallel to the boards, about ten feet out. This was supposed to teach us that wingers stayed between the lines and the boards, while centermen stayed in the middle of the ice and didn't cross over into the wingers' lanes. The fact that many teams were starting to show signs of the European influence and use things like moving picks, criss-crosses and drop passes, totally escaped our coaching staff. Nobody else was skating up and down the old lanes anymore, especially not the teams at the top.

We laughed at the lines, and this was seen as yet another slap in the face for management. By then, though, we were getting tired of recoiling from our own slaps. Lanny and I discovered that we had both been on the NHL waiver list as Punch began cautiously testing our marketability. He was determined to move one or both of us and it made good business sense to indicate to other teams that we might be available, and gauge our market value at the same time. What didn't make sense was that he had started to run us down in public; what really bothered him was the clause in my contract that stipulated that I could veto any trade. (That had been added in 1975, into the second year of an existing five-year deal signed in 1973, when

Jim Gregory sought to sweeten the pot for both Lanny and myself by extending the contract.)

The public harassment began in earnest. On November 7, Imlach was interviewed on radio during the second intermission of a game in St. Louis. He was asked if I had lost a step. After the game, all the media guys came running into the dressing room and shoved their mikes and notepads in my face. I was taken by surprise; I hadn't been particularly outstanding during the contest, a 7-4 win over the Blues.

"Imlach was on radio at intermission and said he'd trade you, that you'd lost half a step. What are your comments?" Dynamite. They were practically salivating. The big showdown had finally come. My mind was racing, but my mouth was in low gear. I hoped my tone of voice was matter-of-fact and controlled.

"If Punch really feels that way, I'd appreciate it if he just came and talked to me," I began, measuring each word carefully. "I'd rather we sat down and discussed it than go to the media. If we have a problem, let's try to resolve it." Punch later said that his response to the question began with him restating the interviewer's question, "If he has lost a step," and *if* was the biggest word in the statement. The reporters had conveniently omitted to mention that. I've never heard the tape, so I couldn't say.

I continued, rationally: "Punch is hurting the team by knocking individual players in this manner. What I can say is team communication has not been good this season; in the past with Red Kelly, Roger Neilson and Jim Gregory, it always had been good."

Even Harold Ballard jumped in, with both feet as usual, and without examining all the facts. "If Sittler thinks he's going to run this hockey club, he's got another think coming," he said. "He wants us to hand him an all-day sucker every time he goes on the ice."

That was on a Wednesday night. We flew directly to Winnipeg and it was all over the headlines. Sittler says this and that and the situation gets heated up. Imlach responds. Ballard interjects. Etc. Etc. This was a week-long road trip, we had almost three full days in the Manitoba capital with the travelling media as a captive audience— or vice versa. There was no getting away from the controversy that kept the reporters gainfully employed.

The guys at *Hockey Night in Canada* know good television when they see it and they wanted me to go on the air in Winnipeg for a national game. Brian MacFarlane asked me on the Friday and I agreed to be interviewed during the first intermission.

On Saturday night, we got on the bus at 5:30 to go to the rink. I was sitting at the back and Floyd Smith came over and sat down beside me. "I just want you to know that you were supposed to go on the air . . ."

"Yeah?"

"Well, I'd suggest to you that you cancel that and don't go on."

"Why?"

"Just tellin' ya for your own good."

That wasn't good enough for me. Was there a veiled threat here; what was going on? "I've been on the air before, every time they've asked me, and I've never had a problem before. I don't see why I can't go on now."

"Well, I'm tellin' ya, ya better not go on."

Later that night, Brian MacFarlane beckoned me over to the boards during the pre-game skate. "Darryl, we've got a big problem out in the mobile. Ballard and Imlach went in there and threatened *Hockey Night in Canada* that if you went on between periods, they'll never get another Toronto Maple Leaf again, and threatened the TV contract and everything. We can't have you on."

"That's your choice. You asked me and I said yes. If you don't want me, you don't want me." To make a long story short, Tiger went on in my spot. That really upset Dave Hodge, that *HNIC* didn't take a stand and let these two geezers control the network.

Imlach's ban didn't cover just that game; it was a long-term banishment from the airwaves, although I didn't know it at the time. As he tells it in Scott Young's *Heaven and Hell in the NHL*:

> More fun for the media, but then I didn't let him on TV for months after that. Why should I, when he was going to go on and blast Leaf management? The result was that that first time, in Winnipeg, my ban made the Leafs madder at me. Reporters told me that and asked me to comment. I just told them, "If the players are mad, let them prove me wrong by going out and winning a lot of hockey games." They did— went out and beat Winnipeg, on to Edmonton for another win, and back to Toronto for their fourth in a row. I think it was their best win streak of the year.
>
> It was around then that a player's quote was printed which at first I misunderstood: "If we keep on trying, we'll win in

the end." I thought, that's the spirit, that's pretty good, maybe I'm getting through to them.

Punch Imlach's philosophy: divide and motivate. Another one for the books. He's right, after the 7-4 win in St. Louis, we waxed the Jets 8-4 on Saturday night and followed up the next night with a 6-3 win over Edmonton, before returning home to beat St. Louis. But we won despite Punch, not because of him.

At this time, the media and the general public didn't know that I'd been banned from going on for TV interviews. Come to think of it, neither did I. Dave Hodge could be a bulldog and he persisted in asking before every televised game: "Can we have Sittler tonight?" Imlach, just as obstinately, would say no.

The *HNIC* intermission host was getting upset, and soon I was bothered by it too. Later on, after Lanny was traded, the ban on my appearances on *Hockey Night in Canada* telecasts would become public knowledge. I always figured it was *HNIC* executive producer Ralph (father of Edmonton's Scott) Mellanby's way of letting the new Leafs management team know just what he thought of them. Added to the bombshell of Lanny's trade, it made Punch's life extra miserable for a few days.

Once the news of my ban became public, Dave Hodge knew that badgering the Leafs daily could not work as a long-term strategy. With the news out, there was no more downside—Punch had already been pilloried for the bush league move, and he had nothing more to lose by maintaining the ban.

Hodge saw a way around things. I would be a featured guest on his phone-in sports show on CFRB, a two-hour program on Monday nights. Imlach had said nothing about radio programs. That phone-in show appearance took place the following February, and I'll discuss it elsewhere in this book.

On Saturday, November 24, two days after Smith had benched Lanny for the third period against Edmonton, we were playing the Black Hawks in Toronto. Up to that point in the season, our line was still leading the Leafs' offense (me 11 goals, 10 assists; Lanny 10-8; Tiger 11-9) and the team was doing well. That night I lasted one shift, crashing into the boards with defenseman Bob Murray. I slid backwards and tried to put out my leg to brace myself, but we both came together and my ankle gave way. The early estimates were anywhere between two and six weeks on the disabled list. The same night, Ian Turnbull went down with a knee injury.

Paul Gardner moved into my spot between Tiger and Lanny and played well, especially the following night in our 4-2 win against the Rangers at Madison Square Gardens. The team followed that up with wins over Atlanta and Montreal, and a tie with Philadelphia, and the stress of our early November road trip was lessened a great deal.

I was out of action for almost three weeks. During that time, the undercurrents of animosity and mistrust touched everyone. I came back with a splash, scoring three goals and garnering a First Star in a Saturday night contest. We were on the road for a Sunday night game and it was "Sittler wins game" all over again. It was nice to be back.

Things settled down, on the surface at least, but every now and then some small gibe or animosity would float up for all to see. It affected everybody, especially Floyd Smith and Dick Duff, who were trapped in the middle. One such example is the story of the Road Trip to Nowhere.

By now, of course, we were all pretty well used to the Imlach crew, especially the Floyd and Dicky show in the dressing room. But they could still surprise us. For example, Smith and Duff had discovered the obvious, that our team's road record at this time was considerably better than our home mark. So one Saturday while we were at the Gardens for the morning skate, they called a team meeting.

Foolish us. We thought we were going to discuss that night's game plan.

Smitty started his speech a little dangerously: "Guys, you might think I'm crazy here, but this is what we're going to do. Our record away from home is much better than when we play here. We seem to be more relaxed on the road, so Duffy and I have decided that we're going to try and make this into a road game tonight. What I've done is I've chartered a bus. It's going to be in Applewood Village Plaza out in Mississauga and we'd like you to come in on the team bus if you can, and we'll all pretend we're coming in for a road game so we can get our record better at home."

The guys were looking at each other, rolling their eyes and snickering . . . "Is this for real?" . . . and as Floyd finished up, he turned the proceedings over to Duff.

While Smitty had been doing his spiel, Duff stood silently at his side, a piece of paper in his hand. Where I sat, I could see that it had the number 1,000 written on it. Maybe it was a memory aid, he didn't want to forget the number or some thought associated with it. I wasn't even close—I had missed the dollar sign.

"Guys, I just want to say that we've been taking a penalty when we're already a man short, and the two-men-down situations have been costing us. From here on in, if a guy takes a penalty when we're a man short, it'll cost you a thousand," he said, brandishing his magic paper with the big $ 1 , 0 0 0 on it. Just as he finished, Ian Turnbull coolly sauntered out of the shower room, dripping wet with a towel wrapped around his waist. He'd caught the last bit of Duff's brilliant strategem.

"Screw 'em," he said, turning to us. Behind him, a pained look flashed across Duff's face.

"Let 'im score! If a guy gets a breakaway, I'm not taking a penalty for a thousand bucks. I'd rather have him score a goal. Mike and Paul, you're on your own!" The room dissolved into laughter.

Duff called Turnbull a prima donna, but the damage had been done. His "great idea" had been ridiculed, as it should have been; but we still had Floyd's brainwave to deal with.

As the meeting broke up and players wandered off singly or in groups, guys were coming up to me asking, "Are you taking the bus in?"

"No, my wife's coming to the game and we're planning on going out for dinner afterwards. I'll probably drive in." In fact, a bunch of us had plans to go out with our wives after the game that night, a rarity because we often flew off immediately after Saturday night games for a Sunday night match in places like New York, Boston, Chicago or Detroit. We had no game scheduled that Sunday and planned to take the opportunity for a little socializing after the game. Four or five of us, including Lanny, Borje and myself, drove in together, and our wives came in another car later.

I remember driving by Applewood Plaza on the way to the game and there was a big Greyhound sitting there with the motor running and the lights on. I figured the driver was all pumped up to drive in the Leafs, probably had an autograph book for his kids. Unfortunately, nobody showed up.

A lot of the players quietly joked about our "road trip" in the dressing room before the game. Neither Floyd nor Dick gave any sign of whether they knew we'd taken the bus in or not. The incident was quickly forgotten, or so I thought. About a month had gone by when

Guy Kinnear came over to me on a commercial flight during a road trip. "Harold wants to see you up in first class."

I made my way up to the front of the plane; Harold was camped out as usual, the seat in front pushed down, his feet up. Chocolate bars and other goodies littered the seat beside him.

"Siddown!" (Where had I heard this before?)

"Do you know anything about a team bus in Toronto? I got this bill for $334 for some team bus out in Mississauga."

I told him the story.

He just shook his head; he couldn't believe that Floyd and Dick could come up with such a scheme. He thought I was kidding at first; but that was the mentality of the people we were dealing with.

That bus story represents the humorous side of the attempts to motivate us. There could be a mean streak in some players as well. We'd had our ups and downs in the first half of that season, but injuries to our defensemen and defensive forwards had cost us dearly. Imlach went back to the old tried-and-true recipe that had worked so well during the glory days of the 1960s when well-travelled veterans like Allan Stanley, Bobby Baun and Red Kelly had backstopped the Leafs to three championships: he started beating the bushes for veteran blueliners, dead or alive. If the corpse was still warm, throw a Maple Leafs sweater on it .

The first such experiment was signing Daryl Maggs, a former NHLer and WHA player who had written Imlach saying that he felt he could still contribute. Later that year, we also signed Larry Carrière, a former Buffalo defenseman. The Maggs experiment failed miserably, but it piqued Punch's curiosity. When Paul Rimstead of the *Toronto Sun* telephoned and said Carl Brewer was aching for another try, Imlach took it seriously. Back in the spring, between jobs, he had coached the Leafs Oldtimers in a charity game and Brewer had stood out. Brewer was signed, and sent down to Moncton to play himself into, or out of, shape. We were flying to Montreal for a mid-week game and the word was that Brewer would join us on the way back. Dave Hutchison was the player who was on the hot seat; he'd been benched and not even dressed on several recent occasions, and Smith led him to believe that he would be the odd man out when Brewer finally showed up.

On that December morning we flew out on a charter and it was raining cats and dogs. Pat Boutette was one of the last guys on the plane and he came back to the rear of the plane to ask us: "Imlach left his car lights on. Should I tell him?" This was early morning. We knew two things: we were coming back after the game that night, and Imlach's battery was going to be deader than dead. It became a typical back-of-the-bus joke—"Nah, don't tell him."

We went into Montreal and lost the game 8-4. With three or four days off over Christmas, we were loose on the way home and the guys had a couple of beers on the plane. Carl Brewer, head completely shaved, sat up front with Punch. He was from a different generation, a stranger to us players, laughing and joking up front with the GM, the scouts and Harold.

A lot of the guys were dead-set against having Brewer on the team. Dave Hutchison was popular with the players, he had a role to play and played it well. Brewer was the guy who was going to take Hutch's spot away and that bothered the players. We respected him for what he had done back in his time, but his time was long gone. We got back into Toronto at about one in the morning, and there were Punch and Carl out in the parking lot, looking for a set of jumper cables. They were still fruitlessly looking for cables when Hutchison tooled up in his Corvette, brandished a set of cables, and sped away out of the parking lot. Several other players also drove by, pretending not to notice the general manager's plight. I wasn't aware of this little scene. At the next practice, Brewer came up to me and asked: "What's goin' on with you guys on this team? Don't you help each other out?"

"What do you mean?"

He told me the story about the parking lot and I told him the guys were ticked off at Imlach and that's the way it was. The feeling that the guys had with Brewer was that he was Imlach's spy; Brewer simply wanted to be a part of us, but we wouldn't open ourselves up to him. Looking at it from his standpoint, it was a golden opportunity for him to make $125,000 a year—but Punch stiffed him anyway. Carl ended up suing the Leafs because of some technicality where the deal wasn't signed on such and such a day and he was entitled to an option year. Or something like that.

Tiger Williams probably summed it up best.

After that, I guess it was just a question of who would go first. Hutchison for waving the booster cables? Sittler and McDonald for being Eagleson men? Me, for being a pal of Sittler's and McDonald's? It was a sick hockey club, and the thing that made you bitter was to think how close we'd come to being a real team. Under Neilson, we had always been beaten out by the eventual Stanley Cup champions. And our closeness as teammates was something a new guy should have gloried in. Instead, Imlach wanted to break us up.

Like a lot of people connected with the Toronto Maple Leafs that year, Carl Brewer just happened to get caught in the middle of somebody else's war.

The final straw for Punch and Harold, indeed for everyone involved, came about a week later and this time it was about Ronald McDonald House and I got caught in the middle. And this time, the fireworks were for real. This is the story, as written by Jim Kernaghan of the *Toronto Star* on December 20, 1979. The new decade was eleven days away, and several of my teammates would be wearing other NHL uniforms before it arrived.

In view of a policy of confrontation that has developed between Toronto Maple Leafs players and management this season, yesterday's rather bizarre turn of events hardly was surprising.

At a press conference to announce a fund-raising hockey game between the Leafs and the Canadian Olympic team, Leaf owner Harold Ballard learned that the players would participate only if they could get a chance to play the Soviet Union next season. Ballard long has been an opponent of playing games against Soviet teams.

"This comes as quite a shock," Ballard said. "When I was approached by McDonald's (a major backer of the project), I thought everything was cleared up." The game is to raise funds for the Ronald McDonald House, a temporary home for parents and their children who are undergoing treatment for cancer.

"If this it the hatchet they're using on us, I'll have to go along with them. I've always been opposed to playing the Russians. It's a waste of money and time. All they can do is come over here and take our money home. But if this is the situation, I'll have to accept it," Ballard added, his voice quaking with anger.

The players were upset that the game was sprung on them without their knowing about it, right in the middle of a heavy part of their regular NHL schedule. The game is to be played Feb. 6.

Team captain Darryl Sittler, honorary chairman of the McDonald House, called NHL Players' Association executive director Alan Eagleson late the previous evening to indicate there was some disagreement among the players about the game. Eagleson addressed the gathering and said the fact that the players were not informed of the game had them upset. He met with the Leafs for an hour yesterday morning.

"They asked that we exchange goaltenders and some defense pairings with the Olympic team and they asked for a chance to play the Russians," Eagleson said. Sittler denied the players tried to blackmail Ballard.

"We just suggested an alternative," he said. "We said that if we played the Olympic team, then why not trade goalies or defense and make it more fun.

"He (Ballard) has said a great deal about not wanting to play the Russians, then goes ahead and schedules this game . . . "We have many players on the team who would like a chance against a Russian team. Tiger Williams, for example, said he'd really like to play the Russians and if the Leafs don't have a game against them, he probably won't get the chance." The Leafs played the Olympic team during their exhibition schedule, minus several stars, and lost 6-5.

"We've played them once to help raise funds," Sittler said. "It's hard for us to get up emotionally about playing an exhibition game that time of year and we know they'll be out to beat us."

Our misgivings had a solid foundation. As mentioned in the story, we had played the Lake Placid-bound team the previous September. That game had almost degenerated into a brawl. Tiger Williams recalled the contest:

We had played the Olympic team in a pre-season contest in Calgary, and the game had been a complete disaster. Ballard had insisted we go in without our best players: Salming, Sittler and McDonald. I captained the team. The kids on the Olympic team had nothing to lose, and they played well. They were leading by about three goals when some of our guys started to get pissed off. Before the game, we had agreed that we would go easy on the kids—soon they would be representing Canada in the Olympics, and we had to do our bit to help. Unfortunately, all the good resolutions went up in smoke when the Olympic team got a little cocky. You couldn't blame the kids. They were doing well against an experienced professional team. But some of our guys got uptight with the situation and started taking runs at the kids. On one shift we were really pounding them, and I skated over to the Olympic team's bench and said to the coach, Tom Watt, "For God's sake, Tom, you gotta do something! Clear the benches!" But Watt refused; he said he was teaching his boys discipline.

Such a game was more a recipe for disaster than anything else. We were in mid-season form, all of our team would be playing, and we'd be playing in front of our fans who, though proud Canadians all, would not take kindly to the suggestion that the national kiddie team could beat their home team in a game, exhibition or not. All we needed to hear would be Maple Leaf Gardens fans urging us on, or laughing at us if we fell behind, and we'd blow the Olympians out of the rink. The last thing they needed a week before they met the Swedes, Finns, Americans and Soviets at Lake Placid was to get their heads handed to them by an NHL team. While they cherished the idea of meeting tough competition as preparation for the Games, they were as aware as us that a big score would not help motivate them for the international arena.

The *Toronto Star* article continued:

Eagleson said that when he met the players yesterday morning, there were five options: (1) since the Leafs are the only Canadian team that has played the Olympians, Toronto would play if Montreal had a game against them; (2) not to play at all; (3) play the game in January rather than in a heavy part of the schedule; (4) play next year; or (5) play in an intra-squad game for the fund-raising.

"Darryl suggested the game to the team and they all agreed it was a bad time of year," Eagleson said. "They have games Feb. 2 against Chicago, Feb. 3 against Chicago, the all-star game is Feb. 5, they play Boston Feb. 7, Los Angeles Feb. 9 and Detroit Feb. 10. But they all want to play the Soviet Union.

"If the proposal had been brought before the players a week

ago, it all would have been a tempest in a teapot," Eagleson said. "They've always been told by management that exhibition games during the season are out. Well, they wanted a chance to play the Russians."

Eagleson said that he probably would go to the players and ask them to change their stand on swapping goaltenders and some defensemen for the game.

Ballard, who said he had sold the game for $30,000 to CHCH Television in Hamilton and to CKFH radio in Toronto for $500 to raise further funds, said he'd "just have to swallow my goddam (sic) pride about the Russians and accept it." Bobby Baun, a former Leaf stalwart, noted that he had never seen Ballard so angry in 20 years.

Bobby Baun was absolutely right, Ballard was embarrassed and hurt by the fiasco and vowed his revenge. But previous public accounts of the affair have had many incorrect elements. This is how it really happened.

I was honorary chairman of Ronald McDonald House when Harold Ballard came to me about three or four weeks ahead of the press conference to ask my opinion on the Leafs playing a charity game for Ronald McDonald House. As I was a vice-president of the NHLPA at the time, and fully conversant with the rules governing exhibition games during the season, I knew he needed permission from the players.

"Before you do anything, Harold, make sure you have the support of the players," I told him. I called Alan Eagleson later that day and recounted our conversation, and nothing more came of it, or so I thought.

It was some weeks later; we had just returned from a road trip when I decided to catch the late sports news one night. Imagine my surprise when sportscaster Brian Williams said that the Leafs would hold a press conference the next day at the Gardens to announce a special charity exhibition game. This was the first time since my previous conversations with Harold Ballard and Alan Eagleson that I had even heard the subject mentioned. Obviously, Harold had ignored my advice to check with the players and gone ahead on his own.

I immediately called Alan Eagleson. It was news to him, too.

"Alan, I know how the players feel about such a game; this can turn into a fiasco because a lot of the guys are still upset about the September game and all the emotional stuff that happened."

He was emphatic. "Call the guys into the Gardens for an early meeting before the morning skate tomorrow," he advised. So on the morning of the press conference, the whole team was in the dressing-room an hour early when Eagleson arrived to meet with us.

"We've got to try and resolve this issue," he began. He then took everybody over our previous conversation, mentioned my talk with Ballard almost a month before, reminded the players that NHL rules meant they had to approve everything, and then left it up to a team vote.

I voted in favor of the game. I was in a very precarious position as both honorary chairman of Ronald McDonald House, vice-president of the NHLPA and team captain. The players then said they were voting against the game, unless Harold Ballard would agree to switching defensemen or forwards in order to defuse a potentially serious situation, and unless he would also agree to a lucrative exhibition game with the Soviets. While this meeting was going on, the media and representatives of McDonald's were filing into the Hot Stove Lounge just across the hallway for the press conference for which the players still hadn't received official notification. Leafs PR Director Stan Obodiac knew we were meeting in the room, and he kept coming in and going out, trying to ascertain whether I would attend the press conference in one or another of my official roles. The suspense was mounting.

After the vote, I left the meeting with the news of the players' decision and walked into the media reception and reported on it. This caught Ballard totally off guard; he was flabbergasted, not knowing what to say. Remember, the cameras were rolling and this was live. Personally, I felt sick about the whole thing. I didn't know how I had let myself get caught in such a position.

Needless to say, George Imlach wasn't going to let this golden opportunity pass him by. Strangely enough, Imlach, the man who was most against exhibition games in which stars could be injured, had remained on the sidelines as this issue blew up. He was home with the 'flu during the December 19 press conference, but had shaken enough of the virus to come into work the next day and head right for Ballard's open wound with a gallon of vinegar. This was his long-awaited opportunity to start dealing away the recalcitrant players.

Gord Stellick, the administrative assistant, was privy to their meeting.

"Do you believe those assholes," Imlach would say to Ballard. "Who do they think they are, pulling that crap with you?"

Imlach normally avoided polishing Ballard's apples, but clearly he was desperate to score a victory. Ballard had been reluctant to make wholesale change. He had always been a fan first, executive second and, thus, his opinion of players like Sittler, McDonald and Williams mirrored those of the man in the street. Any lingering reservations about cleaning house disappeared, when the bitter press conference was followed by four Leafs losses in eight nights. The defeats included a 10-0 embarrassment in Boston and a 5-3 loss to Buffalo, which Imlach interpreted as a deliberate slight in front of his former employers.

Imlach got the carte blanche he had sought since he'd been hired. Within three days, Pat Boutette was on his way to Hartford, in a one-for-one swap for somebody called Bob Stephenson. Pat would play six more seasons and wind up his career (Toronto, Hartford, Pittsburgh) with 171 goals and 282 assists for 453 points in 10 seasons, with another 10 goals and 14 assists for 24 points in 46 playoff games. Stephenson would play 14 games for Toronto, 18 NHL games in all, and disappear before the season was over. The other general managers had to be very careful; they could get trampled in the stampede to take advantage of Imlach.

On the same day Boutette was dispatched to the Whalers, the telephone rang in Imlach's office; it was Ray Miron of Colorado. Don Cherry told me the story:

"Miron had called and inquired about your (my) availability and Imlach came back real fast: 'You don't want Darryl; the guy who can really help you is Lanny McDonald.' Miron had his faults, but he wouldn't look a gift horse in the mouth.

"Who do you want?"

Imlach said he liked Paiement and Hickey, he was looking to get some younger players. Back in Denver, Grapes was licking his chops in anticipation, hardly able to believe his luck.

Obviously, Punch must have "run down to City Hall" sometime in the past two months and discovered that my no-trade clause was solid. He couldn't get rid of me, and there was no way Ballard would pay the $500,000 or so it would take to get me to agree to a trade. In his devious mind, the next best thing would be to trade my best friend and valued linemate. Lanny was an Eagleson client as well; he was killing two birds with one stone.

It was obvious to everyone except Punch Imlach that he was killing the Leafs and it seemed there was nothing anybody could do about it. On Thursday, December 28, Miron and Imlach finalized the trade when Punch agreed to have Joel Quenneville join Lanny in Denver. The next morning, after practice, Lanny and Joel were summoned to Punch's office. I was still in the dressing room when Lanny returned, tears in his eyes.

"I've been traded to the Colorado Rockies," he said. He looked lost.

The shock was so palpable, some of the guys fell back or slumped into their seats as if they'd been struck physically. One of the most shocked was Floyd Smith; Imlach hadn't seen fit to let him in on the news bulletin.

For Punch, the trade war was on in earnest. He'd convinced Harold Ballard that I was a cancer on the team and, if he couldn't excise me, he'd make sure that all the tissue around me was irradiated. The result was what doctors call competing diseases; the attempted cure of one terminal malady can often lead to or promote another.

What Punch didn't know was that the McDonald trade would eventually be his undoing. What we didn't know was that the McDonald trade was just the beginning. There would be more fireworks and fire sales to come as a once-proud franchise lurched into the new decade.

Another little fact seemed to have escaped everyone in the heat of the moment. The Leafs had just completed the 1970s—the first decade in their history in which they had failed to win at least one Stanley Cup. Worse still, the decisions they were making at that moment were going to lead to a similar fate in the 1980s.

11

Showdown, Round Two

FOR THE TORONTO Maple Leafs hockey team, the new decade started three days early. For many of us who remember all that went on, the nightmare decade seems never to have ended.

The Lanny McDonald trade was so wrong that the fans stormed Maple Leaf Gardens. The reaction shook Harold Ballard—he could handle the give-and-take of owner-media and owner-fan relations, and could dish out the insults with the best of them. But even he wasn't ready for the hundreds of protesters outside Maple Leaf Gardens for the *Hockey Night in Canada* telecast against (you guessed it!) the Winnipeg Jets. Ballard had genuinely liked Lanny but had given Imlach a free rein in the heat of the moment. Within forty-eight hours, he already was having second thoughts about that decision.

As for the players and myself, it was a deeply sad time, not only because we were losing a close friend and a truly good person, but also because the signals from the top were not those emanating from someone in touch with hockey reality in the 1980s.

That Friday night we all gathered at Lanny's for a wake, talking quietly and shaking our heads a lot. Ardell was nine months pregnant and due to deliver at any time, and her parents were in town to be with her because we were due to go on a road trip early in the new year. Coincidentally, Wilf Paiement's wife was also in the same situation in Colorado, so only Pat Hickey made it in time for our Winnipeg game. Lanny and Joel had already talked to Don Cherry on the telephone and promised to be in Denver for their Saturday night contest, that team's first sellout of the season. Grapes had promised to take Lanny under his wing.

"Lanny, just come to the games and we'll fly you back home as many times as it takes to have the baby and get your family settled," he said, and the Rockies were true to their word. Ironically, Lanny had been traded from the Leafs and was spending more time in Toronto than we did in those days, it seemed, flying in almost daily to be with Ardell.

But, before all of that was to happen, it was time for official good-byes at the McDonalds'. Wendy and I were the last to go, and we could only stand there and stare at Lanny and Ardell. They stared back and nobody trusted their ability to speak. Finally, we hugged them and left for home. Somewhere on that short ride a couple of streets away in Mississauga, I decided I had had enough. Tomorrow would be my last day as captain of the Maple Leafs.

The next afternoon, I sat down and composed my resignation on my personal stationery (white bond with a white 27 in a blue Maple Leaf and my name under it).

I told my teammates and my coach before the game that I was resigning as captain of the Toronto Maple Leafs. When I was made captain, it was the happiest day of my life. I have tried to handle my duties as captain in an honest and fair manner. I took player complaints to management, and discussed management ideas with players.

At the start of this season, I was personally sued by my own hockey team management. I was told it was nothing personal. I explained my position to Mr. Imlach and Mr. Ballard at that time. I told them that I felt a captain's role was to work with players and management, not just with management.

Mr. Ballard and Mr. Imlach made some negative comments about me and my teammates some weeks ago and I met with them to discuss it. I was told I was being too sensitive. I have had little or no contact with Mr. Imlach and it is clear to me that he and I have different ideas about player and management communication.

I have recently been told that management has prevented me from appearing on *Hockey Night in Canada* telecasts. I am spending more and more time on player-management problems and I don't feel I am accomplishing enough for my teammates.

The war between Mr. Imlach and Mr. Eagleson should not overshadow the main issue—"The Toronto Maple Leafs." I am totally loyal to the Toronto Maple Leafs. I don't want to let my teammates down. But I have to be honest with myself. I will continue to fight for players rights, but not as captain of the team.

All I want to do is give all my energy and all my ability to my team as a player.

Sincerely,
Darryl Sittler

Getting into the rink was more difficult than usual that night. Hundreds of fans were outside picketing Maple Leaf Gardens. The various signs they carried had a very clear message: "Kick Punch's fanny for trading Lanny," "Trade Punch before he destroys the Leafs," "Bad Punch spoils a party," and "Silent protest of Lanny's farewell; fans are asked to remain silent tonight because we're not heard anyway."

After the pre-game skate, I came back to the dressing room and got a scalpel-type knife from the trainer. I went to the washroom, sat down in a cubicle, and began trying to take the "C" off my sweater. It was triple-stitched and I ended up cutting a hole in the sweater. I was emotional, shaking a little bit, and every time I tried to get more off, I ended up making the hole bigger, ripping it and making a mess of my sweater. So when Guy Kinnear happened by, I called him over and explained what I was trying to do.

"Don't say anything. Just try to understand what I'm doing and co-operate. Take the sweater in the back, take the 'C' off, and don't let anybody know what's happening. Please. Just do that for me."

While he worked on the sweater in the back, I returned to the room and, in a very emotional speech to the players, I explained what I was doing, and why I was doing it. Imlach was trying to break down this whole team, didn't want me as captain, didn't look upon me as a captain, and wouldn't let me function as one. All of this outside controversy had gotten too big; all I wanted to do was play hockey. And that's all I was going to do.

Tiger was one of the few players to respond openly, "Whattaya doin'? You can't. Don't do it."

"I have to do it, Tiger."

I went off into the coaches' cubicle off on the side where about thirty hours before, Lanny had received the bad news. Floyd Smith and Dick Duff were in there.

I handed Floyd Smith a copy of my statement, which I had photo-copied earlier. "I've just told the players I no longer want to be the captain of the hockey club. I just want to go out and play hockey to the best of my ability." As I was finishing up talking to Floyd, again I was very, very emotional, Smitty was trying to console me and be supportive when Dick Duff shot right out the door.

Friends in the press box told me later that Duff went flying up the stairs, "Where's Punch? Where's Punch? Sittler's taken the 'C' off!"

Anyway, I went back out into the dressing room, hoping that my timing would be such as to get us out onto the ice and get my mind off what I'd just done. I was waiting for the buzzer to sound. I didn't want to sit there for a long time with these emotions coursing through me.

We waited. And waited. The buzzer didn't ring. We had a clock in the room and it was usually three minutes after eight when it went off. It still didn't ring. Then one of the assistant trainers came in to tell us that the Zamboni had broken down on the ice and that there would be a twenty-minute delay.

My very first thought was: "How could Imlach work so fast? Oh geez, this is a set-up." I sat there looking at the door out of the corner of my eye, fully expecting Punch to come down to tell me to take off my gear and that I was off the team. I had no way of knowing that at this point, Duff still hadn't found Imlach.

It was a very difficult situation. I'd just finished a very emotional speech to the players and all I wanted to do was get out there and play. I didn't know how much of this would spread to the reporters right away. I hadn't planned it that way. At last they got the Zamboni fixed, the ice flooded, and we went out and thrashed the Jets 6-1. I ended up with one assist, on the game's last goal by Tiger, who was acting captain that night. Strangely enough, Bob Stephenson had a goal and an assist in his Leafs debut—a performance that made up forty per cent of his NHL career statistics. Pat Hickey also played but was held scoreless.

Few people noticed my uniform alterations at first, but by the end of the first period, people had gotten wind of it, probably from those who were listening to radio broadcasts in the stands. I never had the habit of looking up into the stands during a hockey game—it's a good way to get knocked on your rear—but the couple of glances I took on this night showed quite a few people pointing at me. The game seemed to drag on and on.

When it finally ended, I knew the reporters would come flying downstairs. I gave Guy Kinnear a stack of photocopied statements. "Give them these; I'm not going to stick around for any statements." Then it was a quick shower and out the door.

As hurt as I felt by Lanny's trade—and this feeling was shared by all of his teammates—I wasn't playing the wounded duck. I sincerely felt that in the circumstances I would contribute more to the team just as a player. Let someone else take over as team leader; someone else who would not quibble with Punch Imlach's definition of team captain.

Perhaps a better way of saying it was that I wanted to play my way back into good mental shape. What helped was the avalanche of protest over the McDonald trade. Punch was definitely on the defensive now, and unable to do much of anything but ride out the storm.

The media chipped in, lambasting him at every turn. "Imlach's style is one of confrontation rather than conciliation," said the cutline under one rather unflattering picture of Imlach in the *Globe and Mail*. The author of the article that accompanied the photo, James Christie, got commentary from two dressing rooms to make his point that this management style was dated.

"I can sympathize with the Toronto players," said Buffalo captain Danny Gare after Sabres' 5-3 victory over Toronto this week.

"I know what we went through. It looks like the disease has set in. They're not as aggressive as I remember them."

In our room, the feeling was mutual.

"Now, I don't feel I can express my gut feelings about things without getting into trouble," said one player. Earlier this season, when Toronto captain Darryl Sittler first said Imlach had not communicated with the players, owner Harold Ballard snapped back that the players were acting like babies and that, under the previous management, they had gotten used to some things they should not have. Ron Ellis, the quietest and probably the most reasonable man on the team, replied: "Sure we got used to something . . . a little common sense."

After the Winnipeg game, Punch was asked to comment on my resignation. He said he had nothing to do with it, had not asked me to give up the captaincy, and added, "If he wants to do that, then it's all right with me. I never threatened Darryl with loss of the captaincy in our argument over *Showdown*, although I expressed my feeling that a team captain was there to deliver management's point of view to the players. I won't say I never considered it [asking for my resignation]. I consider millions of things."

Punch had learned of my resignation only when a *Toronto Star* reporter came up to him in the press box and asked him to comment. "I was up here and didn't know a thing about it until I looked down and saw him," he said.

The radio hotlines were sizzling and gallons of ink were being poured into the headlines that ran in newspapers across the country when we returned to work on Monday. We had enjoyed a rare day off after the Winnipeg game but the price was a two-a-day that Monday. As players, we didn't complain about such a trade-off to get a full Sunday off. When I arrived at the rink that Monday morning, Floyd Smith called me into his office.

Floyd, for all his faults, was a nice guy. It was hard to get mad at him, and even harder to stay mad at him. I had no real quarrel with him.

"Darryl, you've been through a lot this season," he began, the concern evident in his voice and expression.

"Here's a little thought from me to you. You've done a lot for this organization over the years. You know what would be kind of neat? To show their appreciation for you, we get the guys upstairs to give you a trip to Florida to get your mind off all this and get away from it all."

As he spoke, Smith's words triggered memory of the Frank Mahovlich situation a decade ago when Imlach had tried to make it look like the Big M had suffered a nervous breakdown, in order to get him out of town and forgotten.

"Floyd, I appreciate your comments, but I don't need that. I'm just going to play hockey. You pay me well to play hockey, I love to play hockey, I'm just going to go out on the ice and show everybody that I'm still a pretty good hockey player."

"We could make you go if we wanted to. Think about it."

"You can't make me go anywhere."

"Well, think about it anyway. If you decide to do it, I'll go up and talk to Imlach and them about it." That was in the morning and I remember it clearly.

We had lunch after the morning session and returned to the rink at about 1:30. I was skating around when Imlach came down to ice level, something he rarely did. I noticed him near the boards and he called me over. I sat on the players' bench and the other guys kept skating. It was a wonder that there wasn't a five-player pile-up in a corner with all of these guys craning their necks at the two of us as they skated by.

"Smitty talked to ya, eh?"

"Yeah, he did."

"Well, we're sendin' ya to Florida."

"Wait a minute . . . "

"Nah, it's decided. We're sendin' ya to Florida, give ya a break down there. Get some rest." The break was for his benefit, not mine. My presence in Toronto was the focal point of the feeling against Lanny's trade. Every time I skated onto the ice, the fans would automatically look for Lanny on my right side. If Punch could be seen to do something that expressed his concern for the "delicate" state of my mental health in these trying times, it would be a public relations coup.

"You're not sending me anywhere, Punch."

"We're sendin' ya to Florida." His voice started rising like it did when anybody showed even the slightest inclination to disagree with him.

"I'm telling you right now, I'm not going."

The eternal salesman didn't even hear me. He upped the ante.

"You can take your family, your wife and kids, and go." This idea was the product of a panic-driven brainstorm, the kind of idea that feels so good and foolproof that its originator could not possibly conceive of any resistance. Punch was not going to take no for an answer because he saw this as a way out for him and his management team.

"I'm not going." I remained adamant. "I'm going to show you and the Fat Guy up there (Harold was high up in the seats, watching all of this) and everybody in Canada that I'm a good hockey player and I'm paid to play hockey. That's all I want to do. Play hockey. Forget all of this other stuff outside the game, just go play hockey— that's what I love to do and what I'm going to do."

He was in a difficult position. He knew I wasn't going to go anywhere, and that what I was saying would kill him in the media if he tried to pull something. I was home later that day when Alan Eagleson telephoned.

"I got an interesting call today from George Gross." (Gross, executive sports editor of the *Toronto Sun*, was buddies with both Imlach and Eagleson, no mean feat.) "He suggested that I talk to you and said, 'Wouldn't it be great for the Leafs to give Darryl a paid holiday, considering all of this emotional strain he's been through? Wouldn't it be a great gesture on the Leafs' part if they sent him and his family down to Florida for a break?' What's this all about?"

I filled Al in on things. "Floyd talks to me in the morning and suggests it out of the blue like it's his idea. A couple of hours later, Imlach is telling me I have to go, and now George Gross is phoning you and 'suggesting' it. Do you think they just might be working together on this?"

When I came to practice the next day, I was very upset with Smith. To think that I'm that stupid or so naive that I'll be sucked into a transparent deal like that. We were coming off the ice, when Smitty came over to me to strike up a conversation, talking for the sake of talking. He knew that I had him.

"Smitty, through all this crap I've gone through, I'm going to look back and remember which guys are the liars and which guys told the truth, and what side of the fence they were on. As far as I'm concerned, you're nothing but a liar."

"Whattaya mean?"

"What you said to me yesterday morning—that the Florida thing was your idea and you were going to go up there and make the pitch. And then Imlach came down and practically ordered me to go ..."

"Well, I don't know where he got it from. I don't know how Gross got involved."

Then the clincher. Floyd got a real pensive look on his face: "Maybe my room was bugged," he said, looking genuinely perplexed.

It was my first laugh in three days. I just turned and walked away into the showers.

The players heard about this latest episode and their reaction was one of amazement. It was quite something else for the Montreal Canadiens or the Philadelphia Flyers to send a veteran down south for sun and rest during the season when they had their division locked up. It was quite another thing for the Leafs, who were battling Minnesota and Quebec for the last playoff spot in the Adams Division, to do likewise. What is this crap? Doesn't management care about winning? There was so much of that stuff going on that the guys weren't surprised by anything. It was a circus, a soap opera—whatever you wanted to call it.

It showed in the room, and it also showed on the ice. The previous two years we had been beaten by a powerhouse in the Montreal Canadiens. We had a strong work ethic, a strong feeling for each other, and when Punch destroyed all of that, it really ended the team. How in the world were we going to take these new guys and mold them into the strong club that we had before without the critical leadership upstairs? The frustration centered on the feeling that I'd given everything that I could and wanted to give to that organization for so long, and I knew what it would take to build it up all over again if it were destroyed.

Personally, I had no animosity towards Carl Brewer, Pat Hickey, Wilf Paiement or Bob Stephenson; they were victims of circumstances, much like the rest of us. They were players just like myself, making a living playing hockey, who had had somebody come up to them one day and say, "We've traded you." I related to them as professional hockey players, not as guys taking Lanny McDonald's job or Pat Boutette's job. Carl Brewer played occasionally, but several guys went out of their way to ignore him, refusing to pass to him. Pretty soon Floyd had to keep him on the bench.

How did the guys really feel? Tiger Williams described his emotions in his book:

> Sittler was a class guy and he was being treated like dirt. McDonald was a player who could score 50 goals when it was a hell of a challenge, and Imlach schemed him down to the dead men in Colorado. It made your stomach turn when you thought of what was happening to a team that just might have made it in a city which was screaming for success.
>
> Hickey, who had been part of the McDonald trade, said to me later, "Why do you hate me?" and I replied, "I don't hate you, I just think you're a goddamned floater." I had nothing against Hickey as a guy, but I couldn't get it out of my mind that he was part of the McDonald deal. I guess it stuck in my throat.

Punch was steamed about the treatment Brewer was getting and figured he'd nip any further insubordination in the bud: he traded Dave Hutchison to Chicago for Pat Ribble.

A number of players had gone down to Delaney's Bar & Grill after practice that day. Some guys had eaten, had a drink and gone, but a sizeable group stayed around. While we were sitting there, Hutch got called to the phone and was summoned to the Gardens. He was told he had been traded, picked up his equipment and came back to Delaney's. It was our second post-trade wake in a little over two weeks and the spirits were running a little high. Some of the players were playing darts and somebody took Imlach's picture out of the paper and stuck it on the dartboard. Later that afternoon, Jim Kernaghan of the *Toronto Star* was wandering by outside and they spotted him. The players trusted his word on what he was going to write. They called him into the bar and they opened up.

As requested, he promised not to use their names. I found out about the incident the following day; I had business commitments that afternoon and had not been able to stay around after lunch. The next morning I picked up the paper and there was the dartboard and Imlach's head on it. They had taken the worst picture they could find: there were a couple of darts sticking in his face, along with the story about the trade and how the team was unhappy. That incident started a war in the media, with older, pro-Imlach reporters accusing Kernaghan and the players of gutless, cheap shots, saying if they had the courage of their convictions they should have allowed their names to be used.

We lurched through January 1980 like a rudderless ship. Mike Palmateer had injured his ankle two days before Lanny's trade, and Vincent Tremblay and Paul Harrison were being shelled every night. When Palmy tried to come back during a game in Los Angeles in late January, he re-injured the ankle and missed most of the rest of the season. During that late December-January run, we'd given up 105 goals in 20 games. The club called up Curt Ridley, and Harrison was sent to Moncton.

After remaining silent for a month, Harold Ballard blew up during the Vancouver stop of the western road trip. All Leafs were up for grabs, including me, he thundered.

> "We just can't sit still any longer and I've told Punch to get some new faces on this team," Ballard said. "I'm certain we'll have some deals to announce in the next couple of weeks.
>
> "I've been trying to win the Stanley Cup for 10 years, the past few years with the same group of players. Well, we seem

to be getting farther away from it, not closer, so we've got to make changes.

"Imlach is one of the best wheeler-dealers in the game and when he's in Florida with all the other general managers, you can bet that he'll be making deals."

Asked if center and former captain Darryl Sittler was a likely candidate for a trade, as widely rumored in recent weeks, Ballard said: "If we can make deals that will improve the team, then we have no sacred cows, not a single one."

We won that night in Vancouver and all the questions in the post-game interviews dealt with Harold's comments rather than with the game. Ballard had been right in saying that the team was totally disorganized, and now the forwards and defensemen had begun pointing the finger at each other. The changes we had undergone were resented by some, and they showed their frustrations.

A worst-case scenario was developing for the Leafs. Ballard had sounded off in public once again and put all of the league on alert that the Leafs were ready to deal, which is exactly what Punch intended to do. However, by doing so he substantially reduced our bargaining power. The other general managers would see Punch coming from miles away, and exact a telling price in any deal. The most marketable "commodity" we had at the moment was Borje Salming.

The question of my "tradeability" had also resurfaced. John Ziegler, the new league president, was on the record saying that the standard NHL contract did not allow for no-cut, no-trade provisions. Therefore, I could be traded.

However, my contract *did* have a no-trade clause in it, agreed to and signed by all parties. Alan Eagleson was very confident that it would hold up in court. Harold Ballard, no friend of Ziegler, publicly told him to butt out and admitted to the media that we had a no-trade deal in the contract. At worst, it would cost Toronto a lot of money to trade me, or some very expensive concessions relative to where I was going. Despite the turmoil, I reiterated my desire to stay with the Leafs and see us out of this difficult period.

Punch went to Florida for league meetings and discussed several deals, including one with Los Angeles which would see the Kings give up Butch Goring and a first-round draft choice for me, and another with Chicago, where former Leaf captain Bob Pulford was the boss. As expected, Punch came home empty-handed.

This frustrated Harold Ballard even more; Punch had done such a good job on him that Ballard was dead set against me. When Scotty Bowman announced the makeup of the Wales Conference team for the 32nd NHL All-Star game in Detroit, he named me captain. Our squad had two other centers, Marcel Dionne and Gilbert Perreault, and Ballard took Bowman's announcement as a slap in the face. He let his frustrations show the following night at the annual Sports Celebrity Dinner benefit for the Ontario Society for Crippled Children. More than 2,100 people had paid good money to see and meet Bobby Orr, myself, Pat Hickey, Willie Stargell of the World Series champion Pittsburgh Pirates, Bobby Mattick and John Mayberry of the Blue Jays, Gary Carter of the Expos, boxer Clyde Gray, Olympic markswoman Susan Nattress, and Willie Wood and Terry Metcalf of the Argos.

Alison Gordon covered the event for the *Toronto Star*, and captured the essence of the affair. Early in the proceedings, Bobby Orr introduced me as "one of the classiest guys on the ice—Darryl Sittler." This must have stuck in Harold's craw because, when his turn came to speak, he came gunning for the Leafs.

"If you think [the Leafs] is a disaster area, you're wrong," he said, his belligerence plain for all to see. "Most of the players are there because they want to play hockey, and the ones that don't, won't be around that long." A few boos started floating up to the head table. I was sitting in the audience, surrounded by paying customers.

He defended Punch Imlach with "Like it or not, he's going to stay." Several people began chanting, "Sittler, Sittler," and I was getting more and more embarrassed.

"Who? Who?" Ballard was the only person in the place who thought he was witty.

"If he wants to play, he can play. Instead of having Eagleson think for him, let him think for himself."

Naturally, the reporters crowded around me afterwards, looking for my reaction.

"I just take it where it comes from," I sighed. Would this season from hell ever end?

That event took place a week before the All-Star game. I was very grateful for the mid-season break and the chance to fly down to Detroit and play in the game. It was a very special contest, what with

Gordie Howe of the Hartford Whalers coming back to the Motor City and playing in the same game as Wayne Gretzky, a boy who had unabashedly idolized him, and who had replaced him as the reigning superstar of professional hockey. We won the game 6-3. Afterwards we were in the reception area at the Renaissance Plaza hotel when Red Wings owner Bruce Norris told Bill Watters he would pay me a million dollars if I would release myself from my no-trade contract. I didn't speak directly to Bruce Norris—that would be tampering— but Watters got the drift. I told Watters I didn't think it was a serious offer.

I had my mind made up that I wanted to stay in Toronto. More than anything, it was the stubborn German nature coming out in me—I was going to outlast this guy. I didn't deserve any of this, I couldn't understand why it was happening to me, but I could overcome it. I could get through it all; at some point something was going to happen: neither Harold nor Punch could go on forever. Anything. Something would happen for the good, though I didn't know what.

Was I subconsciously wishing misfortune on either man? Not at all. But I knew something was going to happen to straighten things out. It's like anything in life—whether times are great or really bad— things never stay the same. Eventually, the logjam would clear.

The papers were still full of trade (actually non-trade) stories a week or so after the All-Star game when Dave Hodge and I agreed it was time to appear on his radio program. I knew that I'd have to be careful about what I said, so Dave Hodge and I rehearsed the conversation before we went on the air.

One of the points I made early in the program was that I had been personally in favor of playing the exhibition game against the Canadian Olympic team; this statement made news because the Lake Placid Games had begun. I also denied wanting to manage the Leafs. "I don't want to run the team; no player does. But when you see things that can be done to help the club, I think these things should be brought up for discussion."

I also took a shot at those people who had accused Alan Eagleson of trying to run the Leafs; especially those who blamed him for the team's decline. There were two well-known individuals who could take credit for that, and both had offices on the second floor at Maple Leaf Gardens. "When we eliminated New York Islanders in the playoffs two years ago and Atlanta Flames last year, no one went to Al and said, 'Hey Al, you've really got the team moving.'" I also denied Ballard's accusation that my removal of the captain's "C" the day after Lanny got traded had been orchestrated by my agent.

We talked about the Neilson era that had gone by, the type of coaching techniques he used, and why the team was successful then. I purposely didn't hammer Imlach or Smitty; I just said nice things about Neilson and let the public draw its own conclusions. I kept it purposely technical, stuff about the training program and equipment; how practices were different, and strategies Neilson had used.

"He [Roger] was very thorough and very technical. We'd practice things day in and day out. We do that rarely now. It's not enough to know what you should be doing to bring the puck out of your own end, you have to know what everybody else is doing, too. Roger always worked on game conditions. We rarely scrimmaged. A lot of it was on the power play, penalty killing, bringing the puck out of our own end. We were—what was it?—third overall on the power play.

"I think that the best way to correct things that we are doing wrong is to work on them in practice."

Another caller wanted to know if we were trying.

"Despite what anyone may think, the players are trying," I replied. "Hockey games are not won by individuals, but through work as a team. There's a chemistry involved, a feeling as a team, a common drive, and that is something we have not had in the last two months."

Later that week, I was out on the ice, trying to stay in shape, when the trainer came over and said Imlach wanted to see me in the coaches' room. He'd been out of town the night of the radio show.

I skated over and got the familiar "Siddown!"

Déjà vu.

Punch loved the superior position; him standing and looking down on you while you sat. Off he went.

"Just who in hell do ya think y'are?"

"What do you mean?"

"You were on the air the other night, on CFRB. You don't have any right to go on CFRB; I'm the general manager, I say who goes on."

"Wait a minute. This is a free country we live in. I've never had a problem with this before in my career that anybody dictated to me when I could go on the air. If Dave Hodge asked me to go on, I felt it was okay to do it."

"Ya cut up Smitty, and ya cut up the Leafs."

"Wait a minute . . . I didn't cut up anybody . . ."

"I got the tape right upstairs . . ."

"Well, go listen to it again. I know what I said."

"Ya said Smitty was a bad coach . . ."

"No I didn't. I said Roger Neilson was the finest coach that I ever had." Up to this point, I was in control, but I could feel the temperature rising. The *Showdown* situation, Imlach's comments in St. Louis, the veto on the *Hockey Night in Canada* interview, Harold's boorish behavior at the sports celebrity dinner, even the ankle injury I'd suffered in December . . . everything was building up to a boiling point. I could feel it coming.

My feeling was, "Let it go, what do you have to lose at this point?"

Boom.

"You know what's wrong with you?" Punch turned to me and actually listened to one of his players for the first time in his life.

"You think that you're still back in the '40s and '50s. I'm telling you, you can't motivate people today like you did back then. Things have changed. I appreciate the success you've had and the Stanley Cups, but things change. And you're not going to get anything out of your hockey club and your players, motivating the way you did back then." Then, I aimed for his Achilles heel.

"That's what was wrong with your teams in Buffalo. You spread crap all over them . . ." He wouldn't let me continue.

"We had good teams in Buffalo! Good teams! I had good teams in Buffalo!" The temperature was rising.

"Yeah? What did they ever win? You always got beat in the playoffs. They were so sick and tired of you, they just wanted to get out of there and away for the summer—just to get away from your B.S."

Bull's-eye. Punch went nuts. You could have played a lot of rock and roll classics on the vein that popped out in his forehead, it was so taut.

"You'll be gone! You'll be gone! You'll be gone tomorrow!" It was Friday afternoon.

"And furthermore, I went down to City Hall with your supposed no-trade contract. I had my lawyers look it over. Your lawyer Eagleson is leading you down the garden path. So you'd better be careful."

I still puzzle over the "City Hall" aspect of his statement. Maybe he meant the courthouse.

"Well, Punch, you get your lawyers and I'll get mine and we'll meet in court and see what happens." So far in court, it was Sittler 1, Ballard-Imlach 0.

"You'll be gone! You'll be gone!" He stamped out and slammed the door. I was sitting there all by myself with my equipment on in the coaches' office, wondering: "What do I do now? Is he coming back in?" He didn't return.

After a few minutes, I got up and left. I was at home when the phone rang sometime around four or five in the afternoon. It was Bill Watters. "What the heck happened at Maple Leaf Gardens this morning? I've had every general manager in the league calling me. Imlach's on the phone and he's going to get rid of you. He's going to make a deal and he doesn't care if it costs $500,000 to buy out your no-trade clause. You're gone!" I told him what happened.

As it turned out, I outlasted Punch with the Leafs, but that didn't prevent him from substantially altering the team. As Rick Fraser of the *Toronto Sun* wrote after a 6-4 win against the Rangers in New York, "Darryl Sittler isn't making it easy for Punch Imlach to trade him."

After our donnybrook, I began a hot streak, scoring eight points in two games and taking it from there. Within a little more than a month, 17 games, I was on a two-point-a-game clip, with 15 goals and 19 assists for 34 points. That included a three-goals, three-assists night against Detroit and three goals and one assist against Pittsburgh in a comeback 5-3 win. After I scored my third goal into the empty net against the Wings in the 6-3 victory, a lot of fans in Maple Leaf Gardens began pointing to Harold in his private box and chanting, "Keep Sittler, keep Sittler." Every time my name was brought up to him, Ballard would change the subject to my new linemate, Wilf Paiement.

"Wasn't that a great trade? Do you see how he can be tough and score goals, too? That's what we need. I used to think that Darryl Sittler was God. But Alan Eagleson has turned his head around like a corkscrew."

Punch was talking with Minnesota (defenseman Brad Maxwell and the NHL rights to Kevin Maxwell, then with the Canadian

Olympic team), Buffalo (Rick Martin), Chicago (Doug Wilson and others) and the Islanders (Billy Harris). There also was a published report of a Buffalo-Toronto blockbuster that would see myself, Tiger and Mike Palmateer move across Lake Ontario in exchange for Don Edwards, Rick Martin and either winger Ric Seiling or defenseman Bill Hajt.

None of those moves panned out so Punch did what he felt was the next best thing. He traded Tiger Williams and Jerry Butler to Vancouver for Rick Vaive and Bill Derlago. In the long run, it turned out to be a positive trade for Toronto, the only good one made by Punch during his short but destructive tenure, as Vaive went on to become the first-ever Leaf to score 50 goals in a season, a feat he accomplished three straight years from 1981-82 through 1983-84. But at the time, it meant that more of our heart had been painfully removed, especially with the loss of Tiger. Bill and Rick were good guys; it wasn't their fault that Imlach had gone and got them.

There was method to his madness, too. He had Smitty give every new player he brought in a lot of ice time, put him in every situation that would make him look good. Imlach's philosophy was: "I traded for them, let's give them every opportunity."

Floyd Smith tried to have us believe that he was making the calls and running the team. The attitude of the players was that Smitty was Punch's rubber stamp; he was a yes-man to Punch with no backbone.

Long on animosity and short on class, Punch Imlach didn't even tell Butler he had been traded; Jerry found out secondhand from his roommate, who just happened to be Tiger Williams, after we had checked into our hotel in Uniondale. We were heading off to practice the following morning when I met him in the lobby. "Tiger told me I was traded so it must be true," he said quietly.

Meanwhile, I was going to bed and waking up with "Where do you think you'll be traded?" questions and rumors ringing in my ears. I just tried to play my game amid the turmoil, responding to the silliness with good on-ice performance.

In the end, my scoring feats in the second half of that season stopped all trade talk about me. In the second week of March, Harold Ballard publicly admitted that I would remain with the Leafs through the end of the season. He didn't have much choice; a trade for me then might have led to a lynching. His. After a slow first half, I ended the season with 40 goals and 57 assists, good for ninth place overall in the scoring race. Only one player outscored me in the second half of that season; somebody by the name of Wayne Gretzky. Our club was moving upwards in the standings, 15th, 14th, 13th, 12th, 11th ... until we latched onto a playoff berth.

Then yet another tragedy struck, and this was far more serious than hockey players changing teams and cities. At a team meeting on Friday morning, March 21, Floyd Smith mentioned that he was going to Archie Katzman's restaurant in St. Catharines for a birthday party that afternoon. That night on the radio I heard on the news that two people had been killed and Floyd Smith was involved in the accident. He would be laid up in hospital for a long time, at least through the end of the season and the playoffs.

A couple of days later, another Imlach crony, Joe Crozier, was brought up from Moncton to coach the team. His debut was an impressive one, a 9-1 rout of the Jets, and we all were feeling quite confident with the playoffs just around the corner. With a bit of luck, and the momentum we'd built up, a terrific playoff could relegate this nightmare season to the garbage can.

When it comes to the playoffs, your outlook changes. If you've had a good season, you know you've still got to have a good playoff or your season is washed out. If you've had a bad season, it's a chance to make things better.

So we went to Minnesota with an optimistic attitude—"We know a lot of crap went down during the year; let's have a good playoff and fix it."

Then Punch Imlach reared his head yet another time and ruined it all.

Before we left for Bloomington, each player received a trip itinerary which contained our travel route, where we would stay, and a schedule of activities for each day on the road. The itinerary indicated our normal, game-day morning skate at 11:30. All of the teams visiting Bloomington stayed at the Marriott, right across the street from the Metropolitan Sports Center, so the guys were over there early getting their sticks taped and donning their skates and sweats. The other options included staying in bed or going for a walk in the boonies.

We were getting close to the skate when Dick Duff came into the dressing room and announced: "You guys aren't supposed to go on the ice this morning."

"What do you mean?"

"Imlach is superstitious; he doesn't want you on the ice."

A lot of the guys already had their skates on, just waiting for the North Stars to finish. They all looked at me for direction. I always enjoyed the game-day morning skate, just to loosen up and test my equipment and stuff.

Duff said we were going to have a meeting at 11:30, instead of the skate. As it happened, the North Stars came off the ice early, at 11:00, and we had half an hour to kill, so I said: "Let's go on, have a quick skate, and we'll all come off for the meeting at 11:30."

Dan Maloney, who had a broken thumb and wouldn't play that night, was already out on the ice with Mike Kaszycki, the rookie. We'd acquired him from Washington for Pat Ribble five weeks after we got Ribble from Chicago for Dave Hutchison; more evidence of Punch Imlach's trading acumen. Other players were getting ready to join us when Smoky Lemelin, the trainer, came running down to ice level in a panic.

"Boy, you're in trouble. Imlach is up there and is he mad!"

I was thinking to myself, "So what's the big deal?"

A little later, I was walking up the steps that led to the dressing room, and there was Imlach, beet-red in the face with the fedora pushed way back on his head.

"Just what the hell do ya think you're doin'? Didn't Duffy tell ya not to go on the ice?"

I don't know what triggered it in me, but I gave him the gears.

"Punch, I got new blades on my skates. Do ya want me to tell you tonight in the middle of the second period that the blades are no good or do you want me to test them now and find out?"

He couldn't, and didn't say anything. So I just blew by him and continued on into the dressing room.

"What about you?" he bellowed at Kaszycki who was right behind me. "I just followed him, man!" Kaszycki was a rookie but he wasn't stupid.

I walked into the dressing room and the guys were all looking at me; they must have heard the commotion outside. I was standing at the table getting a piece of gum and Imlach walked in muttering, "Sonofabitch, ya think you're running the hockey club around here?" and continued walking by.

Then we had our team meeting. It started something like this. "Duffy told you guys not to go on the ice. I'm runnin' the show here. I know other guys around here think they're runnin' the show, but

I'm runnin' the show. You had no business goin' out on the ice." No explanations.

He went on to talk about the Stanley Cups the Leafs won back whenever.

"We're gonna try somethin' different tonight. It's worked for us before."

"What in the world could this be?" I wondered.

"We're gonna start five defensemen."

Dead silence. You could almost hear Maxwell Smart of Control piping up in his high-pitched voice: "So, the o-o-o-ld five defensemen trick!"

Larry Carrière, who once played for Punch in Buffalo, was going to start at center. Hawk seemed embarrassed by the whole thing, but it was an opportunity for him to make a few extra bucks so he wasn't going to turn it down.

Punch continued: "Burrows, you're up on left wing, Salming up on right." (They weren't going to hurt anybody on wing.) He turned back to Carrière, a look of cunning on his face.

"Hawk, when you line up before the puck's dropped, I want you to go over and tell Bobby Smith [the North Stars' center] that if he touches the puck, he's gonna pay the price."

This was all in the team meeting. The guys were looking at Punch like he had just landed in an alien spaceship. E.T. call home.

Then it was time for Show and Tell.

"Duffy, show 'em the ring."

Dick Duff flashed the hand and showed the Stanley Cup ring he was wearing. With Punch's luck and penchant for showmanship, it probably was a Montreal Canadiens ring, not a Leafs one. Nobody said "Oooooh!"

Larry Carrière actually did pass along Imlach's message and ended up telling Smith to wipe the smirk off his face. Whenever you got Smith mad, he'd look down at you with this little smile. As for the threat, nothing came of it.

After the great strategy session ended, Imlach and Duff left, and Smoky Lemelin came up to me.

"What did you tell Imlach?"

"What do you mean?"

"He just chewed me out for putting new blades on your skates before a playoff game! I didn't put new blades on your skates." He'd actually changed my blades about three weeks earlier. But that was

Punch; first chance he got he started jumping all over the trainer for changing my blades. I apologized to Smoky for getting him in hot water.

The upshot of all this voodoo and mayhem is that we got blown out of the playoffs real quick. I remember that Jiri Crha was the goalie in the first game and we got thumped 6-3. It was more of the same the next night in a 7-2 hammering, and we returned home on the Friday night to expire 4-3. The North Stars outscored us 17-8 in the three-game sweep.

We had been pumped up for the playoffs, and then along came Punch with the histrionics. Two minutes later, we were on the golf course.

Punch used the quick elimination to get back at Harold.

"Sittler is the cancer on this hockey team. We've got to dump him before the next training camp."

But, as things turned out, Punch was not going to be in any shape to trade me.

12

The Long Goodbye

PUNCH IMLACH HAD won.

Every indication had it that I was an ex-Leaf that summer. Harold Ballard had stated publicly that I was a cancer on this team and that I was on my way out. How far was he willing to go? I wasn't even included in the Toronto Maple Leafs 1980-81 Training Camp Media Guide. I had ceased to exist for the blue-and-white.

Harold was an expert at making somebody or something disappear and had all sorts of experience with this crazy stuff. When he and former fellow owner John Bassett got into a fight for control of the team, Harold had had Stan Obodiac doctor an official team picture so that Bassett no longer appeared in it. (John Bassett's head was replaced with Bill Ballard's in the photograph.) Gordie McRae wore a beard during our team photo session one year. There was no team rule stipulating clean cheeks, and Harold didn't even bother to solicit Jim Gregory's or Roger Neilson's opinions on the matter. McRae lost his head, too; luckily for the lanky goaltender, the replacement head was his own, from an earlier, non-bearded era. In the summer of 1980, it was my turn to be symbolically shorn from the Leafs.

The previous season ended in acrimony, with Ballard blasting us after the second loss in Minnesota, saying that the players were getting out their golf clubs and weren't even trying. I fired back to the effect that if he thought he was motivating his players with this kind of talk, he was far behind the times on the subject of group psychology. I used much more basic language: "Statements like that make the players sick. But then, you must understand who comments like that are coming from. He hasn't had his name in the paper for a while."

Harold also castigated the so-called old guard, hinting strongly that such charter members as Dan Maloney, Ian Turnbull and Ron Ellis would join me somewhere as ex-Leafs.

"I guess that just gives management a couple more years to tell the fans the team is going through a rebuilding process," I replied.

Harold retorted that I had been a cancer on the team ever since I had ripped the "C" from my sweater, and he fully expected me to ask for a post-season trade. I'd get one, even if I didn't ask for one, he added.

Instead of going home when we returned from Bloomington during the previous playoffs, we'd checked into the Westbury Hotel, just around the corner from Maple Leaf Gardens, on Thursday night before our Friday home game. It wasn't a bad strategy on the surface. Lots of teams, such as the Montreal Canadiens, routinely stay at a retreat in the Laurentians during playoffs. Punch wanted the team to stay together and focused, and it might have worked if we hadn't had the superstitious silliness before the first game in Bloomington. By now, however, the players were in open revolt and some of them were quoted in the newspapers to the effect that if Punch was doing this to keep them out of bars, hadn't he ever heard of room service?

I didn't endorse that point of view, but understood the season-long litany of frustration that had led up to it. After we lost Game Three in overtime, all I wanted was to get as far away from Maple Leaf Gardens as I could, take a long rest at the cottage and get back into a proper frame of mind to get my career on track.

Before I left, however, it was up to quiet Ron Ellis to put the previous year's tumult in proper perspective. "When the men at the front end of this team consider everything that happened here this season—all the trades and constant personnel changes, the three coaching changes and all the stuff that seemed to surround this team, they have to be pleased with what the team did—and I mean that.

"We won 35 games and if the confusion could have been reduced just a little, we could have won 10 more. They have to be very proud of the kids this team has. They're a good bunch and they're going to get better."

Ron was the senior statesman of the Leafs that season, the only holdover from the previous Imlach administration (I don't include

Carl Brewer in this because of the special circumstances surrounding his return), and his words hit home.

"I've never been through anything like it and I hope I don't have to go through a season like it again. It was no fun at all. For one thing, it's difficult to have three coaches in one year."

We finished 1979-80 with 75 points on 35 wins, 40 losses and 5 ties, and went 0-for-3 in the playoffs. Little did Harold Ballard and Punch Imlach realize that this nightmare season would represent a highwater mark for the Leafs over the next decade. It wasn't until an exact ten years later, the 1989-90 season (38-38-4, 80 points, finishing at the .500 mark for the first time since 1978-79), that a Toronto team would win as many as 35 games, and they would reach the 30-win plateau only once during the 1980s. Finishing as high as first or second in their division was simply out of the question. Punch and Harold seemed not to have realized what destructive forces their lethal management marriage would unleash on a proud hockey city. (In the four seasons prior to that unholy alliance, we had finished above .500 four years running.)

Having set these wheels in motion, Punch was dedicated to finishing off what he called the Toronto Maple Leafs Country Club. The first step was to get rid of the dependable Mike Palmateer. Palmy was dispatched to Washington in an entry draft deal that June—he and our third-round selection in the draft for Tim Coulis, Robert Picard and the Capitals' second-round pick.

This might be the best place to recap Punch's trading year. After officially joining us on July 4, 1979, he:

- acquired Reg Thomas from Edmonton for a sixth-round draft choice on December 13, 1979, and turned right around and dealt Thomas to Quebec for Dave Farrish and Terry Martin;
- traded Pat Boutette to Hartford for Bob Stephenson on December 24;
- traded Lanny McDonald and Joel Quenneville to Colorado for Pat Hickey and Wilf Paiement on December 28;
- traded Dave Hutchison to Chicago for Pat Ribble on January 10, 1980;
- traded Pat Ribble to Washington for Mike Kaszycki on February 16;
- traded Tiger Williams and Jerry Butler to Vancouver for Bill Derlago and Rick Vaive on February 18;

- traded Walt McKechnie to Colorado for a third-round 1980 draft choice on March 3;
- acquired Dave Shand in a three-draft-choice deal on June 10;
- traded Mike Palmateer and a draft choice to Washington for Tim Coulis, Robert Picard and a draft choice.

Punch, the tradin' man! Nine deals involving (including each draft choice as a player) 28 players past, present and future. The Toronto Maple Leafs hockey club made only nine trades in the *entire* 1930s and 1940s, involving 30 players. Punch had done two decades' worth of trading in a little over seven months, considering the fact that he didn't really get going until December 1979. Given an opportunity to move me, Punch would take it. In fact, he and Harold started a squabble over that very issue, with Punch having moved me to Calgary, only to have The Boss botch the deal with some inopportune gum-flapping.

I enjoyed a quiet summer. Harold and Punch's summer wasn't as peaceful because they, especially Harold, had become the targets of a fearful media barrage. A weekend magazine in Toronto had Harold on the cover, standing defiantly, if unwittingly, under the headline: "Portrait of a Bully." Another headline called him "Harold the Terrible." Most of the time, Ballard lived to exchange barbs with the best the media could throw at him. This summer, however, his heart didn't seem to be in it.

I would discover later that he was genuinely upset with Imlach's machinations, not too pleased that his captain had been an early target, and that two of his favorites, Lanny McDonald and Tiger Williams, had been traded. Worse still, I think, was the knowledge that he had brought this all down on himself when he had hired Punch. It didn't help that every time I spoke to the media that summer, at charity golf games or softball matches, I took the high road, swearing allegiance to the team and adding that I wanted to finish my career in Toronto. Every time Harold opened his mouth, it was to change feet, and the media badgered him at every turn.

I even took time out for a quiet visit with Punch at Maple Leaf Gardens on a Saturday morning halfway through the summer. The offices were deserted, there wasn't a writer in sight and that seemed to take the pressure off. Before going down to the meeting, I had spoken with Alan Eagleson and told him that I would deal with Punch Imlach on my own. I took great care to let Alan know that I felt he was blameless in this whole affair, and that Punch Imlach's irrational position on himself and agents in general was at the root of the problem. The Eagle understood, even if he might have been a little hurt by this.

"Punch, I just want you to know that Eagleson is no longer my agent for dealing with the Leafs," I told him. "I'll take care of that myself; he'll be handling all my commercials and endorsement arrangements." I also mentioned that I was willing to let bygones be bygones, and that I didn't want to talk about the previous season.

It was quite unlike any previous conversation between us. Quiet, peaceable, almost respectful. Punch had his renowned temper, and I had my German-Canadian stubbornness. We could easily have gotten into a shouting match, but without saying it, we both recognized the need for at least one conversation between us that didn't degenerate into a verbal brawl. He didn't say he would trade me, although I knew that my name had beeen bandied about in Montreal during the NHL draft. Punch made no promises in that regard. He did, however, promise to set up a meeting between Harold Ballard and me some time in late summer.

A week or so after our conversation, Imlach flew off to Sweden to meet with Borje Salming and his agent at the Stockholm Sheraton. Borje wanted in the neighborhood of $400,000 a year; Imlach characteristically replied that the defenseman had Rosedale tastes and Mississauga talent. Both stuck to their guns and, when Punch returned home empty-handed, he discovered from King Clancy that Harold was upset with his singular lack of success in signing Salming. In hindsight, that may have been the first ominous sign.

Salming was unsigned and my status was still festering. According to Punch, I was included on the training camp roster and in the media guide he had okayed, and my disappearance occurred when Harold saw the official list that had to be submitted to the league. Then came the word that I was being traded to Calgary in some complicated deal involving "future considerations," who might or might not be Guy Chouinard and Bob McMillan, with Chouinard reverting back to the Flames the following year in return for Kent Nilsson. Punch's deal with Cliff Fletcher was contingent on secrecy; once I had reported to Calgary, the "future considerations" would materialize into living, breathing hockey players. If I didn't accept the trade, then the Flames would not be stuck with two players who had been moved, and then returned, a depressing experience.

Five minutes after Punch had left his office, Harold blabbed. It was all over the newspapers the following morning, Monday, August 25. Punch heard about it on his car radio and began to experience chest pains. He knew the feeling well, having suffered a previous heart attack in 1972, during his second season in Buffalo. The pains had eased somewhat when Punch got to Maple Leaf Gardens. Ballard wasn't around, so he lit into King Clancy, telling him to tell their mutual boss that he had probably scotched the deal. A few hours later when the chest pain came back, Punch knew it was time to check into the hospital; he was in intensive care when the heart attack struck at four o'clock the following morning. He was going to be out of the picture for several months.

I'll never know for sure, but I think this new development gave Harold the chance to get out from under the situation, and at the same time make it look like Imlach was the one who was trying to do me in. Punch was barely hooked up to the EKG when Harold gleefully signed Borje Salming to a five-year deal, giving him all of the things that Imlach had refused a month before in Sweden. Punch was in intensive care and on a strict, media-free diet. No radio, no TV, no newspapers. He wouldn't find out about the deal until his return to work in October.

Around Labor Day, I, like many other Canadians, was emotionally drained by the Terry Fox drama. When the Marathon of Hope had passed through Toronto earlier in the year, I had given this extraordinary young man my All-Star team sweater. His plight, and his grace and courage in the face of the most overwhelming odds had touched me deeply.

That weekend, the word came that Terry couldn't continue his run. It appeared that the cancer that had cost him his leg several years before, had returned. When a reporter telephoned me about that piece of news, I suggested taking his place, in a relay run with many other prominent Canadians. Unsure of my official or unofficial training camp status with the Leafs, I was ready to go.

I was still up at the cottage in Orillia when I got a call the following day from Joe Crozier. In one of his last official actions before he set off for the hospital, and true to his word, Punch had asked Joe to pass on my request to Harold that we meet. Harold was expecting my call and we agreed to meet in the Hot Stove Lounge for breakfast the next day, just the two of us with nobody else around. Especially no media. We met on the Tuesday after Labor Day.

That morning Ballard told me that Imlach would not be back as general manager. "I'll give him a job in the organization, maybe he'll drive the Zamboni, I dunno, but he's not comin' back."

Ballard went on to say he'd made a mistake in hiring Punch Imlach. I think Harold had come to the realization that his general manager was past it, and he would use Punch's heart attack as the excuse to get rid of him.

But there were other things to consider. Punch had neatly maneuvered Ballard into the media's bad books. While Imlach took his share of the blame for the trades and bad feelings in the dressing room, let alone our first sub-.500 season in five years, Ballard had become the true media target because of his penchant for dancing all over his tongue. By meeting with me earlier that summer, Punch might have been retreating into a neutral corner.

As Ballard's then-assistant Gord Stellick would later write, "Imlach had a solid reputation and a three-year contract. He also had a knack for stealing the headlines, which perturbed Ballard no end." Had Harold been there when Moses came down from the Mount with the sacred tablets, he would have amended the First Commandment to read: "Thou shalt never get between Harold Ballard and his beloved media coverage." Punch transgressed against that commandment daily.

Two days after our Hot Stove Lounge meeting, we were back in the same room and this time the media were in attendance. Harold announced my return to the team.

But, even on this good news day, the state of his relations with the working press was dismal. Frank Orr, the veteran *Toronto Star* beat man who was respected by everybody in the league and rarely took a cheap shot, described an uncomfortable Ballard wearing a tan three-piece suit that "made him look like a retired Man from Glad." The reporters, grateful for a chance to pin Harold's hide to the wall, fired away.

"You called him a cancer . . ."

"You were gonna trade Darryl . . ."

"We were never going to see him again in a Leafs sweater . . ."

"He's a coach killer."

Harold, never at a loss for words, offered lamely: "I was just kidding. Just trying to keep things stirred up. I can't have the Blue Jays hoggin' all the headlines, can I?"

"Is Darryl Sittler being invited to training camp?"

"Of course."

"Any chance of Darryl wearing the 'C' again?"

"I'd seriously reconsider it," said Ballard. Each word was another brush stroke, painting him deeper and deeper into a corner.

"What about you, Darryl? Would you be captain again if they offered it to you?"

"I'd seriously reconsider it," I mimicked Harold.

A couple of weeks later, the "C" was back on my sweater.

We started the 1980-81 season with a much better attitude and improved on-ice performance ... no *Showdown* squabble, no upheavals with the coaching staff, no heated three-way exchanges with the media. However, as the season pressed on, it became readily apparent that, despite the infusion of youth, we were not the club we had been, and very little could be done in this area. Punch and Joe Crozier had been high on the Czechoslovakian goalie Jiri Crha the previous season, starting him ahead of Mike Palmateer, and eventually trading Palmy because they figured Crha could handle the load. Crha, Curt Ridley and Paul Harrison were our goalies and, unfortunately, all three were good backups, or journeymen, but none was a reliable starter. To fill that gaping hole, Punch had acquired Jimmy Rutherford from Detroit for Mark Kirton, but that wouldn't work out either. A lot of our veterans were gone and, even though Dan Maloney was still with the team and kids like Wilf Paiement and Robert Picard could take care of themselves, we had lost that toughness we had enjoyed with veteran players like McKechnie, McDonald, Hutchison, Butler and Williams. (At the trading deadline in March, we'd pick up René Robert from Colorado and send Picard to the Canadiens for Michel Larocque, a competent professional goaltender. The first move did nothing to help our game in the corners, but the latter certainly helped between the pipes.)

By the time 1980 turned into 1981, I'd been in and out of a slump, we were heading for last place in the Adams Division, and Joe Crozier was on his last legs. Harold Ballard, anxious to undermine Punch Imlach but not brave enough to do it head on, had been taking shots at Punch's underling since the start of training camp. It didn't take long for the players to notice, and Crozier lost all credibility in the dressing room. He responded by increasing the volume on his tirades, but his exhortations fell on deaf ears. In January, after an embarrassing 8-2 loss to Winnipeg at Maple Leaf Gardens—only that team's fourth win of the season—Crozier was fired. We were 13-

22-5 at the 40-game halfway point and going nowhere when Joe left. To be fair, very little of this was purely his fault.

Crozier's departure was bizarre, like that of other Maple Leafs before him. We had gone to practice at North York Centennial Arena, but instead of going on the ice, Crozier called the players into a closed-door meeting.

"Everybody tell all, don't be afraid to get things off your chest," was his surprising opener. He then went from player to player, soliciting opinions. I sensed that something wasn't right. I couldn't say for sure what it was, but when my turn to speak came I said very little. However, we had other players who were young and eager and wanted to help, like Rocky Saganiuk, and they were forthright. The meeting turned quickly into a litany of criticism of Joe.

After the meeting was over, Crozier spoke:

"I sense the feeling here is that I'm not doing a good job and some of you believe I'm not able to, either," he said. "I'm going down to Maple Leaf Gardens to resign my position as coach of the Maple Leafs hockey club." And he left. There wasn't much to be said after that bombshell.

As the players left the room and went out onto the ice, I went to the washroom. Harold Ballard came in.

"What's going on, Harold? I smell a rat."

Ballard was taken aback. "Whattaya mean?"

I told him about the Crozier meeting that had just ended, and Crozier's vow to go down to Maple Leaf Gardens, hand in his pink slip and retire.

"Hand in his pink slip? What's he talking about? We fired the guy last night. What's he doing around here? After practice is over, I want to see you downtown."

I ran the practice and then went to the Gardens, where I waited in the reception area outside Ballard's office. Joe Crozier's office was kitty-corner to where I was sitting. I could see him in there cleaning out his office of books and things. He spotted me, came out of his office with an armful of books, and dumped them on the secretary's desk in front of me without a word. He went back into the office, grabbed another pile of stuff, and did it again. Neither of us said anything. The secretary sat watching this little vignette, amazement on her face.

Nothing was ever said. To this day I don't know if this was

Crozier's way of telling me to stick it, or if he was recommending some decent reading.

Imlach couldn't prevent Crozier's firing, although he had tried to prevent it. He was back in the saddle though when it came time to replace Joe, and he and Ballard reached into the broadcast booth for our new coach. Mike Nykoluk, a former bosom buddy of Fred Shero and assistant to Freddie the Fogg at both Philadelphia and New York, stepped down from his job as color man on the Leafs' radio broadcasts and into the coach's shoes. That winter, those shoes fit him well as we turned it around and finished 15-15-10 in the second half. Nykoluk had no pressure on him, and this took the pressure off us. We responded well to his quiet demeanor and solid support of our efforts. After a bad start, I finished the season strongly, setting a personal best with five hat tricks in one year, my 14th through 18th career three-goal games with Toronto.

The playoffs probably best revealed the weak underbelly that Punch had left unprotected in the blue-and-white. In 1978, when we had upset the Islanders in overtime in the seventh game, we had done so with a solid defensive effort and timely scoring. People like Maloney, McDonald, Williams and Butler pounded the boards and the Islanders at every opportunity and they proved to be the team that flinched. In 1981, we barely edged into the playoffs at the end of the season (beating the Nordiques 4-2 in Quebec on the last night of the season) and faced the Islanders again. This time they had too much for us in every department: offense, defense, size, speed, work ethic and determination. The scores were 9-2, 5-1 and 6-2 and we were on the first tee.

The media now added two new charter members to the Take An Old Leaf, Please! Trade Exchange—the other remaining members of the original Big Six, Ian Turnbull and Borje Salming. At least I had company.

I also had lost faith in the ability of the Toronto Maple Leafs hockey team to compete. Two short summers before, I had been champing at the bit to return to training camp and get back about my business of winning the Stanley Cup. We were good, getting better, and were a couple of judicious drafts or trades away from challenging even the Canadiens and Islanders for league supremacy. I believed that totally, and so did people like Lanny, Tiger, Borje, Ian and Palmy. Punch Imlach didn't believe it and he was in a position to express his dissenting opinion in very concrete terms.

By the summer of 1981, I was a very different person as far as the
Leafs were concerned. I would be turning thirty-one on September
18 and moving into the last year of the seven-year contract extension
I had signed in 1976-77. The next contract I would sign might very
well prove to be my last and I had my financial well-being and my
family to think about. As well, I had come to the unhappy but clear-
eyed realization that my opportunity to see my name on the Stanley
Cup, the real dream of every NHL player, could only happen if I was
playing somewhere else. The Leafs had won only 28 games the
previous season, while losing 37, the first time the team had failed to
win at least 30 games since the NHL had instituted the 80-game
schedule in 1974-75. My pessimism would prove to be well-founded;
the Leafs would finish 1981-82 with a 20-44-16 mark.

When Jim Gregory had signed Lanny and me to the contract
extensions, we both were happy with the vote of confidence and
financial security they represented. My deal called for $160,000 a
year in that first season and annual increases that would have me
earning $190,000 before bonuses in the last year of the pact. Alan
Eagleson had counselled us to play out our options just prior to
signing that deal, because he knew that we could get a lot more
money on the open market, or even if there was a threat of an open
market. Jim Gregory, of course, knew it was in his best interest to
lock us up for the long haul. In the end, we went against Eagleson's
advice and opted for the long-term security.

There was one proviso. The deal was that we would be paid on a
scale commensurate with our membership in the league's elite. A
year later, when the New York Rangers offered Ulf Nilsson and
Anders Hedberg a combined $1.6 million U.S. to leave the WHA and
Portage and Main for the bright lights of Broadway, top stars in the
NHL began scrambling to renegotiate their deals. When approached
by the media, Lanny and I held firm—we were happy with our
contracts and the Leafs and weren't seeking extra money.

By the summer of 1981, I had lost a lot of ground. Both Pat
Hickey and Wilf Paiement were making in excess of $200,000, and
Borje Salming was earning well over $300,000. The picture was the
same among my major competition across the league; Marcel
Dionne, Guy Lafleur, Bryan Trottier, Gilbert Perreault, Bobby
Clarke, Larry Robinson and Denis Potvin were on a different pay
scale than I was. In fact, Guy Lafleur would hold out the following

season: his current salary of $375,000 a year, or twice what I was making, was not enough.

Consider these comparisons (1976-77 through 1980-81 seasons):

Player	GP	G	A	Pts
Marcel Dionne	390	259	344	603
Guy Lafleur	363	245	347	592
Bryan Trottier	380	196	340	536
Darryl Sittler	376	202	285	487
Gilbert Perreault	366	167	267	434
Denis Potvin	338	114	278	392

Obviously, I had delivered the kinds of numbers that merited financial recognition from the Toronto Maple Leafs. The major problem was, how to sell Imlach and Ballard? I pondered that question during the summer and discussed it several times with Alan Eagleson. In September, I went in to talk to Harold. I didn't ask him to renegotiate my contract; rather I wanted him to reconsider what I had done for the hockey club, the number of years I'd played, and the fact that my 1,000th point and 1,000th games were not far off on the horizon. Both would be firsts for the Maple Leafs. If he didn't want to consider a contract extension, maybe he'd do something around those two events.

There was another factor. In the October budget speech, Finance Minister Allan MacEachen announced the cancellation of income-averaging annuities. These annuities, or income-deferral programs, allowed professional athletes, entertainers and others making high wages over a short career to spread out the tax bite over a longer period. This announcement set off a mad rush for the United States by hockey and baseball players. Harold promised to take this discussion to the board of directors in October and get back to me. He bought more time for himself when he announced a couple of weeks later that the meeting had been moved to November 30.

Meanwhile, back on the second floor, Ballard was continuing his campaign to oust Punch. Imlach still had a third year and an option year remaining on his contract. Worse still, Imlach's tentacles—or so Harold thought—reached far and wide in the world of hockey. Ballard could not be sure that Punch wouldn't come back and haunt

him if they parted amid hostilities. His feeble attempt to get rid of
Imlach the previous season ("I don't want to be the guy who puts
him in a box") had proved to be a dismal failure. Though stung over
the Salming salary affair and my return, especially the return of the
"C" to my sweater, Punch had taken up residence quietly in his
office in October and, by Christmas, was running the team again.

He and Ballard quibbled and squabbled but it was essentially a
stalemate. Then, Punch went and solved Ballard's problem for him
by having a recurrence of his heart problems. He was in St.
Catharines checking out our rookie camp in early September 1981
when his chest pains returned. Punch later admitted it was his own
fault; he had ignored doctors' instructions to take it easy after the
previous coronary and found himself in hospital for the second time
in thirteen months. He would need a triple bypass operation.

Barely ten days after the complicated operation, he read in the
newspapers that Ballard did not want him back as general manager.
During his entire stay in hospital, he had received the best wishes of
many people, including myself, but not a word from Ballard. Punch
was out of hospital in a month and spent the last half of October and
the first half of November walking miles, exercising his "new" heart
and getting himself into the best physical shape he'd enjoyed in
years. Harold, on the other hand, spent his month feuding with
reporters over the Imlach situation and stirring up all sorts of
Ballardian baloney.

Midway through this mess, Ian Turnbull decided he had had
enough. He missed curfew the night before a game in Colorado, was
sent home by Mike Nykoluk, and patiently and happily awaited a
trade. On Remembrance Day he got his wish and was traded to Los
Angeles for John Gibson and Billy Harris.

When Punch finally was cleared to return to work for November
17, the first sign that things had changed came when he discovered
his parking spot at the Gardens had been "reassigned." He went
straight to Harold and challenged him, and Ballard did not have the
intestinal fortitude to tell his employee that he had been fired.
Instead, he suggested that Punch resign, for his own good. Punch
refused. Punch still had two years on his contract and finished the
conversation: "I'll be at home if you need me."

As it turned out, Harold could have used Imlach's NHL contacts
and smarts, but chose to surround himself with yes-men. While
Punch's battle was carried on for him by media friends, Ballard

summoned Gerry McNamara into his office and told him he would be acting general manager. "Acting" was a very good description; everybody in Toronto knew that Harold had finally decided that he would run the team himself, pulling all the strings. While the puppets behind the bench would occasionally be replaced, the puppeteer would remain. This situation would continue throughout the 1980s and go a long way to explaining the Leafs disheartening string of failures.

McNamara, who had played less than half a dozen games with the Leafs in the 1960s, was Toronto's head scout in 1981, and had made his reputation a decade earlier when he had returned from Sweden with Inge Hammarström and Borje Salming in tow. He was perfect for the job—the Toronto hockey media hated him as much as they did Ballard because of his constant complaints, insults and tantrums in the press box and elsewhere, and, like his boss, he returned the "mutual admiration" in spades. Things got so bad that even-tempered Mike Nykoluk joined into the "us versus them" fray and alternated with McNamara in confrontations with reporters, especially those of the *Globe and Mail*. "Maple Laffs" or "Maple Loafs" became common descriptions of the team, both in the media and on signs carried by the paying customers. When confronted by the Unholy Trinity, the players could do little but shake their heads in total bewilderment.

Like most of the players, I was content to let Punch and Harold play out their own little drama without getting involved. My deadline with Harold was drawing near. Things were fairly quiet, although I had received an indication early in the season that perhaps my days were numbered. Mike Nykoluk and his assistant coach, Dan Maloney, came to me and asked if I might consider accepting a position as an assistant playing coach, and giving up my captaincy.

"We'd like to give the 'C' to Rick Vaive because we think that the added responsibility will mature him," Nykoluk explained. I could take this two ways; they knew that Harold wanted to move me out, or they honestly felt that I would be honored by the offer and happy to help ease Vaive into the post. I turned them down. I wasn't ready to become part of management. I had too much to contribute as a player.

Another indication that Toronto was no longer the place to be had nothing to do with my personal concerns or salary conflict; instead, it had to do with another player, Laurie Boschman. Laurie was a feisty little native of Major, Saskatchewan, who was playing junior hockey with the Brandon Wheat Kings when we drafted him in the first round, ninth overall, in 1979. He made the team on his first try but, new to the big city and the fast pace of the NHL, he was already drinking a lot and living the wild life in his rookie season. He was following in the footsteps of Borje Salming, the original party animal, and having a good time. But like many young professional athletes, it didn't take long before he realized that something was missing in his life. He got to know Mel Stevens and the people at the Teen Ranch and eventually made a commitment as a Christian.

It would have surprised him to learn that Harold Ballard would have been more comfortable with his original lifestyle than with his reformation. The first indication that Ballard was unhappy with Boschman's born-again Christianity was out of the public eye. Mel Stevens would often come to the games because several players, including myself, frequently left him tickets. This showed our appreciation for the many things he had done for us and our families— things I describe in detail in a later chapter. Harold knew Mel a bit and the two would occasionally exchange a few civil words.

Laurie took a phone call in the dressing room one night and came right over to me: "I've just got a call from the special ticket office. Mel came to pick up tickets I'd left and they said there weren't any. I went up there and found out that they won't let me leave any tickets for him. That's not fair; they're my tickets, why can't I leave them for who I want?" Apparently, Ballard had left word that nobody was allowed to leave tickets for Mel Stevens.

"Go and call Mel and tell him you'll leave them in another name so he can pick them up," I advised, and helped Laurie arrange for some backup tickets. Harold's edict puzzled me. I brought this up to Harold on a team charter, the time when we discussed the infamous "Mississauga road trip" bus bill.

"Why can't Laurie Boschman leave tickets for Mel Stevens?"

Harold immediately got all bearish. "I don't want those people in my building!"

I could sense that I'd caught him off guard and that he wasn't at all comfortable with the question. I wanted to hit home on the point: "Those people? What are you really trying to say to the kid?"

"I don't want 'em in my building!"

"Wouldn't it be nice if we made a public statement that you didn't want any Christians in the stands to watch the Leafs play?" He couldn't even look at me. I'd made my point and it was time to get out of there.

But Harold wouldn't leave well enough alone, or his prejudices private. About ten days after his 1981 meeting with Imlach, during a game, he told Dick Beddoes that Laurie's Christianity was interfering with his play and that he was going to be demoted to the minors. Beddoes immediately reported Harold's words on the post-game TV show he did on CHCH, and once again it hit the fan.

Laurie was so upset with his mistreatment that he wrote a letter to "acting" general manager Gerry McNamara that said the happiest day of his life had been August 9, 1979, the day the Leafs had drafted him. However, as proud as he was to play for the Leafs, he couldn't remain with a team that publicly belittled his religious convictions. How sick was the atmosphere in Toronto? Nykoluk took that letter and tacked it up on the club bulletin board to prove that Laurie was a quitter who was turning his back on his teammates. McNamara, a staunch Roman Catholic, uttered not a peep of protest at the actions of the owner and the coach.

Two days after the Boschman affair hit the news, it was time for Harold and me to get together. The deal was we'd meet in his office right after practice that morning, but he wasn't there when I stopped by. I decided to join several teammates for lunch, right down the street from Maple Leaf Gardens at Grapes, Ian Turnbull's restaurant. I wanted to be able to return quickly to the building when I tracked down Ballard. Midway through lunch I called Harold's office and he grabbed the phone.

Harold put on the rough-gruff-let's-bluff-him voice. "Well Darryl, there's nothin' I can do for ya on more money, but I'll tell ya what I'll do. I'll trade ya to whatever hockey club ya want."

I got that sick feeling in the pit of my stomach that said it's really over. Sure, I had consciously thought of leaving the team, and probably welcomed the opportunity to go to a winner. But this was the first time I had been confronted by the possibility that I would soon be moving. It was a very unsettling experience.

"If that's all I deserve after the years of loyalty to this team, get me out of here," I replied. What bothered me was that he hadn't had the courage to invite me over to say this to my face; he had to do it semi-anonymously over the phone. I wasn't going to let it go this easily: "Mr. Ballard, I'll be right over." I didn't return to my table at lunch.

I went straight into Gerry McNamara's office and explained what Ballard had said.

"You're going to have to move me," I told him.

He looked non-plussed.

"Wait a minute! Let's get Harold in here . . ." He didn't even finish the sentence before Ballard came sailing through the door.

"Harold, you didn't really mean it like it sounded?" He was almost pleading; say it ain't so, Joe!

"Damn right I did! If he wants to be traded, I'll trade him. I'll trade him to the city he wants to go to."

I think Harold felt he was calling my bluff. After the no-trade clause controversy and all that had gone on, and the fact that I had several lucrative endorsement deals with Toronto area businesses and companies, he felt that I would choose to stay there. His insensitivity to people around him blinded him to the fact that his cavalier attitude was the straw that broke the camel's back for me. It was time to do something for myself and my family.

With McNamara looking on, totally overtaken by events, I dictated the trade terms to Ballard. "I'm going to leave this office and call around the National Hockey League to a number of general managers and find out who is interested in me, and I'll be back here tomorrow morning to tell you. And you can trade me to one of those cities; I want to decide where I'll go."

McNamara jumped in. "Wait a minute! We're going to need some time to scout these teams."

I just looked at him. Harold nodded to me and I left. When I got home, I called the Flyers and the North Stars. Without tampering, a league offense, both clubs let it be known to me that they would welcome me with open arms. I had selected them for several reasons; both were young, up-and-coming teams with great possibilities in the short- and medium-term, and both, it seemed to me, were desperate for a quality, veteran center. And they paid in U.S. dollars. Both Keith Allen and Lou Nanne expressed a serious interest, and I reported this to McNamara the following morning. I wanted to make sure that I had a contract in place with each team, and each agreed verbally to a four-year deal at $250,000 per, or a million dollars.

McNamara and I arranged to keep negotiations quiet, and agreed that a deal would take place in two weeks. This gave them the opportunity to quietly scout both clubs and make the arrangements they felt they had to make. I went to practice and acted like it was business as usual, fully believing that they were going to trade me. The two-week grace period was going to end December 15, a Tuesday. On the previous Friday night, we were playing in Washington and Harold came to the game. He had spent most of that week at Board of Governors meetings in Florida and had mentioned to reporters covering the meetings that there was no question of me being traded.

This word got back to me and I called Alan Eagleson the next morning when we had returned to Toronto. After we lost 6-2 to the Montreal Canadiens before a coast-to-coast audience on that Saturday night, Eagleson went on *Hockey Night in Canada* unbeknownst to me, and announced that I might have played my last game as a member of the Toronto Maple Leafs.

The following Monday, I went to see Dr. Charles Bull. He had served as team physician to Team Canada in 1976 and on other occasions. He took one look at me and volunteered, "If you keep this up, you'll have a breakdown. Why don't you let me write something up for you, recommending about ten days of rest?"

Today they call it burnout, or job-related depression. Back then, some of the media called it quitting, turning my back on my teammates and fans. I thanked Dr. Bull but refused, saying I just needed for the Leafs to know that I had sought medical advice.

"It's for your own benefit," he added.

"That's not why I'm here," I replied. "I just want to go on record that I did consult a doctor. I'm going to play because I'm confident they will trade me."

Then Leafs management started complaining that the Flyers and North Stars weren't serious with their offers, and would I recommend any other favored teams? I mentioned Buffalo and the Islanders. Nothing seemed to happen, and then it was Christmas.

If Harold had learned anything two years before, it was that you don't trade a team hero during the holiday period. McNamara begged off for him—"We don't want to cause this upheaval in your family life at this time of the year, but we'll do something on the other side of New Year's." For some reason, people under siege always seem to believe that they operate in a vacuum. There were several telephones in the Sittler residence in Mississauga. I used one and called Long Island and Buffalo and heard the same story: the Leafs are asking for the moon and the stars. Bill Torrey of the Islanders told me that the Stanley Cup champions had mentioned six top players they would protect, and the Leafs could pick anyone else off the roster, and receive several draft picks as well.

"You're never going to get out of there," Torrey told me. "No team's going to give the Leafs what they're asking for."

I was dogged everywhere by the media, at practices and games, as McNamara continued to work out a deal for me. Lou Nanne came close twice, but couldn't swing a deal. Flyers GM Keith Allen and team president Robert Butera had lunch with Ballard at the Hot Stove Lounge—I was the blue-plate special—only to emerge and say "no deal" to the assembled media hordes.

I went back to Dr. Bull, and I must have looked worse than I had during my first visit two weeks before.

"If you don't take some time off, you'll get sick. You'll make yourself sick, Darryl."

I admitted defeat. "Okay doc, do what you have to do."

He wrote a letter stating that I should be rested for ten days to two weeks, for medical reasons. I went to Dr. Murray Urowitz, our team doctor, for a second opinion and he agreed with Dr. Bull.

The next stop was McNamara's office. The team was leaving later that afternoon for Minnesota. I put the letter down in front of him and he read it.

"Does this mean you're not going on the trip to Minnesota?"

"Yeah. The doctors say I need the time off for my health. I've lived up to my part of the deal; and the two-week trade deadline is now a month old. It seems to me that you had no intentions of trading me."

"We'll have to suspend you," he countered.

"Do whatever you have to do," I said.

I left his office and returned home. Shortly after the charter took off, the phone started ringing at home. The beat reporters had noticed my absence at the airport and had called their offices with instructions to track me down. The next day I read with no little amusement McNamara's comments in the newspaper that the Leafs had no intention of suspending me because of my loyalty to the organization. Some reporters who didn't know me well claimed that this was a set-up, that I'd convinced a friendly doctor to write out a sweetheart prescription. The few who knew me well were well aware that I was burned out and had to get away from this stifling atmosphere.

Dick Beddoes and Brian MacFarlane even went on the CHCH Overtime post-game show after the North Stars game to debate the issue in a point-counterpoint setting. Beddoes asserted that I had done the team an injustice and my place was with the team, while MacFarlane argued that I had been treated badly and I should have long ago been delivered from this misery. Ballard's response was to get Brian banned from working Leafs telecasts. Beddoes' reward for being Harold's house broadcaster was to get permission to write Ballard's "official" biography a few years later. To this day, I appreciate the support and courage demonstrated by Brian, support which probably cost him his career with *Hockey Night in Canada*.

The next day, the reporters camped out at my place; I made some of them mad by refusing to file daily updates on the story, but like them, I was awaiting events. Other people were involved in this decision-making process. I refused to go out and make a statement.

At about eleven o'clock that morning, the telephone rang. Nancy Martin, Terry's wife, had fallen down the stairs backwards while doing laundry at their home and had very seriously injured her back. It had taken her almost two hours of pure agony to get to the telephone. Knowing I was the only player not on the road trip, and that we lived nearby, she called me. I sped out of the house, with a posse of press people in tow, and zoomed over to her place. She was lying on the floor when I got there and I called an ambulance. I went along with her to the hospital, and got the impression that some of the reporters were miffed because I had turned my back on the serious story to help out Nancy.

When I returned home, the phone was still ringing off the hook. Some of the senior writers tried everything, including threats to blackball me if I didn't give them the story. It got so bad for us, especially for Wendy, who was handling the phone calls, that we went up north for a few days to get away from it all. Nobody in Toronto knew that I was skating to stay in shape up in Orillia.

We returned home a week or so later.

Finally, the telephone rang at 2:00 a.m. on January 20, 1982. It was McNamara calling from the NHL general managers' meetings in Palm Springs. The magic words came: "You've been traded to Philadelphia."

January 20 would prove to be a very special date on my personal calendar: two years later to the day, I would score my 1,000th NHL point, a goal, in a 5-2 win over Calgary.

Right now, however, a new day beckoned.

13

Orange and Black Look Good on You

WEDNESDAY, JANUARY 21, 1982. Day 1, A.B., of my professional hockey career. A.B., of course, stands for After Ballard.

I slept fitfully after Gerry McNamara's telephone call, only because I was too full of nervous energy. My first task as a Philadelphia Flyer was to head down to Maple Leaf Gardens, clean out my locker and get my equipment. I got there about ten o'clock and discovered my popularity in a sort of backhanded fashion; all of my sticks were gone. I was under contract with Titan and I normally had a couple of dozen sticks in the Leafs equipment room at any given time during the season. What had probably happened was that they had become hot collectors' items during my two-week sit out at home. When I got to Philly, I had no sticks.

I brushed by the reporters who had gathered at the Gardens that morning for regular practice, essentially telling them that I would clear up my side of the story a little later down the road. Maybe I acted too mysterious; a lot of the guys on the beat got it in their minds that I had some bombshell revelations to make, while the truth was that Harold Ballard had seen a chance to move me, with my agreement, and taken it. When I got to Philadelphia, there was a press conference which answered most of those questions, if there were any questions left to answer, and I turned a page in my hockey life.

As luck would have it, the Flyers had finished with their Toronto visit for that season, and weren't scheduled to play at Maple Leaf Gardens until March 2 and April 2 of the following year. I wouldn't be back in Toronto as a hockey player for fourteen months, and by that time my story would be old.

My first Philly press conference was my first purely positive press encounter in about a year; which is not an indictment of the Toronto media, so much as a description of how bad things had gotten with the Maple Leafs hockey club. I was glad to be with a contender like the Flyers, I told the Philadelphia media, and even happier to have the luxury to concentrate on playing, period.

Pat Quinn was coach of the Flyers when I arrived. A couple of years before, he had led the Flyers to an NHL record for the longest undefeated streak in one season, 35 games without a defeat, from October 14, 1979, to January 6, 1980 (25 wins and 10 ties). That streak paced Philadelphia to a league-best 116 points, though they fell to the Islanders in the Stanley Cup final.

The rumbling began the following year when the club slipped to 97 points, 13 behind the Islanders in the Patrick Division. The team I joined would slip another 10 points, and Quinn would be gone before the season was over. When I arrived the team was struggling, and continued to do so until Quinn got fired and his assistant coaches, Bobby Clarke and Bob Boucher, were relieved of their duties. Clarke remained as a player, of course, when Bob McCammon returned from Maine for his second stint as head coach of the team.

I started to wonder if I was jinxed: here I had left the Leafs after three years of turmoil, only to find myself in Philadelphia just as the Flyers started having their problems. The temptation was to keep sneaking peeks behind me to see if it was following me around.

A lot of veteran players were upset by Quinn's dismissal, guys like Clarke, Bill Barber and Paul Holmgren. Pat was not only a coach, but a friend to them. He also was good, honest, hard-working, and I think the players felt they had let him down. You do feel guilty when somebody loses his job, especially a guy whom you like and who you know is giving to the best of his ability. We assumed that team management felt that Pat Quinn had run his course in Philadelphia, and that a change was needed because they couldn't see us going anywhere in the playoffs.

Bob McCammon has an ability to evaluate character and talent in players; he's always been excellent at spotting the players who can go the farthest for him, those who want it and those who don't want it. He had done a terrific job with the Maine Mariners and the handwriting on the wall was that if this club didn't do well in the playoffs, next year's team would have a lot of Mariners on it, so McCammon was the ideal choice to replace Quinn.

He was a known quantity, and if he hadn't been available, Quinn would probably have lasted out the season. But this was the kind of decision that is sometimes made by owners to spark fan interest, because they feel that something, anything, has to be done.

We finished the regular season at home against the Maple Leafs on April 4, 1982, and blew them out 7-1. I got one assist. (That evened me out for the year as earlier in the season I'd had one assist in two games for Toronto against the Flyers.) The Leafs had been out of playoff contention for more than a month when they came into the Spectrum, and played like it; the talk among the former teammates I met after the game was all about their team trip to Atlantic City once the game was out of the way. The charter was staying over for a couple of days before returning to Toronto.

Strangely enough, I don't recall much about that game, my first-ever against the Leafs in the NHL. It didn't count for anything in the standings because our impending match-up with the Rangers had already been settled and the Leafs' failure to make the playoffs had also taken any edge out of their participation. I spent a lot of time with the Toronto media and our conversations and interviews were in a positive vein, more about how I was enjoying my new team and new city and very little about not being a Leaf anymore. I think the reporters were pretty tired of all the negativity and needed to get away from it themselves if they could.

Late in the 1981-82 season, the Flyers took a long step toward future success when they called up Pelle Lindbergh from Maine. In the off-season, they made two moves that solidified our defense even more and started us back on the way up to the NHL's penthouse. At the June meetings, we sent Pete Peeters to Boston for sophomore defenseman Brad McCrimmon; two months later, we traded Ken Linseman, Greg Adams and a draft choice to Hartford Whalers for Mark Howe.

I didn't really start to feel comfortable with my new team and city until I started my first full season with them. The turmoil and circumstances of my trade had left their marks on me; I wasn't my regular self right then. More than anything, I wanted to prove my worth and show the Flyers that they had gotten a good player. I just couldn't get untracked, even though the record book shows I had 14 goals and 18 assists for 32 points in the 35 regular-season games I played with Philadelphia. (I finished 1981-82 with 32 goals and 38 assists in 73 games, which wasn't bad considering what I had gone through, but which just didn't *feel* like a Darryl Sittler year to me.)

I even scored my 400th career goal on March 18, with 22 seconds remaining to give us a 4-4 tie in Chicago. I personally appreciated the milestone and the Flyers, first-class organization that they were, made certain that it was honored; just as they would celebrate my 1,000th career point and my 1,000th career game in the coming seasons.

There was some talk in the local media that the Flyers had brought me in as a quick-fix for some of their problems. The team had been so close to the top, and had then started fading, and was looking to get a talented veteran who could help right away—the kind of trade usually made right before the March deadline to move a team up a couple of strides in the stretch run. I didn't get that impression from the players, though. They were a great bunch of guys in a situation where everything was team-oriented, there was a strong group atmosphere and not one of these guys would think of pointing the finger at another. That made it very different from what I had been used to back home.

Management, obviously, had expectations of me because of my record in the league up to that point, and also because Philadelphia had built a tradition of winning. However, I didn't really sense that I was seen as the guy who would make the difference between third place, where we finished, or first or second where the Islanders and Rangers ended up. An indication along this line is the fact that the Flyers didn't lose a regular player or someone off their roster when they traded for me.

I might also have been an insurance policy because the team was having a disagreement with one of its top scorers. Reggie Leach was feuding with management and ended up getting suspended after missing a practice. That led to his move to Detroit shortly thereafter.

The media coverage in Philadelphia was nothing like the coverage back in Toronto. It's a totally different environment playing in Montreal or Toronto from that in an American city. Hockey is just as important to you, it's your livelihood and you want to do well, but it's not there every waking moment of your life. If you go down to the corner store, you are not confronted with the fan worship or criticism you might have had back in Canada. It's not as stressful. In

Philadelphia, we shared the sports pages with the Phillies, the Eagles, the 76ers, Temple University and Penn State, a varied collection of professional, university and even high school sports.

As I say that, I don't want to downplay players' attitudes to their sport just because they are in a rich sports market. As a player your attitude shouldn't be any different and you should be as motivated to do as well at your job whether one newspaper covers your games, or ten. The Philadelphia difference was that the pressure or hassles away from the rink weren't there. I really enjoyed this new-found freedom, especially after three years under the intense media microscope in Toronto.

We opened the playoffs in the spring of 1982 with a 4-1 win in New York, but the Rangers quickly drew even with a 7-3 victory the following night. They then came into the Spectrum and dumped us 4-3 and 7-5. The Rangers were coached by Herb Brooks that year, hero of the 1980 Olympic Games at Lake Placid, and they played a very international, skating game with players like Reijo Ruotsalinen, Mike Rogers, Mikko Leinonen, Jere Gillis, Tom Laidlaw, and U.S. Olympians like Mark Pavelich, Dave Silk, and Rob McClanahan, and Team USA Canada Cup veterans Robby Ftorek and Dean Talafous. Ed Mio played great in nets for them and I soon found myself en route to Europe to join the Canadian national team at the World Championships.

I was the second-highest scorer on the national team with three goals, one fewer than Bobby Clarke, but that was little consolation for a player who had looked forward to a long and successful postseason when he left Toronto. Bill Barber, Calgary's Paul Reinhart and I were selected Canada's top three players at the tournament and that put me in a more positive frame of mind for the flight home and the season that beckoned.

The following summer, the Sittler family got settled and rested and planned to make a serious contribution to the Philadelphia Flyers hockey club. When Wendy and I had originally arrived in the City of Brotherly Love, we were greeted by Bill and Jenny Barber. We all became friends during the 1976 Canada Cup and they invited me to move in with them in Cherry Hill, New Jersey, until we could find a house and schools for Ryan and Meaghan. We settled on a place in Voorhees, N.J., the next suburb over from Cherry Hill, and moved in just before the playoffs. But it wasn't really a home until I returned from Europe.

Bob McCammon was head coach and assistant general manager when we reported for training camp in the late summer of 1982. Bernie Parent was our only assistant coach, which was unusual; by the early 1980s, most NHL teams had two or even three assistants and Quinn had had two the year before. Training camp represented a clean slate for me. I trained very hard that summer, determined to show the Flyers and the rest of the league that I still had a major contribution to make to a major team.

Right from the beginning, the 1982-83 season went right for me. Three weeks into it, I was honored in Philadelphia with the NHL Milestone Award for my 400th goal (which I had scored near the end of the previous season) and it carried over into a selection to the Wales Conference team for the All-Star game.

One thing that made me very happy was the fact that McCammon gave lots of ice time and responsibility to his veterans. For me, hockey was fun again. Although Tim Kerr was injured and played only 24 games, with guys like Barber (27) , Ilkka Sinisalo (21) Clarke (23), Ron Flockhart (29), Holmgren (19), Brian Propp (40) and myself (43) doing the scoring, and the defense of Brad Marsh, Brad McCrimmon, Miroslav Dvorak, Glen Cochrane, Bob Hoffmeyer, Behn Wilson and Mark Howe playing in front of Lindbergh and Bob Froese, we jumped right back up to the top of the standings in the Patrick with 106 points. That tied Edmonton for second overall in the league behind Boston's 110 and ahead of Chicago, Montreal and the Islanders.

So it was hard to figure that we would again lose in the first round of the playoffs, and still harder to believe that we'd be blitzed three straight by the fourth-place Rangers, 5-3 and 4-3 at the Spectrum, and 9-3 in New York. The season had been successful, but the playoff result was devastating.

The following season, Tim Kerr, Dave Poulin and Brian Propp again got a lot of the ice time, but I played less. It showed in my statistics; I had finished with 43 goals and 40 assists in 1982-83, but that dropped off to 27 goals and 36 assists for 20 fewer points in 1983-84. The Flyers, very conscious of our poor playoff performance the previous two years, decided that one of the major reasons was that the older players had been worn down by the wear and tear of the long season. Their solution was to order veterans like Clarke, Barber and myself to take some time off in March, stay away from the rink and recharge the batteries.

Wendy and I went to Florida for almost a week, all expenses paid by the Flyers. Pat Croce, the team's physical conditioning and rehabilitation consultant, gave us a set of exercises to do while on the beach. I had mixed feelings about the vacation, however, because I wasn't convinced that we had lost the previous playoffs due to the veterans' fatigue. Also, from a personal standpoint, I had had a string of ten consecutive 30-goal seasons, and this late-season break might prevent me from making it eleven. It turned into a great holiday, though; once I had resigned myself to the fact that they insisted on my going, it was time to enjoy. I can't remember where Bobby Clarke took his break, but Billy Barber took Jenny to Pennsylvania's Pocono Mountains. He screwed up his knee and claimed it had happened while doing one of Pat Croce's exercises, the leapfrog. Many other people mentioned the coincidence of a pro hockey player sustaining an injury that was highly common to a popular ski area and drew their own conclusions. I don't know how he hurt himself, but that was the knee injury that led to major surgery and eventually ended his career. Billy underwent total knee reconstruction.

Clarke and I were rested, Barber was out for the season—and we got blitzed by the Rangers for the second straight year. You knew that big changes were coming.

In the early off-season, from our ouster in the playoffs until school ended in June and we headed back to Orillia from the summer, Clarke, Poulin, Bob Froese and I worked out almost every morning at a gym not far from where we all lived, and where a lot of state troopers and weightlifters usually trained. The two consecutive first-round playoff exits weighed heavily on the organization. Clarke was at a crossroads after fifteen years with the Flyers as a player; but as captain of the team that had won two Stanley Cups, he wasn't really going to have to worry about his future. He was Mr. Flyer, close to Ed Snider and everyone else in the organization.

While we were jogging and working out, we speculated on what might happen, but there was never any suggestion that he might become the team's next general manager. On the morning of May 15, a Tuesday, Clarke wasn't there for our workout, and left word that he had to go into Philadelphia for a meeting. That afternoon, the Flyers announced that he had retired as a player and accepted the post of general manager. Bobby Clarke, my teammate and someone

I worked out with all the time, had just become (call me Bob, not Bobby) Clarke my boss, a first in my career. Nine days later, he appointed Mike Keenan coach of the Flyers.

After he became GM, and before we returned to Canada for the summer, he called me in for a short meeting. I was going into the option year of my contract and back then I would have been allowed to sign with another team. Whatever I was offered, Philadelphia had first chance to match if they desired to keep me. But there was no other compensation due to them for my classification of free agent. If they had refused to match another offer and I signed with someone else, they wouldn't have been entitled to any players or draft choices.

We discussed this situation and a few other things. He was pretty certain that Bill Barber's injury was going to force him out of hockey, and recalled that Paul Holmgren had been traded (in February). That meant he would be looking to me for more leadership as captain to help lead the younger guys. We talked about my contract and realized there was a potential problem there. I even recalled the letter that Keith Allen had written to me when I joined the team which had said that when my playing days were over, there would be a place in the organization for me. That letter, and Clarke's mood that day, led me to believe that the Sittlers were well on their way to becoming permanent fixtures in the Philadelphia area.

Clarke was interested in me as a player for another year or two, and Wendy and the kids loved living in the Philadelphia suburbs, so we agreed that to revoke my free-agency status and prevent the media from blowing the story out of proportion, the Flyers would pay me $100,000 in five annual installments of $20,000, on top of my existing option year in the contract which was for $250,000. That $100,000 and the team captaincy convinced me to stay in Philadelphia. Although no other NHL team had made any approaches to me, Alan Eagleson told me that moving to another city would be no problem, that he had received feelers from several clubs.

I was up north that summer when I got a telephone call from the front office. The team had drafted Ron Sutter in the first round and was thinking of having a press conference to introduce the new draft picks. Could I come down for it? It would be a great opportunity to introduce the new captain. A day or two later, the team called me back and said the Sutter family had an obligation out west and the timing wasn't good for Ron. They would introduce him and the other draft choices, as well as their new captain, at training camp. I was under orders to enjoy my summer.

That summer, I had lunch with Mike Keenan in a Yorkville restaurant, since we both lived in the Toronto area. We talked about where the team was going, individual players, and other issues that dealt with the Flyers, and I felt that we had established a good line of communication. I came away feeling very positive, and looking forward to the next season. Keenan impressed me as a very thorough guy, with a lot of control and ideas. He reminded me somewhat of Roger Neilson in terms of his depth of thinking and hockey ideas— he had a game plan and an idea of how he would make everything work, a ray of sunshine compared to some of my previous coaches. Even McCammon hadn't shown that kind of depth; he was more of a motivator and rah-rah guy who depended on a set routine and didn't demonstrate a gift for innovation. I felt that Keenan had a lot of respect for me and what I had done in my career, and he was especially interested in my leadership qualities. This meeting was a stark contrast to a similar pre-season lunch in Toronto with Floyd Smith in July 1979.

Still, Keenan did represent change and new directions in the coming season, some unknowns; but the anticipation was strictly positive. I was looking forward to the 1984-85 season, even though I knew that two key on-ice contributors, Clarke and Barber, were gone from the dressing room. My projected contribution and the Flyers naming me captain meant they were ready to give me some responsibilities and room to prove that I could handle it. I thrive on that kind of challenge; Roger Neilson had been excellent at motivating me in this way. I might not go around looking for responsibility, but when it's there, I grab it with both hands.

There was a Canada Cup that summer and I was asked by CTV to do color commentary for the games. I called the Flyers for clearance, realizing that I would have to miss the first few days of training camp because the final series games in Calgary and Edmonton would pose a conflict. Clarke said there was no problem, he knew the type of guy I was and that I would report to camp ready to go. I had my skates with me and skated between Team Canada practice sessions and games.

The Canada Cup over, I returned to training camp and didn't skip a beat, blending in right away. During the training camp, Ed Snider and Keith Allen came to me and said the club was going to have a special retirement night for Clarke in November, and asked me to take charge of the players' gift to him.

Towards the end of the training camp, a day before the press conference to introduce the team at a special Chamber of Commerce luncheon that they have every year in a downtown hotel, Keenan had all the players in for a team meeting. He announced the cuts and the regular roster of twenty-five guys who were staying. He talked about the team, its strengths and weaknesses, and then we broke off into smaller work groups. I led discussion in one, Dave Poulin in another, and we talked about the season that was going to start in three or four days. At evening's end, Keenan drew me aside and asked if I had my acceptance speech ready for the captain's announcement at the Chamber luncheon at noon the next day.

"No problem," I replied, and went home and stayed up until after eleven o'clock that night to put it together.

The next morning we left early for practice so we'd have plenty of time to get to the luncheon. We left the Coliseum, our practice facility in Voorhees, and took a team bus to the luncheon. All the media had been alerted, and they started to interview me upon arrival about what a captain means and does for a team. The reporters wanted to get their stories, sound bites, and film and get out of there rather than stay until two-thirty or three o'clock that afternoon. People congratulated me during the dinner, and afterwards on the ride in the team bus back to Voorhees. Strangely enough, the official announcement hadn't been made during the lunch, and I was puzzled about this on the bus ride back to our practice rink.

I got off the team bus and Mike Keenan was waiting for me. "Darryl, can I see you in my office?"

We adjourned to his office and found Bobby Clarke already there. He had been at the head table at the luncheon and had returned by private automobile. There was a gaunt, faraway look on his face, and I suddenly felt very nervous. His voice sounded like he was speaking out of the bottom of a well, but the words were as clear as a bell.

"Darryl, we've just traded you to Detroit."

"You *what*?" My stomach felt like it was heaving.

"A good deal came up and we traded you to Detroit." He couldn't look me straight in the eye, he was giving me a sideways glance as he spoke.

Did it happen earlier that day and had they tried unsuccessfully to stop me from going to the luncheon? Had they completed the trade between courses at the lunch? Had this thing been in the works for days or weeks? It was a tense situation for the three of us in the room.

Clarke hurried to explain the trade; the deal had come up quickly, and with all of the young players on the team, management wasn't looking at the present; instead, they were looking three or four years down the road and building a dynasty with a new GM and a new coach.

Now I had trouble hearing myself speak. "That's it; I'm going to hang 'em up, bronze 'em, put a suit on and go to work," I quipped, paraphrasing Clarke's own retirement announcement from four months earlier.

"I'll get Jimmy Devellano on the phone . . ." he said, probably hoping that the Detroit GM who had just traded for me could say the right kinds of things to make me comfortable again.

"Don't bother getting Jimmy Devellano on the line," I retorted. "I'm not going. I can't believe this is happening."

He ignored my comment and dialled Detroit. He handed me the telephone.

"Jimmy, before you go on, I just want to let you know that this is very disappointing for me and I think I'm going to retire. If you could nix this trade, it would be in your best interest, because I don't think you'll get anything for the players you've sent here [Joe Paterson and Murray Craven]," I said, barely containing the emotion in my voice.

"Darryl, do you really mean that? We'll give you a better contract with another year on it." Jimmy went into the sales pitch automatically, which led me to believe that he and Clarke might have rehearsed this scene.

"Maybe it's time for me to go into something else," I replied. "If I'm going to go to Detroit, I want to do so in a good frame of mind. This announcement has just floored me, and I'm telling you if you can get out of the deal, get out of the deal."

I gave the receiver back to Clarke and left Keenan's office for the parking lot. Then I remembered that I didn't have a ride home; I'd come in with a teammate and had expected to return home with him. By now, though, everybody was long gone. I went to a public telephone and called Alan Eagleson long distance. He was flabbergasted when I told him the news. He had had no inkling of an impending deal, even though by then, GMs were in the habit of contacting agents in cases like this.

Mike Keenan eventually drove me home. The doors were locked, Wendy and the kids were out somewhere, so the two of us sat there in my driveway. I was really upset and very emotional; Keenan was very quiet, but sympathethic to my plight. Whether he was directly involved in my trade wasn't even a consideration under these very special circumstances. I simply appreciated the fact that he was there and had given me a lift home.

Wendy returned about thirty minutes later and found me sitting in the driveway with the coach, which wouldn't be so unusual considering I had been named captain that day. When I told her I'd been traded to Detroit, it was such a ludicrous and unreal piece of news that she wouldn't believe it at first. A lady who that very morning at breakfast had said goodbye to the new captain of the Flyers only to be greeted by a Red Wing at suppertime, and who loved the greater Philadelphia area with a passion, didn't know what to believe. When it finally sank in that this was true—and I was still having trouble myself believing the events of the day—Wendy was so upset she started crying.

The telephone calls started. Ed Snider, the owner, and then his son Jay Snider, the Flyers' team president, called and tried to console me, vowing that they cared about me as a person and wished me well, personally and on behalf of the organization. I heard them, but I was in such a state of shock that little of this really penetrated. I turned on the sports news later that evening, and the first question the reporters asked Clarke was: "Weren't you going to name Sittler captain?" I'll never forget his reply.

"Darryl was one of the candidates. I don't pick the captain, Mike Keenan does." That led people to believe that my trade might have been purely a coaching decision, which I don't think was the case. When Bobby Clarke came in as GM, I don't think he had the same powers Keith Allen had enjoyed before him. The Flyers had exited early twice from the playoffs and that bothered the people upstairs. When Clarke signed on as GM, he became part of a management committee, or at least that's the impression I got. Ed and Jay Snider, Keith Allen, and Gary Darling were all part of that group of "advisers" and I don't know who had the final say. Even when Bobby was negotiating my $100,000 "non-free-agency bonus," he would have to get up and leave his office, go in and see Jay Snider about it, come back out and continue the negotiation.

I saw red when I heard Clarke's comments on television. Why

couldn't he stand up and say it the way it was? He traded me, it was untimely and he regretted it, whatever he had to say to clear the air, but forget the cop-out.

I refused to report to Detroit, but I didn't publicly announce my retirement. Alan Eagleson and I had decided that we'd wait for a while and see how the trade winds blew. Meanwhile, I was skating every day by myself at the Coliseum.

Who should walk in three or four days later but Clarke.

When I was in Toronto, I knew Bobby Clarke as an opponent and always recognized him to be one of the most dedicated competitors you could ever run into in the NHL. I was under the impression that his teammates held him in high esteem, and they showed it on the ice by protecting him when the action got hot and heavy.

However, when I got to Philadelphia I discovered that some of the veterans had a quite different feeling about the guy off the ice. There were stories about his buddy-buddy relationship with Ed Snider, and how a lot of the other Flyers stars had salary caps that didn't exist on other teams. The players felt he was being paid a lot more than he admitted to, and that when they went in to renegotiate, management prefaced all conversations with, "Well, we only paid Bobby Clarke such-and-such an amount. How can we pay you more?"

Dave Schultz by then had burst a bit of the Bobby bubble with his book, and I could remember some of the veterans telling me, "Watch out, because the guy will get you, somewhere along the line. He can turn on you; he's turned on other guys." The players telling me this had been there a long time and had shared two Stanley Cups with Clarke. They believed that he had been in management's pocket all along, and that suspicion increased when he forsook the team captaincy and became a playing assistant in 1979.

When I heard this for the first time, I put it down to normal team squabbling and personality conflicts. I believed in Clarke's competitiveness and work ethic; we had been teammates in the Canada Cup and Challenge Cup and a two-man mutual admiration society for a long time. I had a lot of respect for him, especially because of the fact that he was a diabetic who had overcome that handicap and become one of the best in the world at what he did. He was the type who did whatever he had to do to win, and was a respected opponent around the league.

I always enjoyed playing against him. When I heard those comments, I was taken aback, and thought things like, "How can these guys say this about this guy? They must have brought it upon themselves; there must be a reason for him to turn on them." Now, almost three years later, I wasn't so naive on the subject and here we were, just the two of us, at the Coliseum.

I let him know those feelings; that this whole Flyer family thing had been overblown; it was made out to be a lot more than it actually was. When they were winning, it probably had been a tight-knit family thing. But anybody can tell you, every family has its strengths and weaknesses and one of the weaknesses of the current Flyers was that they were still feeding off the glory of their winning years. There was an underlying feeling with a lot of the players that this wasn't a family. I also told him that I was disappointed in his TV announcement; all he had to do was tell the truth about why the club had traded me minutes before or after they were going to announce my appointment as team captain. Then I left.

As captain-to-be I had been charged with finding a players' gift to Clarke for his retirement night. Instead, I sent him a telegram, as a former teammate and former opponent. I worded it very carefully. It was read out that night, and a lot of people in attendance apparently couldn't believe that I would send such a positive message.

Especially Wendy. She couldn't understand why I would do something nice to someone who, in her own words, "had knifed me and my family in the back."

I said nice things about him as a player and competitor, the Bobby Clarke I knew and respected on the ice. I also tried to put myself in his shoes, as an inexperienced GM in his first days in the office. He was going to make mistakes along the way, and in my case, he ran into a situation that he probably would never again face as a general manager.

Maybe the trade happened moments before, or during the luncheon, and they either couldn't get to me in time before the bus left the practice facility in Voorhees, or before the luncheon started. Or, maybe the trade had happened earlier that day and they didn't want to hurt attendance at their luncheon, or face media coverage on the evening news with me angrily reacting to the trade on TV. The way things went, the media didn't have much of an opportunity to get to me before their evening deadlines had passed.

A lot of things had changed in that organization in the short time I was there. Ed Snider had handed over the reins to his son Jay, who obviously didn't have the experience of his father and yet, because he had been around the team so long, presumed he did know a lot about the sport. Ed had remarried and his life was focused on his new wife and child and their move to California.

In the long run, Bob Clarke the GM would have one too many run-ins with Jay Snider over hockey matters, and even Mr. Flyer left Philadelphia. To be fair, any Clarke knockers have to admit that he took that team to two Stanley Cup finals in his six years there. And, if there were any doubts about his managerial abilities, they might have been dispelled by the performance of the Minnesota North Stars in the 1990-91 Stanley Cup playoffs.

I have heard some people say that Bob Gainey did it all for the North Stars under extremely difficult circumstances, with his wife suffering from brain cancer. However, Clarke had the good sense to hire Gainey as his coach, and to bring in people like Brian Propp, Bobby Smith, Brian Hayward, Chris Dahlquist and Jimmy Johnson to solidify that team. Bobby Clarke is a hard-working guy, and being a general manager is not something you learn overnight. If you are smart enough to learn from your mistakes, adapt, and hire good people around you, you'll look good.

Bob Clarke is probably a different GM today than he was in his first several months in that position, and that's called maturity. He might admit today that my trade was handled badly, I don't know. But considering the fact that I lasted one year in Detroit and as we went to press Murray Craven was still playing for Philadelphia, he probably would make the trade again.

Despite the sad parting of the ways, I prefer to end this chapter on a positive note because the memories I retain from Philadelphia are primarily ones of happiness. I enjoyed the city, the team, my team-mates and most of all, the people. Whoever said Philadelphia sports fans would boo a funeral is nuts.

I had been at a fan club party in March 1983, signing autographs after the formal part of the evening had ended, when a young woman came up to me. She had short, dark hair, and was about 20 or so.

"Can I have your autograph?" she asked, one of several dozen similar requests in the minutes before and after.

I signed her autograph book.

"Thanks. When you have a quiet moment, could I have a few minutes of your time?" The woman was very polite and it would have been difficult to say no. Several minutes later, I went over to her.

"I just wanted to share this with you. I had a brain aneurysm and I was in hospital in a coma; and the nurses knew my family and I are real die-hard Flyers fans," she began.

"They had a TV monitor at the foot of my bed, and a radio right beside me, to get the Flyers games when they were on air. At the exact moment that you scored your 1,000th point against Calgary, I came out of my coma." A tingle went down my spine when she told me that; and there was something in the way she said it and the way she was quietly, almost shyly talking, that made me believe it without question. The magic moment had come on the first anniversary of my trade from Toronto, January 20, 1983. What made it even more special was that I scored a second-period goal in a 5-2 win over Calgary and my buddy Lanny McDonald was there to see it.

I tell stories like this one when I am asked to speak publicly or privately on matters like team building and working together toward a common goal. I don't tell stories like this to build myself up, but rather to illustrate the point that sometimes you can influence other people's lives without ever realizing it. And if you try to lead your life in a positive way, and try to do things right, there are other people out there watching and looking for something to grab onto.

I never got the girl's name.

Being with the Flyers reminded me of the teams we'd had in Toronto under Roger Neilson. Guys came to play every night. As well, I had left Toronto which had gotten used to having weak teams in the last three years I was there, and come to a city where having strong teams was the norm. Most nights with the Flyers, you walked away from the building with the feeling that you'd done something right. In Toronto it was, "Man, another one; third or fourth in a row."

The Flyers system was team-oriented. They had removed all individual player bonuses from contracts and replaced them with team bonuses based on ten-game segments. Roger Neilson also had divided everything into ten-game segments, but that didn't figure in the bonuses players could earn. In Philadelphia, it did. We'd assess our next ten games, trying to figure out how many points we could realistically get out of the available twenty, and work toward that goal. That kept us focused all season long.

Also, we had bonuses for limiting goals against. If we were up 5-2 and trying to get the sixth goal—and we couldn't have more than two goals a game against us if we were to reach the bonus in that segment—we'd work harder on our defense. Penalty-killing percent-age, power play percentage . . . if we finished in the top three in any of the special teams categories, there would be bonuses.

The team even extended the bonus system to include the wives. Rather than paying them money, they could earn shopping sprees at Bloomingdale's at the end of the season. The whole idea was that the wives were interested in your career and the team's success, and if that meant going on the road a day early or not seeing us while we practiced a little longer, everybody understood and pitched in. The Flyers actually called in incentive consultants who normally worked in large corporations to design these programs for us. They were light-years ahead of most other NHL teams in motivation.

Philadelphia's off-ice programs were excellent, and the training facilities were first-rate. I remembered Punch Imlach, Floyd Smith and Dick Duff taking equipment out of our gym and then saw the Flyers with their circuit-training program. Again, there was no com-parison. It was easy to understand why they were so successful.

This kind of management support was something you wanted as a player. Players on teams which had no faith in the people upstairs to solve big or small problems would find more ways to lose than to win. Would this management team be able to do something around trade deadline while your arch-rivals were stocking up for the playoff run? Would your management team be smart enough to spend a little more money on travel and accommodations sometimes, so you can come into a certain city rested and prepare properly for a big game?

We saw encouraging signs when they brought in Ted Sator as an assistant in Philadelphia. He was a thinker from the new school, and had coached in Finland and at Bowling Green University and was up with the times. He contributed a lot to the Flyers.

The man who was named captain after I was traded to Detroit, Dave Poulin, would have been my choice too. A very nice guy, the Notre Dame University alumnus was one of the most dedicated players I've ever seen in the NHL. Nobody was ever in better shape than him. I remember they put us through a battery of physical tests the first day of that fateful training camp and Poulin came in first; Mark Taylor, a college guy, was second, and I was third. I had always been a fanatic for conditioning.

I had met Dave many years before, without knowing it. When we beat the Islanders in the seventh game of the 1978 Stanley Cup quarter-final, a huge crowd met us at Toronto airport late that night upon our return from Long Island. Poulin was a teenager living in Oakville, and he and some buddies went out to greet the team. I invited all the players back to my place in Mississauga for a little overnight celebration and the Poulin gang followed us home, hanging around outside waiting and watching the comings and goings. Sometime before dawn, Dan Maloney went out and confronted them: "What are you guys doing here?" Maloney, who had a lot of facial scars and didn't shave much to look fierce, was a menacing sight for fully grown NHL bruisers; looming in front of this gang, he probably caused more than one voice to change right on the spot.

"We're just hangin' around watching the guys [Leafs]," some kid replied. Very respectfully. He might even have said Sir several times.

Maloney's reply was uniquely Canadian.

"Better take off, eh."

Five years later, Poulin was on my team. When a young teammate tells you a story like that, you suddenly feel a whole lot older. Another young Flyer I recall fondly is Glen Cochrane. The tall native of Cranbrook, B.C., was a rugged defensive defenseman, a solid contributor and consummate team player who led the Flyers in penalties for four straight seasons. During Mark Howe's first year with us, Cochrane was his regular defense partner and ended the season with an amazing plus 42, which was second only to Howe's plus 47. He was a tough guy to play against, that much I remembered from my Toronto days. He was also a pretty funny guy.

One night, I got clipped and found myself in the Spectrum clinic for repairs. Cochrane had suffered a concussion earlier in the game and was still in the clinic, lying quietly in full gear. A team doctor was stitching me up on one bed, while another examined Cochrane on the other, to determine whether he should be sent to hospital for overnight observation. The answer was obvious: Cochrane still showed signs of having had his bell rung.

"Glen, you have to fill out these forms. You should do it now before we go over to the hospital," he said.

Cochrane sat up on the side of the bed while the doctor put him through a series of questions.

"Do you have high blood pressure?"

"No."

"Any history of heart disease in your family?"

"No."

"Diabetes?"

"No."

"Kidney problems? Nervous disorders? Lung disorders?"

"No. No. No."

The doctor looked up at Glen.

"Anything else we should know?"

Cochrane didn't hesitate. "My mom and dad split up last summer."

The two doctors and I looked up at each other at the same time, trying hard not to crack up. The same thought was going through our minds—"This guy's an old hand at concussions, isn't he?" I filed this story away for future reference. Cochrane was a very tough guy, and I was going to find out if he could take a joke before I told the story. I was itching to tell it, that's for sure.

Ironically, we roomed together for most of that year and I got to know him as a very nice guy. The story made the rounds and his teammates were quite merciless, me in the lead. He tried to slough it off as something he had said as a joke.

I drove him nuts when we roomed together because I always like the room real fresh—or, as he used to say, ice cold—and Glen was just the opposite; he liked to pretend he lived in the Brazilian jungle. We were in Minnesota one midwinter night at the Bloomington Marriott, across the parking lot from the Metropolitan Sports Center. Minnesota, as they say, can get a little cold, eh.

Cochrane covered all the bases as we prepared to sack out.

"Sittler, if you open the window tonight, I'll kill ya," he said. I believe he was quite serious.

After he fell asleep, I got up and opened the window. It might have been twenty-below. When I awoke the next morning, my nose was freezing and I could see my breath when I exhaled. I got up and went to the bathroom. I heard his voice from the main room. "I'll kill ya. I can't believe you opened the window when I told you not to."

I started laughing. Knowing that he was going to come in after me to ease the pressure on his bladder, I decided to cover the bathroom floor with water. If he waited long enough, we could paint red and blue lines on it and we'd have our own indoor rink.

To my surprise, he was sitting on the edge of the bed when I came out, already fully dressed in shirt and tie, three-piece suit and socks . . . but no shoes. He rushed into the bathroom, sploosh, splash into the water. That did it. He flew back out, grabbed me, flipped me down on the bed and took his beard and gave me a third-degree whisker burn on both cheeks. I was laughing so hard I couldn't move.

Moving to a team like the Flyers meant changing alliances for a veteran like me. Remember, this was the Broad Street Bullies who had gone to war against the Carlton Street Chickens in three straight playoff series in the mid-1970s. When I got to Philadelphia, I noticed that other teams that had played tough against Toronto, did not have the same game plan when they faced the Flyers. They underwent a total attitudinal change because they knew they were up against the Holmgrens, Cochranes and Behn Wilsons. They didn't take any liberties. But you don't realize that until you change teams.

In NHL hockey fights, you rarely ever realize what damage you've done to the other guy. One night, we were milling about in a scrum when somebody's stick came out of nowhere and hit me on the top of the head. Blood spurted copiously. The Toronto media thought it was Clarke, but if you looked carefully at game films you would discover that it was Brian Propp. Now these guys were my team-mates.

Propp was a very consistent player, good penalty killer and a good scorer, who would have made the NHL's under-rated players All-Star team. You appreciated him when you saw him play every night. Others who turned out great included Tim Kerr, the Sutter twins, and our two young goalies, Pelle Lindbergh and Bob Froese.

Ron Sutter was our first draft choice in 1982, while his twin, Rich, went to Pittsburgh, but we later acquired him in a six-player trade. I played on the same line with Rich and Ronnie my last year in Philly; Ronnie was center and Rich was right wing. I really enjoyed those two kids. They were very competitive, very down-to-earth kids and you could see that the Sutter parents had done something very special raising their boys—all six who made the NHL were players who made their teams better by their presence.

Rich and Ronnie spent a lot of that season over at my house as Wendy and I became their unofficial den parents. It was amazing to watch the twins together, the interaction. In a way, they were almost playing mascots, because they lifted up a whole team just by their presence. They both weighed about 165 or 170 pounds, but played like 200-pounders. They'd go flying into the corners like nothing could hurt them, and bodies would be flying everywhere. If you knocked one of them down, he'd get right back up and knock you down. Twice. And then the other one might stop by and repeat the procedure. They reminded me of guys like Jerry Butler or Pat Boutette in Toronto; guys who would play any role you gave them. Add skilled Europeans like Miroslav Dvorak, Thomas Eriksson and Ilkka Sinisalo, goalies like Lindbergh and Froese, and you had a team that could play several styles of hockey. That, in large part, explained our success.

Lindbergh was extremely competitive, but aloof at times, like many of the Scandinavian players I'd known. I never really got to know him very well. Froese, on the other hand, was a practical joker who had a habit of barking like a dog in the middle of games. A Philadelphia television station even did a feature on it for the supper-time news; I have it on tape.

Of course, there was Mark Howe, one of those players just a cut above the rest, like a Borje Salming or a Larry Robinson. You had to play with a guy like Mark Howe to appreciate all of the things he could do; he made the game look so easy with his effortless skating style, his great wristshot and the way he saw the entire ice surface and made those perfect passes. You have to wonder why he doesn't have a Norris Trophy on his mantelpiece. Maybe he was too quiet and self-effacing. But he belonged in that class, and it is amazing that an all-star with a surname of Howe could go unnoticed or unrewarded in the National Hockey League.

When I think about guys like Mark Howe, or talk about my two-and-a-half seasons with the Philadelphia Flyers, the positives will always outnumber the negatives, by a long shot.

Still, there are bitter memories, because the day I was traded to Detroit still ranks as the biggest disappointment of my life. Even today, Bob Clarke can't come close to realizing how much he hurt me, and my family, that day.

My feeling at the time was, "Why are these things always happening to me? Do I have some kind of disease?" In Toronto under Imlach, you always expected that kind of behavior from team management and prepared for it.

In Philadelphia, I never saw it coming.

14

Life After Hockey

I REMEMBER ONCE seeing a book with the title, *Been Down So Long It Looks Like Up To Me*. I never read it, but I think I lived it at the end of my hockey career and in the transition period that led to my life and career of today. For me, getting out of hockey was even more difficult than getting in, even though when it came time to make choices, the decision was easy enough.

It all started, of course, with the difficult decision to move on to Detroit after Bobby Clarke's bombshell trade. I took the trade very hard, but this time Wendy and the kids took it harder. It got so bad that, for the longest time, I thought my marriage might be over. And although the sociologists and psychologists will tell you that marriage break-up is common among couples when a professional athlete is wrapping up that career and going through a transition to the rest of his life, you never feel more alone than when all of these emotional factors all come together.

The near breakup of my marriage was the culmination of a lot of things. One was the shock of the trade from Philadelphia to Detroit. After the upheaval in Toronto, Wendy was settled in Philadelphia and wanted to stay there. The suburb of Voorhees, N.J., was our home and, although the Flyers had a large following in the greater Philadelphia area, the fishbowl existence of being Mrs. Darryl Sittler or the children of Darryl Sittler in southwestern Ontario was a thing of the past.

There were many other factors as well; this kind of situation doesn't develop overnight. It was a long process that had built up over time and a major reason for it was my single-minded concentration on my career. Anybody who spends a lot of time away from his or her family realizes that no matter how strong you or your family feelings are, this absence fosters a dual independence, which is not like mutual interdependence. Mom adopts the roles of both parents because for long periods of time, Dad can't be there. And even when he is there, he is so focused on his career that he may develop a blind spot in the area of his own family contributions.

At the same time, Mom realizes that this focus and concentration will contribute to success on the ice and so she will make a conscious effort to shield Dad from all but the more serious family crises. The downside of this is that eventually the husband might start thinking that "she doesn't need me there." Like when he phones up from the road and asks, "How's everything going?" and it's always "Fine, everything's going great!" He might begin to feel he isn't being taken seriously as a parent. Sometimes when you're on the road and feeling lonely, you want to hear all about the kids or that you're needed at home.

If both partners are trying to keep it light and positive, a dissociation results, where what you're both saying inside is, "I wish you were here," but you don't want to get too emotional over the phone because you know it will make you both feel miserable the moment you hang up, so you leave a lot of things unsaid. You both try to tough it out.

In professional sports, a lot of independence develops within a couple because of the unique circumstances. You're away and she's running the house, and when you come home you want to take over or assume your fair share of the responsibilities. But she's got things running her way and might not want to change, or maybe she sees your input as interference. And you don't know that. You might be full of goodwill, ready to pitch in and be the dad, only to discover that the two of you are giving mixed signals to the kids. And kids, being kids, will try to manipulate the person they perceive as the weak or most easily swayed parent. "Mom said no? Let's go ask Dad."

During your career, you can sacrifice the father role to the necessities of making your living in a highly competitive environment that takes uncommon concentration and effort. As that career wanes, however, it is time for re-entry into the family as a full-time member. That takes a very special effort for all involved.

When I was traded to Detroit, I spent three or four days thinking it over before deciding to move. Wendy, Ryan, Meaghan and Ashley stayed in Philadelphia until school break at Christmas, reluctant to move. When they did move, I was in the midst of a difficult season with the Red Wings, not playing a lot, and that complicated matters. A year that was supposed to start out with me being named captain of the Philadelphia Flyers, serious contenders for the Stanley Cup, turned out with me as a part-time player on a team that might not even make the playoffs.

Now, though, I had to make up my mind about moving to the Red Wings. While I was deliberating, I got calls from Danny Gare and Tiger Williams. Danny I knew well from our days together in the Superstars competition and in the Canada Cup series; Tiger by then had moved over to the Red Wings from Vancouver. They spoke to me separately, without knowing that the other had called, and yet the conversations were distressingly similar. They both wanted me to join them in Detroit because they knew I had something to contribute, and Detroit had potential. Conversely, they both went out of their way to give me their views of head coach Nick Polano, just so I knew what I was getting into. Duly advised, and still feeling deeply that I had something to contribute to the sport and to my career, I negotiated a two-year deal with the Red Wings and moved into the Ponchartrain Hotel in Detroit.

On the ice, it proved to be a nightmare season. In concrete terms, it led to crucial decisions that resolved many things for me and my family, and opened the way for the rest of my life. That year was a long time in the building.

The process of placing myself on a laboratory slide and slipping it under a microscope began on Wednesday, October 24, 1984, at Maple Leaf Gardens. It was my second or third game of the season with the Red Wings and my first return to Toronto in red-and-white. I didn't last the game. Early in the third period, I got hit from behind by Jim Korn. I had had a couple of fights with Korn earlier in my career; he was one of those players I never liked. He caught me in a vulnerable position and hit me into the boards. But, rather than leaving it at that, he took his arm and drove my head into the top of the boards, just where the glass and railing meet.

I was down briefly, and confronted with the scariest injury of my career when I got up. My upper cheekbone and bone around my eye socket had been broken in three places and my eye had slipped down further into the socket. It was the equivalent of a pair of binoculars with one lens a couple inches higher than the other. I still had the wherewithal to skate after Korn, who by then was standing next to the Toronto bench, and with a "Why did you do that, you jerk?" I punched him in the face with my glove on. (While I was in hospital, he dropped off a bottle of scotch and a note of apology at the front desk. I was in no mood to accept his apology; I tore up the note and the Crown Royal went home with an orderly. You don't excuse such an action with a note—he could have ended my career.)

Skating off the ice, I knew I was hurt seriously, so I signalled for team doctors and Dr. Leith Douglas, the Toronto plastic surgeon, and headed straight for the Gardens clinic. By this time, I was probably in shock. If I wasn't in shock, I certainly was shocked a few moments later when I got to see my new face in the clinic mirror.

"You're going straight to the hospital, Darryl; we've got to check this out," Dr. Douglas said. Experience had taught me that sports team doctors never let on to you how bad an injury might be right there on the spot. They wanted you relaxed and in a positive frame of mind for the important treatment and diagnosis phase. Afterwards, when you had stabilized or they had had an opportunity to close the wound or put the broken limb in a cast, they would level with you as to the gravity or true nature of your injury. There wasn't anything else to talk about so off I went to hospital in an ambulance.

About an hour later, I was coming out of the radiology department at Wellesley Hospital when I happened upon my dad, lying in emergency. The ambulance that had delivered me to the hospital from Maple Leaf Gardens had turned right around and picked up my father less than thirty minutes later. He'd been at the game at Maple Leaf Gardens with my brother-in-law, George Cescon, and had suffered a heart attack sometime during the game.

When I arrived at emergency, I called Wendy back in Voorhees to tell her I was injured and at the hospital, and explain about my dad. I was crying and scared, both for myself and my father, and Wendy later told me she had never ever heard or seen me like that. She was very concerned for the both of us. I was scheduled for surgery the next morning, and Dad was a floor above in intensive care. This would have been deemed a preposterous a script idea for a soap opera, but there we were.

My dad and I had always been close and I had appreciated his low-key way of encouraging me in my youth, without pushing me too hard in hockey. A few years earlier, my mother had shocked me and the rest of the family by leaving my father, and that had hurt Dad deeply. It had taken him a couple of years to recover and he finally did so with the help and support of a beautiful lady named Marilyn. In later years, it was so great for us to see how happy he was with Marilyn, a truly wonderful lady.

Life had been unpredictable, to say the least, in recent years, and this episode probably summed up my personal disarray better than anything—I couldn't ever remember feeling so alone.

The next morning, after I had been prepped for the operation, I was lying on the gurney and feeling very drowsy because they had already given me a needle.

Someone took my hand. "Darryl, it's me, Mel . . . Mel Stevens." I stirred and I think I croaked something original like "Hi, Mel."

"I'd like to pray with you before you go in." So we said a little prayer while I was lying there, which was nice. He had been visiting the Princess Margaret Hospital down the street because his wife Janet had cancer and was undergoing chemotherapy. After he finished the prayer, he said, "I'll go up and see your dad." While I was under the knife, he was in with my dad. They sat and talked, and Mel left him a book on professional athletes who had become Christians.

I didn't know all of this at the time. I was released three days after my operation and returned to Detroit. Each day that Janet was in having her chemotherapy, Mel would visit my father. They got into deep discussions on Christianity and larger questions like where we're all going, and things like that.

Two months later, in early December, Janet Stevens passed away. We were back in Toronto for a December 5 game and her funeral was the next day, so I stayed over. Although I knew the Ellises and other friends at the ceremony, I decided to sit quietly in the back, alone with my thoughts. Mel spoke about Janet, their relationship and shared faith, and his words had a lasting impact on me. It wasn't about a sense of loss, but on what death was all about: life in heaven afterwards. Something in Mel's words, and those of the other people who had also spoken, stirred me. There was a curious sense of peace and purpose in them, one which I certainly wasn't feeling.

Also, I think, there was a heightened overall sense of reality, one I wished intensely that I could have shared at that moment with my own family, so that those people who were closest to me would have this experience in common. I've heard it said that this is a pretty common phenomenon for people from very close families who spend a lot of time on the road.

My father died the next February. I spoke at his funeral; it was probably the toughest thing I've ever had to do in my life—talk to a church full of people at my dad's funeral. My father was lying in his coffin at the front of the church, when I made a comment to Marilyn about good people going to heaven. Mel's words about his wife a couple of months before had had a profound effect on me.

Marilyn took me by the hand. "Darryl, you don't have to worry. He became a Christian through Mel." Our family had never shown outward signs of great commitment to Christianity. Late in his life, my dad decided the time had come from his personal decision.

My feeling was, "Here it is again, touching me." I found out from Mel after that, that it was his visits and his time at the hospital with my dad that had led to my dad's decision.

This gave me immense peace of mind. As I've mentioned before, the Sittlers were of German stock that had settled the Kitchener-Waterloo area of southwestern Ontario back in the 1800s. (In fact, until the First World War, Kitchener had been called Berlin. That changed when the Dominion of Canada joined the rest of the British Commonwealth in the war against Kaiser Wilhelm.) Most of the settlers of German descent were Mennonite or Lutheran—we had both in our family tree—decent, God-fearing Christians all. My great-grandfather had been a Mennonite with a horse-and-buggy and no electricity on his farm near St. Jacobs. We were Evangelical and believed in a very practical, everyday kind of Christianity.

I had prayed regularly as a young boy and, although I had never shown it or professed it to anybody else, I always said a silent prayer before each game in my career. However, I was not an avowed Christian, or "born-again" like many hockey players are, even though a vague sort of commitment was always on the periphery of my life. Without realizing it, I had been moved by the commitment and faith of others, and the sense of peace they had found internally and externally.

Paul Henderson was a great example. When fame was thrust upon him after the 1972 Soviet-Canada Hockey Summit, he found he could not handle it. Wendy and I were close to Paul and Nora Henderson at the time; in fact, we babysat the three Henderson girls, Heather, Jennifer and Jill, while their parents were making history overseas.

The following spring, after the Leafs failed to make the playoffs, several of us went on a Florida vacation—the Sittlers, Hendersons,

Glennies and Ellises. I can't quite remember how it came about, but we were all together one evening when Wendy severely upbraided Paul for some comment or attitude and it built into a critique of his behavior in the past year. It was something which probably had been brewing for a while, but which blew up so suddenly that it took us all by surprise. Perhaps what touched Paul the most was the fact that this was uncharacteristic behavior for Wendy, she was just not the type of person who would act this way. Deep down Paul accepted Wendy's comments and the need for him to get his life back on an even keel, for several of his closest friends and teammates spoke up that day and agreed with Wendy's assessment.

Shortly thereafter, he was introduced to Mel Stevens and came to know Mel as a friend and learn what Mel's life and Christianity were all about. At some point, he made a commitment. Today, Christianity is a very large part of his life and he has helped many other players turn to Jesus as head of Athletes in Action, a group of Christian athletes who go out and share the work. I met Mel Stevens through Paul.

Paul's close friendship with Mel eventually brought many of the Leafs close to Mel and Janet and the Christian Teen Ranch in Orangeville. Even today, some twenty years later, I'm periodically involved with the Teen Ranch in the summertime and our kids have gone up there for summer tennis or hockey school for many years. We're very close to Mel, his new wife Betty, and others at the ranch. When I say that, I don't mean that I get out and talk about it to the public as frequently as Paul Henderson does, or minister as he does. But in the quietness of my own heart, or our own home and our family, I believe in Jesus and Christianity.

It wasn't necessarily Paul's example that got me closer to my Christian roots. Our Florida group, the Hendersons, Ellises, Glennies and Sittlers, were always welcome at the Teen Ranch for a day of relaxation and activities such as horseback riding. Later, as Leafs captain, I would invite the guys on the team to come up on a Sunday off and most of the team would show up—they have more than a hundred acres up there—and we'd ride horses, perhaps have a bowl of chili, and relax, away from the grind and pressures of hockey. This had nothing to do with trying to expose or push any beliefs on anybody; it was just a day's outing away from it all.

Over a period of time, this became a place of personal comfort for me. When Laurie Boschman was overwhelmed by the good life in the big city in his rookie year, Mel took him under his wing and set him back on course. The Teen Ranch then, and still, had always given Maple Leafs players beautiful leather-bound Bibles with the Maple Leaf insignia and their own names inscribed on them. And strangely, as much as some players might have trouble coming forward or standing up for what they believed in—because it's always much easier not to say anything—when a player didn't get a Bible it bothered him. They now give Bibles to many teams in the NHL, which is a great undertaking for the ranch, but they do it.

Although many people around me had made commitments to faith, I always seemed to be subconsciously rejecting this road. It might have been something about feeling that I had made it this far on my own talent and drive, and the fear that I might belittle myself and my talents by using religion as a crutch. The straight-ahead purposefulness of the ego-driven athlete—who usually has become that way by necessity—rarely leaves any room for God and such things. Or he only seems to need God and the afterlife when his career seems destined for an afterlife of its own. Consciously or subconsciously, I must have fought the urge and this resistance showed up in the strangest ways.

I remember standing at the blueline of the Montreal Forum after my overtime goal against Czechoslovakia in the 1976 Canada Cup. "O Canada" was about to be played when I turned to Gerry Cheevers and, in the best tradition of Super Bowl stars who say, "I'm going to DisneyWorld," cracked: "Well, now I can become a born-again Christian just like Paul Henderson."

It was a cheap shot that just popped out, with me not really thinking about what I was saying; but it stuck with me that I had said that. Deep down, I felt ashamed of it; it nagged at my conscience.

Religion touched my life in strange ways. One night Wendy and I were lying in bed at about eleven-thirty at our home in Mississauga, during the problem year with Imlach and Ballard, and there was a knock at the door. It was a man in his late thirties or early forties, and to this day I don't know who he was. He was well dressed, jacket, shirt and tie, and spoke with a pronounced Southern accent.

"I was up in this area and I was reading articles in the newspapers on Darryl Sittler's problems and it came to me that I had to see this guy; I had to talk to him," he drawled in the kind of voice that constantly turns up on evangelical TV.

He talked his way in, and the three of us sat in the living room as he shared his belief in Jesus with us.

"I don't know where I got this feeling from, I don't know you from Adam, but I just happened to be here and I felt I had to come over," he said. To this day, I don't know how he tracked down my address.

We spoke for about forty-five minutes. On his way out, standing by the door, he said a little prayer with us. He left Wendy and me looking at each other with "did this really happen?" expressions on our faces. Whatever possessed us to let him in? Whatever possessed him to end up on my doorstep? I still can't answer that. These anecdotes serve to set the scene for my last year in hockey and my transition back to the real world.

After recovering from my cheek injury, I returned to the ice and regular play with the team. I was looking forward to a couple of milestones, scoring my 500th goal, and playing my 1,100th game. If I stayed healthy I could achieve both late in this season, or early in the next.

Wendy and the kids joined me at Christmas. We had bought a home in Bloomfield Hills, and the holiday period was a rush for all of us, moving house, trying to get the kids and their schooling organized, and trying to keep my career on track. However, I sensed a wall between Wendy and myself, and hoped that once the season was over, we'd have time to talk it out.

Again, Lady Luck conspired against me.

We were a curious mix of young and old in Detroit; older players like myself and Ivan Boldirev, Brad Park, Danny Gare, John Barrett, Greg Smith, Reed Larson and Tiger Williams; and youngsters like Kelly Kisio, Gerard Gallant and Steve Yzerman. Our goaltenders were quite young and unreliable, but we seemed to have enough talent to do more.

Part of the problem might have been the fact that we were in the Norris Division, the good old Snorris, where mediocrity was rewarded. We finished 14 points under .500 that year, and still managed to get third place, four points ahead of Minnesota's 62. (Toronto was in a league by itself, with 48 points.) In the Adams and Smythe divisions, it took 82 points to clinch fourth that season, and while the Rangers made it in the Patrick with 62 points, they were light-years removed from the Islanders' 86 points in third.

Nick Polano and Jim Devellano brought up the big question: "Why aren't we doing any better?"

I had been with the team barely a week when we were divided into two groups and asked to meet with a pair of sports psychologists that the Red Wings had hired to get us out of our funk. We all knew the answer to the question; we just needed a forum for presenting this opinion to team management.

As I mentioned, I was new to the team but already I was plugged into our team dynamics. This was a team of unhappy players who questioned their coach's competence; and having played under Floyd Smith and Punch Imlach in Toronto, I knew exactly what this was all about. The two sports psychologists handed us all pieces of paper and asked us to list problems with the team that they might be able to rectify.

They got a lot more than they bargained for. It has always been my philosophy to deal with problems openly or head-on, rather than beating around the bush. Some people might call this a lack of tact or diplomacy; I call it facing life honestly. So I wrote on my piece of paper something to the effect that "the players on the team would like to know how they can handle playing for a person whom they feel is incompetent. How do you deal with such a situation?" I wrote a few other suggestions down, and then we folded the pieces of paper and threw them into a pile in the middle of the table. Anonymity was the key to honest discussion, the psychologists had told us.

It just so happened that the first paper picked up was mine. As the first consultant read it aloud, he looked at his partner with a pained expression on his face that seemed to say, "What is *this*?" I think they had expected self-motivational stuff, like what players were supposed to do on game day and how they were prepared to face the opposition. Instead, they got heavy-duty criticism of team management, especially the coach, and it was team management that had hired these two guys. The subject of my comments took over the rest of the session as our half of the team jumped in with their personal variations on the theme.

"That hit the nail right on the head!" and "That's the problem, exactly!" and a simple "Amen" were among the first comments as we launched into our group session. The psychologist who had read my comments stood up, took off his sports jacket and draped it over the back of the chair. You could tell he was reluctant to dip into this fine kettle of fish, but he and his partner were trapped. They weren't doing their jobs if they tried to deflect us from this track.

The second group came in after us, went through the same exercise, and had the same result.

We didn't have much to do with the psychologists after that. They decided to go to the root of the problem and spent most of their time with Nick Polano, figuring it was much easier to change him than to change twenty-five of his hockey players.

Later on in the season, we were in Minnesota for a Saturday night game on January 26. During the morning skate, assistant coach Danny Belisle came over to me. "Nick would like to see you in the coaches' room."

A player has a sense of when he's going to get canned or benched, you can feel it. And this little invitation had my antennae working overtime. Whether it is at practice, during a game, in the dressing room, getting on a bus, or on the bench, the coach suddenly starts treating you differently, even if he's doing his best not to treat you badly. You notice a very subtle change, even though you might not be able to put your finger on it.

With all of the things that had happened during this season, I knew that I had been distracted and had not given my best effort. Though I was off for only two weeks after the triple fracture of my cheekbone, I had to wear a special Itech face mask for protection, and that may have contributed to my lack of concentration.

"I'm probably not going to dress tonight, and he'll probably lecture me on my play," I thought as I walked up the ramp to the coaches' room.

To his everlasting credit, Nick Polano started out with a great deal of sensitivity. "Darryl, Danny and I have been giving it a lot of thought and we feel that you can't play three games in four nights, your conditioning is a factor. You might have a half-decent game but the next night it will show; you can't play back-to-back. We're going to sit you out tonight because of that." We had come into Minnesota fresh off a quick blitz of New York, beating the Islanders 5-4 on Tuesday and dropping a 3-1 loss to the Rangers on Thursday.

While conscious of the fact that I hadn't been playing great hockey, I knew for certain that conditioning wasn't a factor; I'd finished third among all players in special conditioning measurement tests at the Flyers' camp in September and I worked hard every day to maintain that high level.

Maybe the conditioning line was the wrong opener, I don't know, but I reacted poorly and threw it all back at Polano.

"Talking to you is like talking to a cement wall." And then I walked out.

"Wait a minute! Where are you going? Get back here and let's talk this out."

"All right, maybe it's time everybody around here knew what was going on," I countered. The talk of the organization revolved about how Jim Devellano and Nick Polano had maneuvered owner Mike Ilitch into a corner, shielding him from the real hockey operations. Devellano had started out as a scout with St. Louis Blues, moved over to the New York Islanders for ten years, and was assistant general manager there when the Red Wings reached out for him in 1982.

Earlier in the year, while I was still in Polano's good books, he had come over to me during a practice quite perplexed. "Darryl, you've just come over from Philadelphia and they're a top team. Are they that much better than us? Is their personnel that much better?"

The answer was no. We weren't far apart in talent. I gave Nick Polano a direct answer why Philadelphia was doing much better. "All we do in practice here is skate around a bit and do some real simple drills," I said. "In Philadelphia, we worked on all aspects of the game over and over again. The guys who were on the regular power play practiced it all of the time and got to the point that they'd know where the other guys were without even looking. Here, we don't do any of that." He got real quiet after that. In fact, the meeting in the coaches' room in Bloomington was probably our first real conversation in a couple months.

The upshot of the morning talk with Polano was that I didn't play that night, and I also sat out the following week against Washington, St. Louis, Quebec and New Jersey. Then my father died and I left the team for several days to attend to the funeral and other family matters. Driving back to Detroit after the funeral, I made up my mind to speak to Devellano and rectify the situation; I didn't want to end my career this way. Devellano passed me right back to Polano and I ended up apologizing to him.

"Look, put me back into the lineup and I'll keep my mouth shut and play where you want me to," I vowed. I was back in the lineup the next night, but for the rest of the season I saw only spot duty, banished as I was to the outer reaches of the fourth line. Strangely enough, when we went to Toronto, Polano played me all night and I was the star of the game, scoring two goals. In other words, my conditioning was fine and my performance was linked directly to my ice time. But the game after Toronto, I was back on the fourth line, barely playing enough to break a sweat. These performances proved to me that I still could play the game; all I needed now was the opportunity.

The season lurched to a conclusion in this fashion, and in 61 games played, I had only 11 goals and 16 assists. Nobody in Toronto could understand it; every time I went in there it seemed I scored a couple of goals.

In the first round of the playoffs, we were up against the Chicago Black Hawks in a best-of-five series. I hardly played as we lost both games there 9-5 and 6-1; and as I was skating off the ice in the Stadium, a weird feeling came over me.

"This might be the last game I play as a professional player," my sixth sense seemed to be telling me. The old radar proved right. Playoff veteran or not, Polano had me in the black sweater during the next practice back home and I wasn't dressed for the third and final game of the series, an 8-2 shellacking at home. It was a slap in my face from a coach who appeared to feel comfortable blaming his players for his shortcomings.

I felt a strange kind of responsibility to the Detroit ownership for the way things had turned out, but also suspected that owner Mike Ilitch wasn't aware of everything going on with his team. Partially out of loyalty to him, but mostly out of loyalty to the players, I put my feelings and comments on paper and personally delivered the letter to his home. I received no response from him. I wonder, in fact, if that letter might have precipitated my departure from the Red Wings, or even the replacement of Polano behind the bench.

While all of this was happening on the ice, Wendy and I were experiencing our differences, and it got to a point where we weren't sure whether our marriage was going to make it or not. We both agreed that the first major step was to set up a semblance of family order in Detroit. In early May, Wendy returned to Philadelphia to organize moving our furniture which we'd left in our other home. The market was bad so we had decided to leave the house empty and try to sell it later. The most important thing was to get everything settled so we could enjoy our summer and I could get ready for the next training camp in Detroit.

I had a meeting set up with Jimmy Devellano and I gave it a lot of thought going in. The Darryl Sittler they had traded for wasn't the same player who had reported in. With the broken cheekbone, the death of my father, and the marital strains at home, I had been sidetracked most of the year. But now I was going to walk in there and tell him, "Let's clean the slate over what happened last year; I'm going to come to training camp and show you guys what the player you traded for can really do."

When I got to the office, I didn't even get a chance to recite my prepared speech. Devellano did all the talking.

"Darryl, we've made a decision. We're buying you out of your contract. You're no longer a Red Wing." This floored me, and something in the way it was said told me that there was no way of talking them out of it. The Red Wings had decided to buy me and some of the older players out of our contracts and sign a bunch of young guys with all of the money they saved.

There was a discrepancy over what they were buying me out for; I believed that I would be paid full salary, $260,000. I'd given Alan Eagleson instructions before I left Philadelphia that I wanted two years guaranteed—$250,000 and $260,000. I was paid $250,000 in my last year in Philly so unless the Detroit money was guaranteed, I wasn't going to accept the trade from the Flyers and move. Devellano had a different opinion: "We're going to buy you out under the Collective Bargaining Agreement stipulations." That was two-thirds of the contract paid off in $50,000 annual increments. So I phoned Eagleson and he assured me that this wasn't the deal and he would sue the Red Wings if he had to.

While this was going on, Wendy was in New Jersey organizing our move. Our furniture already was in a moving van somewhere between New Jersey and Detroit.

When I got home, I told her the latest development and it was the last straw. "Why wouldn't they tell us they were going to do that? Why would they spend the $10,000 to move our furniture here if this is what they planned?" If we decided to move back to Voorhees and keep our home, it would have cost us another $10,000. We kept the New Jersey house on the market and moved up to the cottage in Orillia.

This was my first summer in my life during which I wasn't sure where I'd be in September. There was an offer on the table— Vancouver wanted me and I could have signed a one-year deal with them. The Detroit problem hadn't been settled and Devellano was saying, "If you sign with another team, we aren't going to pay you your money." What was the sense of signing if I had a guaranteed $260,000? I might as well not play and take the money, rather than play for somebody else and maybe make less.

It finally came down to the middle of August, and I had to make up my mind. It was time to retire. If I wanted to keep playing, I would have had to move the family to Vancouver, and Wendy didn't want to come. The kids were in school in Detroit and they'd already had a pair of moves in the past few years. Enough was enough.

The downside was the possibility of going through another season like the last one. On the upside was the attraction of scoring my 500th goal—I had 484—something very few players get to accomplish. Vancouver represented a very real chance to score my 500th, and do it in Canada where it would get the attention it deserved as a major milestone. But the Vancouver offer was for a year only, and would entail a third move in three years for my wife and kids after the season.

In reality, there was no decision to make. "I've got to do what is right for Wendy, the kids and myself. It's time to retire."

To this day, I've never regretted it.

That August, with all of these still-unanswered questions and problems roiling up inside me, I was out jogging one day near the cottage and it felt like the whole world was coming down around my ears. I remember it like it was yesterday.

I started praying. "Hey, I can't do all of this on my own. All of these problems are ganging up on me. Come into my heart and help me."

A variety of images assailed me: Paul Henderson and the misery his fame brought him in 1972; a similar road I travelled after my incredible successes of 1976; regularly attending Bible studies with the Leafs on Sundays when we were on the road or going to see Norman Vincent Peale in New York with teammates; my family's involvement with the Teen Ranch; my parents' breakup, and my father's death. All of these images, and many others, finally came together to form one big picture.

From that point on, I had a real commitment to my beliefs and who I really was. I had been close to this all my life it seems, but unable to take that final step until then. It felt good to feel certain of at least something. My trials weren't over, however. Not by a long shot.

The first step was to let people close to me in on it; among them

Dave Burrows, Mel Stevens and Wendy. After speaking to Wendy about this, I began to notice a change in our relationship. I feel I had become more humble, more approachable and more aware of what my real priorities were. The irony of the whole struggle through the marital difficulties, career change and the number of things that happened in my life, was that I could easily imagine people on the outside saying: "Darryl Sittler has got it all, beautiful home, wife and kids, career. Man, wouldn't I love to be him!"

Even though I was now retired from hockey, I was on the road as much as I had been when I was playing. I was up in Toronto a lot on business, working with a couple of companies I'm involved with. During my hockey career, I had begun working "outside" on endorsements, and then expanded that to representation deals. I also did a lot of public speaking and motivational work with a variety of companies. This kept me very busy after I hung up my skates.

What our marital situation basically boiled down to was a mutual lack of understanding—though we had to go through a lot of counselling to analyze it and get it back to where it is today. Wendy had tried for years to talk to me about her feelings and explain her concerns, but I was so busy with things that I just hadn't heard her. As I write this it sounds so simple, but of course it's not; I wouldn't wish this on anybody. It's the toughest thing one could go through in a life; you think your wife and kids and everything is going to be gone and all because you lost your true focus.

Wendy had lost her love and feeling for me. This was the culmination of many things, among them the fact that she felt I never could give her the love and attention she needed because I was focusing all my efforts on hockey, endorsements and charities. It also was related to the pressure of constantly being my backbone, and the frustrations that grew out of our difficult departure from Toronto. But most of all, my unconscious turning away from Wendy and her needs led her to build a wall of indifference around her. I found myself on the outside of that wall because she no longer needed me.

Wendy and I began counselling together at the end of 1985. It got down to crunch time, whether it was going to go or whether it wasn't, and seeing how this was affecting the children, Wendy decided to re-commit to our marriage. Nothing spectacular happened overnight, there was a whole building process that would take a long time.

It wasn't as if she or I suddenly felt married again; but there was a very real feeling of turning a corner, or reaching another, higher plateau in our relationship. For me, there was the realization that something had been missing in my life until I also made this re-commitment. I knew there was a change in me. I can't fully explain it to people. I just try to live it.

The hardest aspect in this was dealing with my children. I don't care what some of the experts say, when you live in a troubled home your kids will sense the friction. Even if we both gave them as much love as we could as individuals, it wasn't the same for them. The stress of potential, permanent marital breakup is not something I'd want my children to go through ever again. I can remember even as a child the times when my mother and father argued and there was that underlying threat of one or the other leaving. It scares you to death as a child because you sense that your entire world is caving in.

Rod Wilson, a committed Christian, was our marriage counsellor and he took us both through some intense sessions, trying to get into all the reasons for our estrangement. Sometimes you have to go right back into your own childhood to understand your behavior and how you might change that behavior. We had to try to understand our-selves, each other and the overall picture. We realized we both had to change, especially me, for this to work. How much change would it take? Had you said to either one of us back there that our marriage would come back and be stronger than it's ever been, we probably wouldn't have believed it.

A last point, just to clarify my personal feelings towards Christianity. When the word gets out in Christian circles that you are a high-profile athlete or celebrity and a self-professed Christian, people automatically want to use that and would like you to get involved with them and share your experiences. At the beginning I was very hesitant to get involved with that, and still am, not that my belief is any weaker for it. The main reason is that my life with my family and kids is paramount, and even the most worthy causes tend to take away from the quality of family life because they demand so much of your time. That is why I really have to reflect on my participation in even very good causes. The only way to decide is to trust my own feelings.

Paul Henderson believes strongly in the evangelical message, and in passing it on to as many people as he can. I think that this is great because that's what Paul wants and feels in his heart. It's really positive. If somebody wants to broach the subject privately with me,

I would be delighted to share my beliefs. The point is that my commitment to Christianity is highly personal and private.

People often ask me about living in Buffalo or why I'm not jumping at the chance to get back into the Leaf organization. But I look at what my priorities are in my life. On the one hand, I'm an achiever; I've always got to be going and doing something, making a deal here or there, I can't sit still. Wendy, on the other hand, is a homebody, who's into bringing up the kids and being an excellent mother and wife.

I'm focused on tomorrow and she's looking at today. As well, there's my need to provide my family with its needs: good schools and the lifestyle we've become accustomed to. I wouldn't be satisfied sitting at home. When you go through the exercise of trying to understand what makes the two of you tick, individually and as partners, you strive to find that harmonious balance.

A hockey career takes a lot of prisoners—the player, his wife and his kids. You tend to prefix each description with the word "hockey," as in "hockey player," "hockey wife," and "hockey family." That can wear you down as a player, wife or child, because you are expected to play the role assigned to you by circumstance. To my mind, Wendy had concluded that she could do without the conflict, and that she preferred family duties over hockey duties. She would prefer to spend her time with her children or doing something for herself. After thirteen or fourteen years of hockey life together, Wendy had breathed in that atmosphere for so long that she needed to get away from it. Other wives might love it, thrive on it, and want always to be a part of it. Wendy didn't. It took a long time for both of us to confront our different feelings because public recognition enhanced my career and I sought public opportunities or forums to express my gratitude. That's why I had always been involved with charity work and other volunteer activities.

With our marriage back on track, Wendy and I wanted to make a clean break with hockey and decided that if we were going to put this marriage back together, we'd almost have to start a new life. We originally looked out in Colorado. I had confidence in myself to start a career in something else. But when we got out there and looked around—and Wendy was ready to buy the house and move—something inside, a gut feeling, told me that this wasn't the place. So we had to find a compromise. Wendy wanted to stay in the States and enjoy the lifestyle that comes with it, or better still, the lifestyle she experienced away from Toronto and the public attention. The official duties of hockey wife and, even more, the unofficial demands are very wearing.

I don't want to give the wrong impression when I say this because I realize that public attention is inevitable for sports stars. But when we lived in Toronto, family excursions were impossible. One thing parents love to do is enjoy family outings, as a couple, or with their children. Wendy and I might finally get that rare night off, a chance to catch up on things and enjoy each other's company—but it couldn't happen, just the two of us alone. If we were at a restaurant, there would be a steady stream of well-wishers and autograph seekers throughout the meal. I didn't resent it as an individual, because I knew what celebrity as captain of the Maple Leafs meant. But we grew to resent it as a couple, because it came between us.

A simple thing like Christmas shopping became an impossibility. I couldn't take my kids to see Santa Claus at the mall because we'd be mobbed. In the end, I had to do my Christmas shopping alone, just after the stores opened in the morning. We enjoyed the Canadian National Exhibition in August, but could hardly ever go for the same reason. I remember one ill-fated visit to the CNE, me in floppy hat and big sunglasses, and crowds following us everywhere.

Even these were fairly positive experiences; there were many negative ones too. One of my reasons for living near, but not in, the metro Toronto area, was I wanted my kids to grow up and enjoy hockey and not have know-it-alls or troublemakers in the stands yelling, "Sittler, you suck!" or worse, at Ryan or Meaghan. Though we have been fortunate—Ryan has turned out to be a big, talented forward who was pursued by every junior team in the Ontario Hockey League before the Detroit Ambassadors made him their second-round draft choice last spring. As well, all the major hockey universities in the NCAA have pursued him. He has made a place for himself in hockey and has had to deal with some pressure as the son of a former pro, but probably nothing like what he might have faced in southwestern Ontario or in Toronto. Meaghan has played AAA elite hockey in the Buffalo area; imagine what a circus it might have been had "Darryl's daughter" grown up in the MTHL!

These two, and kid sister Ashley, are three normal, everyday kids and the pride of their parents. So you have some reasons why Wendy, to this day, doesn't want to move back to Toronto. I had to weigh all of these factors when we were in Detroit. I was driving back and forth to Toronto, a back-breaker of a commute, and spending more time driving than with either my clients or my family. Something had to be done.

The last consideration dealt with extended family ties. Most of my brothers and sisters still lived in the Kitchener-Waterloo area; Wendy's parents and her sister were still in London. While I sought freedom for my wife and kids, I didn't want to lose the advantages of my proximity to Toronto. So Buffalo it was. Terry and Nancy Martin lived there, as did a large number of other former players, and everyone liked it.

This September will be our fifth year in the Buffalo suburbs, and we call it home.

The supreme irony in all this is that I do a great deal of work in Toronto while I live in the Buffalo area. My great nemesis, the late Punch Imlach, worked down here for almost a decade and always kept his home in Scarborough.

Maybe we were always diametrically opposed, and just didn't realize it.

15

"My Brother's Keeper"

PROFESSIONAL ATHLETES AND other celebrities often get requests to visit hospitals and similar institutions during the Christmas season to spread a little cheer. The Maple Leafs were no different, and staged an annual visit to the Toronto Hospital for Sick Children, known universally as Sick Kids'.

I always felt a responsibility to do this and it was something I felt good about doing, first as a young Leafs rookie, and later as team captain. In my captain's role, I tried to organize functions to get other players actively involved in those requests, instead of shying away from them. I knew from my own experiences that this was well worth the energy and the time invested. I also tried to impress on the younger players that we'd all get our own rewards from this type of activity and I'm proud to say that the players responded superbly. These memories never leave you.

During one visit to Sick Kids' Hospital, I met a boy from Sudbury who was dying of leukemia. I spent some time with him alone, and after I left his room, I met his mother in the hallway. She was extremely upset, which is very understandable, and I discovered during the course of our conversation that she had been in Toronto for a number of weeks to be with her son and that she was staying at a hotel. The family couldn't afford the hotel bill and they had sold some of the animals on their farm, and then had put their farm up for sale, so that the husband could pay for these bills that were piling up in Toronto because the mother needed to be with their dying son.

It wasn't too long after that conversation that I got a call from Peter Beresford of McDonald's Restaurants. He told me about the Ronald McDonald House concept that had been initiated in Philadelphia with the Eagles football team. Ronald McDonald House was a place for the families of sick children from out of town to stay and be near a child while he or she underwent treatment. Beresford was vice-president of marketing for McDonald's at the time and the company was looking at building a Ronald McDonald House in Toronto and needed a spokesperson for it.

"Could you get involved?" he asked.

"Yeah, I'd be proud to," I jumped right in. I could still see the faces of the sick little boy from Sudbury and his distraught mother. Nobody had to convince me that there was a need for this; I'd seen it.

I did some commercials for McDonald's and we raised more than $1 million toward construction of a Ronald McDonald House in Toronto. At last count, there were twelve Ronald McDonald Houses throughout Canada. I really feel good about the small part I could play in such an important project.

When I spoke at the press conference to announce the program's fund drive, I told the story about the Sudbury woman and her boy. There wasn't a dry eye in the house, mine included. I began to cry about halfway through the story, and the retelling of it made me realize how deeply I had been moved by that woman's courage and that family's plight; how she watched her boy waste away, and how her husband back home tried to keep what was left of the farm going, selling animals to meet her hotel bills, and having to hear his son die over the telephone.

"I hope," I told the people in attendance, "that nobody else will ever have to go through what that family did, once we have our own Ronald McDonald House here in Toronto."

I have met many interesting people in my experiences with various charitable groups and associations. Some I met through events like hospital visits and fund drives; others I met through normal fan-player channels. I always felt that a fan who put a lot of time and effort into sending me something in the mail deserved some sort of response. I did a lot of my fan mail on the airplane on road trips. One day I was going through my mail on a team charter to some NHL city, when I happened upon a letter from a girl named Lena Pang who was eleven or twelve. As I read on, I learned that this girl was very concerned that she was going to die from a blood disorder. I wrote some words of encouragement on the back of one of my pictures, talked about the great advances in medicine we enjoyed, and encouraged her to keep the faith and to be strong.

Shortly after she received the letter she went into remission. She credits the timing of that letter to the change in her life. She really believed in her own heart that this did it for her. Lena started up a long correspondence with me at that point; a poet and an artist, she'd send me things she drew, poems, pictures for the kids. I'd attend autograph sessions all over southern Ontario and Lena would show up with cookies and chocolates and little presents for the kids. She became a big part of our lives for a number of years.

When I got traded to Philadelphia we didn't correspond as much, but we haven't been out of contact entirely. Recently I attended a dinner for the Special Olympics Program in Toronto and there was a message at the hotel that Lena had called. We had a good conversation and caught up on things; she's now married and very successful.

The point of this story is that sometimes, when you really make the effort and take the time to help people, you can hardly believe the impact you have, and how much you've touched somebody. Meeting Lena Pang has been a memorable and rewarding experience for me.

My association with Terry Fox, which I referred to in an earlier chapter, began when I picked up the *Toronto Sun* one day, and there on the cover was a color picture of a young Canadian boy with a big smile on his face, freckles, full of life, whose dream was to run across Canada. It was one of those times in my life when a newspaper article really touched me. I was bowled over by his courage and guts. I used to jog myself, and to think that he was going to run twenty-six miles a day on one leg, every day, was phenomenal.

I followed his run right from the point where he dipped his leg in the Atlantic Ocean, and then across the Maritimes and into Quebec. When he arrived at the Quebec-Ontario border, Ontario Cancer Society organizers asked if there was anything special they could do for him when he arrived in Toronto, because they were planning a big ceremony down at City Hall. He said he'd love to have the opportunity to meet Darryl Sittler and Bobby Orr, because as a youngster growing up in Port Coquitlam, we were his favorite players.

He was amazed that I wanted to meet him as much as he wanted to meet me. On the day of the meeting, I drove down from Orillia. It was a beautiful sunny day and the car ate up the miles on Highway 400 while I tried to decide what kind of memento I could leave with him. What could I do that would be special for this kid, that would show my appreciation for his special effort? It came to me; I'd played in the All-Star Game that year—I would give him my All-Star sweater. I stopped off at home, picked it up, put it in a brown paper bag, and went down to the Four Seasons Hotel. I met the Marathon of Hope organizers in the lobby.

"Terry's up in his room resting," one of them told me. "He's just done thirteen miles so far today. Why don't you go up and surprise him, ask him if there's anybody there who might want to go for a run?"

I followed that script, and entered his room. He was there with several of his escort party. I can still see the expression on Terry's face when he turned and recognized me. He was the biggest ongoing story and celebrity in Canada at the time, and he couldn't believe that I'd want to be there to meet him. It was a very special moment.

A little while later, he led me and several other people through the streets of Toronto, lined with people, down to City Hall for a short ceremony commemorating his visit. At the beginning, I ran beside him, but when I felt the incredible emotion from the people in the streets, and their cries of "Run for us, Terry" and things like that, I pulled back because I didn't want to detract from the real hero of the day. We ran down University Avenue to City Hall, where thousands of people had gathered. Several politicians were in attendance and they all welcomed Terry and praised his courage and dedication.

When it was my turn to speak, I mumbled a few words about having played in the All-Star Game that year, and how he was the real All-Star there that day. I reached into the brown paper bag I was carrying and pulled out my sweater. We both had tears in our eyes when he put it on in front of downtown Toronto.

After that, I got to know Terry as a person. We kept in touch as his run continued. Unfortunately, the cancer spread to his lungs and stopped him near Thunder Bay just after Labor Day. Later that year, we were out in Vancouver and I called him up and had him down to the rink to meet the team. The ravages of cancer shocked me; it had sucked the life out of a young man who just months before was brimming with it.

When he went to hospital, a Terry Fox Telethon was organized and I took part. It raised something like $25 million for cancer research. Not too long afterward, Terry passed away. I can't and won't forget this young man, not only for his guts and determination, but because he was a kid with a goal and a dream—to find a cure for cancer, the disease that took his life. He may have lost his life, but he did immeasurable things for people suffering from cancer, and other diseases, in this country.

His picture hangs in our family room. Canadian artist Ken Danby did a special painting commemorating Terry's Marathon of Hope, and in it Terry is wearing my All-Star sweater. This has always touched me deeply. His dream still lives; subsequent annual Terry Fox runs have now raised a total of $75 million.

I am proud to say that Terry Fox turned the tables on me. Somebody who was inspired by my hockey career and feats on the ice, turned it around through his actions to become my hero and inspiration. I am happy I was able to tell him and show him how I felt before he died.

A year earlier, I had met a courageous little girl who shared Terry's plight—osteogenic sarcoma. Her name was Ann Lillian Jewel Phipps and she was just ten years old and a figure skater when doctors had to remove her right leg. She had fallen from a bicycle in her hometown of Tillsonburg, Ontario, in September 1980 and broken the femur in her left leg. A routine X-ray taken after the leg was set turned up a cloudy area which, biopsies showed, was bone cancer. That October, her leg was amputated about six inches below her hip.

A special trip was arranged in December so that she could visit Maple Leaf Gardens, meet some of her favorite players, and scoop up a bunch of souvenir pucks, sticks and posters and, by special request, a sweater from the captain of the Leafs. She was a spunky little kid, uncomfortable with the fact that she had to wear a wig because cancer treatment had made her hair fall out. Ann told me she would need a pair of custom-made skates, but that she was going to pick up on her skating as soon as she could be outfitted with an artificial limb.

"It's going to take a lot of practice and hard work," I told her.

"I'm going to do it," she replied.

On the tenth anniversary of the Marathon of Hope, in August 1990, Ann's parents met with Roland and Betty Fox to tell them how Terry had become Ann's greatest hero, and had taught her how to live, and how to die. She passed away about a month before Terry did.

Sometimes, involvement with awareness campaigns, fund drives, special health associations and groups comes about in a more personal way.

In one case, it again began with my reading of a newspaper, the Saturday *Star*, up at the cottage. It was the first weekend in August, 1987. The *Star*'s health reporter, Lillian Newbery, had written a story about skin cancer, melanoma, that got my attention. It talked about the dangers of too much sun in the summer and how small moles could get malignant. If you had suspicions in this area, you should check them out. Ever since I was young, and especially when I was in London as a junior and building swimming pools for my summer job, I would go shirtless a lot of the time in the sun. I had carried that habit to my activities around the cottage every summer.

I had a funny-looking mole on my shoulder that sounded suspiciously like the moles described in the newspaper piece.

A few weeks later I drove over to Don Stoutt's place for a visit. I had just parked in his driveway when Dave Collins, another acquaintance, drove up. Dave is a GP and coroner in Orillia. I mentioned the article and the mole I was worried about.

"Come and see me tomorrow," he said, "and we'll have a look at it." I was in his office bright and early on Monday. He took one look at the mole and said, "That's coming out right now."

Two days later, he called me at home. "You were right to worry, the biopsy showed stage II melanoma. You'll have to come in for more surgery." I was flattened; Wendy and I just held each other and cried. A little thing like this could end a life, disrupt a happy family? It wasn't possible. It couldn't be possible. All five of us were very scared.

They went in and found nothing else, but I underwent a lot of tests. That October, I went in to Sunnybrook Hospital in Toronto and was tested thoroughly. I passed with flying colors.

What really got me where I live was the randomness of the whole thing. I just happened to read a newspaper article about melanomas and thought about seeing a doctor. But I might not have done anything about it if Dave Collins and I hadn't visited Don Stoutt on the same afternoon, met in the driveway, and talked about it before joining the others inside.

The doctors scared me even more after they pronounced me cancer-free. I was lucky I found this when I did, because melanoma can spread like wildfire throughout the body and pop up all over the place, in all kinds of terrible ways. And it was just millimeters away from spreading when they caught it. The other thing I learned was that I am still at risk and should be checked out every year. And to keep my shirt on whenever I'm out in the sun. Wendy and the kids, all tanners like I was, have learned that lesson, too.

With all this background, I couldn't very well say no the following year when the Canadian Dermatology Association asked if I would participate as a spokesman in Sun Awareness Week, an annual, early-summer event during which the association tries to sensitize people to the dangers of over-exposure to the sun and ultraviolet radiation. Joining me was jockey Sandy Hawley, who had had a much more frightening experience. He went to see his doctor after the racing season about a nasty-looking mole on his back, and stage V melanoma (the most advanced) was diagnosed. A large patch of skin on his back was removed, as well as 32 lymph nodes from his armpit. A month and a half later, a malignant melanoma was discovered on his neck, but his neck lymph nodes tested positive. He was on immunotherapy the last I heard.

That was one awareness week I had a personal stake in. And I certainly hope that the people out there got the message.

Hockey players and other professional athletes don't get involved in such activities lightly, or by accident. A hockey team with a history, like the Montreal Canadiens or the Toronto Maple Leafs, comes to mean a lot more to a city and its fans than just what happens on the ice during the season.

What do the Maple Leafs mean to Toronto?

In the summer of 1989, the *Toronto Star* ran a fans poll on Great Moments in Toronto Sports. The 1985 pennant win by the Blue Jays came first, and that's understandable because it was still a recent championship. No. 2 was the Grey Cup parade in 1983, after the Argos had ended a thirty-one-year drought in the Canadian Football League. In third place was the 1967, and last, Stanley Cup victory by the Leafs, twenty-two years before. No. 6 was my ten-point night and No. 7 was the Toronto game in the Canada–Soviet Union Hockey Summit. It is very significant that the three hockey moments in the top ten had all taken place in the 1970s or earlier. Hockey did not merit a Toronto sports moment in the 1980s, even though our team won the Canada Cup twice in a row, the second time in 1987 just down the road in Hamilton.

Another survey in the same newspaper in 1990 was a surprise to me. One of the questions was, "Who is the greatest athlete of all time to represent Toronto?" I finished first with 20.8 per cent of the vote, ahead of Ben Johnson at 14.7 per cent, Lionel Conacher at 11.3 per cent, Dave Keon at 7.3 per cent, Ned Hanlon at 6.6 per cent, and Frank Mahovlich at 5.4 per cent. Four Leafs in the top six, and I was the last one to play in Toronto, leaving in the first month of 1982. That response was highly significant; no Blue Jays nor Argos were in the top seven and, although those teams have strong followings, they have not been as deeply woven into the fabric of the city.

And when the *Toronto Sun* ran its own survey in 1991, I finished third behind Tom Watt and Jacques Demers when readers were asked: "Who should be coach [of the Leafs] next season?" That's highly flattering when I've never even coached a period of hockey in my life. What it makes me believe, however, is that fans know when players have a genuine feeling for what the home city is, and represents, to the rest of North America and the world. Toronto and Montreal have long been attuned to that mutual relationship between fan and player.

The Canadiens and the Leafs have long been institutions in their cities and that speaks to the pride and emotions of their constituencies in their home provinces and elsewhere. Many sociological studies show that fans identify with and vicariously live the feats of their heroes, because they reflect positively on the quality of life in their cities. Syl Apps, George Armstrong, Jean Béliveau, Maurice Richard and people like them knew exactly what wearing the "C" meant with those teams.

When I was named Leafs captain on Wednesday, September 10, 1975, just as training camp began for a new season, I was honored to be following in the footsteps of Apps, Armstrong, Teeder Kennedy, Hap Day, Charlie Conacher and Bob Davidson. It was Davidson himself who gave me my new jersey. The fact that, at twenty-four, I was the second-youngest captain in Leafs history (Kennedy was twenty-three when appointed) was a great confidence booster and I vowed to be the best captain possible during my tenure.

That meant increased demand on my time and availability and, although personal and family ties sometimes suffered or were placed on the back burner, I felt this position was important enough to the organization to put in the extra effort. That meant meeting people like Martha Jackson. In 1978 I met her at a Leafs practice at Maple Leaf Gardens; the practice was her ninety-seventh birthday treat. Three years later, we both sat over a cake decorated with plastic hockey players at Mapleview Lodge in Acton, Ontario, and talked about hockey and what it was like to be one hundred years old. The cake was a replica of a hockey rink and the scoreboard read "Martha 100, Darryl 32" (actually I was 31). I had driven up right after practice that Thursday, after back-to-back games in Philadelphia and New York on Tuesday and Wednesday.

Being captain also meant summer softball exhibitions. I knew better than most that the arrival of summertime did not quench the thirst of Torontonians for all things Maple Leaf. In 1974 I was instrumental in getting the Leaf players together as the Molson's ProStars and we played a number of softball exhibitions for charity, in this case the Ontario Society for Crippled Children.

Some of the guys were out to play serious ball, others just to have a good time—which was guaranteed every time Eddie Shack participated—and we gathered large crowds all over southern Ontario. It was not unusual for us to attract more than 25,000 fans to Exhibition Stadium to "play ball for Timmy" against other NHLers like Phil Esposito, Pete Mahovlich, Bob Gainey, Mike Walton, Lorne Henning, Danny Gare, Marcel Dionne, Rick Martin and Larry Robinson. We did all right, too, because George Ferguson and Jack Valiquette were a heck of a battery.

The guys really enjoyed the chance to get together as a group and with our fans in a less stressful environment than we usually faced during hockey season. We got precious little privacy in the off-season anyway, so this represented an opportunity to do something positive rather than complaining about having no private life.

Win or lose, the attention Leaf players received 365 days a year always clearly indicated to me exactly how much this team meant to the city.

And that is still the case today.

16

Going Home

A FAMOUS AUTHOR once wrote: "You can never go home."

He was wrong, as the last year in the lives of Darryl Sittler, his family, his closest friends and the Toronto Maple Leafs has proved.

At this time a year ago, as we were preparing to put the hardcover version of my autobiography to bed, I remember the uncertainty that faced me. There had been some preliminary talks with the Maple Leafs about a possible return in some capacity, but these were at what could be called the "feeler" stage. Nothing was certain, from offer to definition of duties through obligations and other such requirements. What was certain was that the ideal arrangement for me would still allow our family to live in East Amherst in upstate New York which had become home to us in all meanings of the term.

All of the events of the pivotal summer of 1991—pivotal in the sense that a lot of very positive things were going to happen for my family and me—had, in fact, begun fourteen months before.

In each lifetime there are milestones or signposts that mark the way for us. People who cannot remember what they had for lunch two days ago, or what they wore last Friday, can remember in minute detail what they were doing shortly after 2:00 p.m. Eastern Standard Time on Friday, November 22, 1963, when President John Fitzgerald Kennedy was shot. Others can recall with similar crystal clarity who sat with them in front of the family television in the wee hours of July 24, 1969 when a man named Neil Armstrong took "one small step for man, one giant step for mankind."

Anyone remotely affiliated with the Toronto Maple Leafs hockey club, past or present, can tell you exactly what they were doing on the afternoon of Wednesday, April 11, 1990. At 2:50 p.m. that day, a little more than twenty- four hours after he had asked to be taken off a respirator at Wellesley Hospital, Edwin Harold Ballard breathed his last at age eighty-six.

I heard about it within minutes, during a radio newscast, while driving just outside St. Catharines en route home to Buffalo from Toronto. Within seconds, my car telephone was ringing. The *Toronto Sun* wanted a reaction piece. I could almost picture Harold looking down with Clancy and Imlach at his side, muttering, "Damn vultures. Body ain't even cold yet!"

I wanted to give more thought to it before I started to talk about Harold. Here it was, finally, after months, even years of speculation. What impressed me the most was how it felt so final. Six months before, a sportswriter had asked me to do an interview on the subject so he could have it "in the can" when Harold finally died. I said no way, I could never do it even though I understood that it was a matter of journalistic convenience and a common practice.

Prepared or not, I spent much of the rest of that day and the next after Harold died talking to reporters. I felt a sadness in his passing. This was a guy who lived on the front pages, a colorful man who was a part of everybody's life almost every day. That was the character of the man, good or bad. In his two decades with the Leafs he had been larger than life and so there was a large void now that he had finally gone. I had mixed feelings about Harold, but I was certain about one thing: an era had ended.

Reporter Mike Zeisberger first asked the question that a lot of reporters would ask in the ensuing days: "The man called you a cancer to the Maple Leafs, hounded you out of Toronto and made your last few years with the Leafs pretty miserable. How can you defend him?"

Even now, well over a year after that, I don't have a rationale for my answer. All I can say now is what I said then: "I've never felt bitter toward Harold Ballard. He loved his Leafs and really wanted them to do well. He just had a lot of trouble with the decisions he made."

If there was any bitterness between the two of us, it was long forgotten before Harold died. In fact, in1989 there were discussions about my possible return to the team. Early that summer I was driving up to Toronto on business and called Harold on my car phone to chat. We spoke occasionally by phone, several times a year, so my call wasn't a surprise to him. On this day we gossiped about several things and the conversation got around to re-connecting with the Leafs. I had spoken with Gord Stellick once or twice to tell him I was interested in getting back in the organization, and Gord had suggested I call Harold. Harold was warming to the idea, I can remember him joking when the signal broke up as I drove through a tunnel: "Why don't you pay your phone bill so we won't have this problem."

During the conversation he was receptive and bounced me back to Gord. I knew Gord Stellick from my days with the Leafs just before I was traded to Philadelphia. I'd always liked him as a person, even though I didn't know if he was qualified or not from a hockey standpoint. I say that because there was a lot of flack in Toronto when Ballard appointed him to succeed Gerry McNamara as Leafs general manager. Many Toronto media types felt he didn't have the kind of experience or personality to run such an organization. I remembered Gord as the second floor's go-fer and, later, as assistant to Punch Imlach and other GMs. He had been part of the organization for many years and certainly knew his way around the NHL. When he was named Leafs GM, I dropped him a note of congratulations and wished him well.

He had been GM for about a year or so when we started serious talk. Gord always had indicated to me that he was interested in bringing some of the older ex-Leafs back into the fold. He felt their estrangement was a shortcoming of the organization. However, he also explained that he was on thin ice whenever he mentioned the idea to Harold, and would have to work on the owner in the long term.

We kept in touch. We met once to discuss what I felt I could contribute to the Leafs. I had been a part of the organization for so long and we both felt—just from a public relations standpoint—it would be a positive move on his behalf to bring me back if he could. I felt I could contribute from my hockey experience, both on the ice and away from the game. We discussed off-ice and on-ice scenarios. I always felt it important that management should provide players with a full range of services, from tips on dealing with the media and handling investments away from the rink, to solving personal problems and managing all the stresses that come with the game. I'd been through it all before and could help counsel the current players. Or, if Gord preferred, I might work with the coaches, going on the ice and helping with face-offs. If a coach wanted to discuss a powerplay situation, I could tell him what Lanny and I did. Whatever input, in short, that I could give that would be of benefit to them, I was ready to offer it.

One major point in my favor, I thought, was that I still was "fresh" in terms of my retirement. I was still close to the game and young enough to relate to both management and players. It was my generation's time to move into the executive suite, as proved by the number of players I'd played with who were now general managers—Serge Savard, Bobby Clarke, Glen Sather, or coaches like Bob Murdoch, Brian Sutter, Mike Milbury, Doug Risebrough and Rick Ley. It almost sounds like a graduating class or Old Boys' network. I had contacts and connections that Gord could not tap, not being an ex-player or ex-teammate. We agreed that I could help him out in that capacity.

Gord was very receptive. He wanted to do it but again he indicated to me the importance of timing and process. The only question was how he could put it together and sell it to Harold. I got together with George Armstrong, Garry Lariviere, and Gord and went out to lunch just down the street from Maple Leaf Gardens to discuss the situation.

When I walked up the stairwell after lunch to go to the Maple Leafs offices, Harold was there with Rudy Pilous. That was the first time I met Yolanda, who was out in the hallway also.

After that meeting, the whole idea seemed to die on the vine. Harold always had a bad habit of listening to the last guy to catch his ear. Gord Stellick and I both believe that Pilous must have said something negative. Gord later wrote in his book *Hockey, Heartaches and Hal* (co-author: Jim O'Leary; Prentice-Hall, 1990):

> He never explained what changed his mind, but I suspected that the reversal was rooted in his growing paranoia and in a conversation with Rudy Pilous, a long-time hockey buddy of Ballard's. The day I met with Sittler, we bumped into Ballard and Pilous outside the Gardens. Sittler and Ballard chatted briefly, and there seemed to be no problem. By the time I returned, however, Ballard had soured on Sittler. Over the course of that summer, Ballard had been growing more protective of his hockey empire and more wary of me. He came to view my Sittler initiative with suspicion. I suspected that,

while Sittler and I dined, Pilous was strumming the chords of Ballard's anxieties. In any event, the opportunity was lost.

When I left that day I didn't have any intuition about whether it would happen or not. I felt good about the vibrations during my lunch with Stellick, Chief and Lariviere; but at the same time I can recall feeling that there wasn't a sense of organizational direction with Lariviere and Chief. George Armstrong was in a bind; he'd been brought in to coach the team against his wishes when Ballard finally agreed to fire John Brophy. Chief had to take it; if he didn't, he felt his job would be in jeopardy. Ballard had told Stellick when he had been brought in as assistant GM that Chief was insurance against Brophy acting up. He hadn't said anything of this nature to Armstrong, who wanted a place in management and specifically didn't want to find himself behind the bench.

In the end, the project died when Stellick resigned and went to the Rangers. Harold, highly displeased over this perceived treason, took some shots at Stellick, which laid to rest any plans or initiatives Gord might have been working on before he left. That was typical Ballard: anything that happened to go right, he took credit for; anything that went wrong was always somebody else's fault. The smallest little thing or perceived slight could result in his abandoning a long-time employee. Yet he demanded one hundred per cent undivided loyalty from everyone. And he would love you until the next conversation he might have with someone who didn't like you. This attitude could even be seen within his family—he demanded loyalty from his children, but turned on them over perceived slights, only to see them later turn on him.

The upshot was that after Stellick left, I had no contact with the Leafs at all. Harold was deep into what some journalists called the Yolanda era, where the only way to get to the man was to smuggle a message past her. After that, things accelerated, he got very sick down in Florida and everybody pretty well knew then that his chances of survival were very small.

I can remember bumping into Don Giffin during this period. I was down at the Gardens for a game and Giffin said: "Why don't you come and see Harold; I'm sure he'd like to see you." I never did do it. I guess one of the reasons was that I didn't quite know how comfortable that whole scene might be. I didn't want to make it a public thing, the media might grab hold of it and I'd be seen as one more in a line of guys hanging around the death bed for crumbs. It was a delicate situation.

More importantly, I didn't really know how Harold would react. Don Giffin might be telling me that Harold might like to see me, when in fact I might upset him. When he was healthy, we had usually been polite with each other, but I had never spent much time in face-to-face conversation with him.

After Harold passed away, somebody made a comment I heard— it wasn't in the paper—that Ballard's true relationship with his management and players over the years was reflected in the number of ex-Leafs who came to the wake. Apparently, they were conspicuous by their absence. The story going around was that the guys who showed had jobs in the organization, and those who had no such financial obligation stayed away. That may not necessarily be accurate, because attending a funeral or a memorial service is a very personal thing.

I couldn't be there. I was out in Vancouver with Wendy at the Purolator Courier bantam championships. But I did send flowers and a telegram to his family, to Bill Ballard personally, and to the public relations department at the Gardens.

I got the impression from some of the news reports that a lot of reporters questioned my judgment in being polite and for saying nothing particularly negative about Harold Ballard. I have thought about that a lot in the writing of this book. I am comfortable with that stance in that it expresses clearly what happened as seen from my eyes during my career in the National Hockey League.

I also am very sensitive to the issue of speaking about persons who have passed away. Harold Ballard, King Clancy, Punch Imlach, my father, are no longer with us. However, these people were very much alive and active during my career and I have endeavored to represent them fairly and dispassionately in these pages. It's not a question of raking over old coals or poking at bones with a stick. I lived it, day by day, as they did. Harold did some good things and bad things and hurt some people. Others may have reacted differently; I recognize that. But I drew my own conclusions on the man.

As for my opinion of myself, what I want to say, without apology, is that I believe I have been loyal to what being a Toronto Maple Leaf represented. In some instances, the other side of what is needed for a mutual relationship to thrive has been ripped away from me. But even that has not dissolved my strong attachment.

That is why it has hurt me to see what happened to the Leafs after I left.

I remember thinking during the spring and early summer of 1991 that if the Toronto Maple Leafs were going to rebound, they would have to link their past with a new future. The result eventually would be success in the present. I spoke about this in Chapter Two when I mentioned the team's poor record with its veterans and retired players, and such things as Oldtimers Lounges and sweater retirements. One great motivator for today's athlete, beyond money, of course, is the knowledge that his hockey contribution has something of value beyond simple game results, that the organization has a place and an appreciation for him beyond his playing days; and that he can be of value within the larger community, both during and after his hockey career. Oldtimers with a direct link to the current team represent a most valuable human resource, especially for a team that's trying to get back on its feet after an entire generation of poor performance.

It goes far beyond simple public relations gimmicks, however. If the team was going to be successful, it would have to be the result of a long-term program. Toronto Maple Leafs would have to be completely restructured and run like a modern corporation.

The crucial first step was taken when Cliff Fletcher joined the Toronto Maple Leafs as top man. He would need to build the organization from the bottom up, and have carte blanche to spend the kind of money it takes.

Scouting is one area he'll have to upgrade. In the past two decades the Leafs have tried to make do with the reports from the Central Scouting Bureau and a handful of paid scouts, George Armstrong, Johnny Bower and Dick Duff, and six or seven part-timers covering the various leagues or geographical areas. The Calgary Flames and Montreal Canadiens have always far outnumbered Toronto in this area and have the results to show for it.

There's an old adage in the business world: You have to spend money to make money. Harold Ballard didn't believe in it because he didn't have to: win or lose, he made money. He wasn't judged on the same business principles as everyone else in this area because as the Leafs' on-ice performance became more dismal, as he made life more difficult for Toronto season-ticket holders, the more his investment accrued and the value of his club increased. Harold Ballard didn't need to join the rest of us in the second half of the twentieth century in hockey matters because he could prove that winning wasn't necessary in order to make money in Toronto.

Now it will be. As I wrote the last chapter of the hard cover edition a year ago, the world of modern NHL hockey had been stood on its ear. The Pittsburgh Penguins had just won their first Stanley Cup after a valiant battle with the Minnesota North Stars. Both teams were object lessons to front offices everywhere in the league. Each had gone out and hired professionals in the front office, let them work, and saw it pay off handsomely. Craig Patrick hired Scotty Bowman and the late Bob Johnson, men with years of experience in professional hockey, and had the courage to make a big blockbuster trade that put his team over the top. (So far over the top that, after a mediocre season characterized by injuries to major contributors, the Penguins repeated in 1992, after yet another well-considered late-season trade.) And Bob Clarke found his man in Bob Gainey, as two men nurtured in two successful organizations, Philadelphia and Montreal, built a team that went to the Stanley Cup final.

The opening step in any rebuilding is to get those bird dogs out there working for you who are proud to have a Maple Leafs jacket and sit in a cold rink, not necessarily for a paycheque, but to help the organization—wherever they might be, northern Quebec or southern Saskatchewan. And they have to report to a staff of permanent scouts who can fly in and check and re-check the reports on coveted players at a moment's notice. And you need somebody with the experience to evaluate and collate all of this input so the Leafs aren't outgunned or out-thought on draft day.

Most importantly, the front office must have a game plan for the 1990s that reflects today's NHL realities and not a nostalgia for how it was in the good old days. That includes inter-club and league relations, communications, community relations, marketing the team and its image, player-management relations, international contacts and more.

If you look at the top organizations and what they do to stay on top, teams like Calgary and the Canadiens, you see the courage to innovate, but within a context of consistency, and the will to be competitive.

If there was something positive in Harold Ballard's passing it is that it opened the doors to a more modern organization capable of giving the people the type of hockey entertainment and the type of team they want but haven't had for so long. There have been so many fans so loyal to the Maple Leafs who have suffered through the lean times. It was tough for them to go to work every day and to take the constant crap from non- Leafs supporters and some wise guys in the media.

These were all of the things I wanted to say to Cliff Fletcher when we met to discuss my contribution to the team in the summer of 1991. But I didn't get a chance—he said them all to me. Talk about being on the same wavelength! After some talk, the Leafs and I agreed that I would be a special assistant to Cliff Fletcher in charge of community relations, much like Jean Béliveau is in Montreal and Lanny McDonald in Calgary. True, the Leafs' 1991-92 season was a disappointment but you don't build a Stanley Cup contender in one year or two. It takes five years at least.

At the start of the 1991-92 season, when I joined the team, the Leafs were in bad shape, with hardly any top-drawer players. At the end of the year, even though we didn't make the play-offs, the team was one with a future. Thanks to the trades that Cliff Fletcher made with Edmonton and Calgary, the addition of guys like Grant Fuhr, Glenn Anderson, Doug Gilmour, Ric Nattress, Jamie Macoun, Rick Wamsley and Kent Manderville gave us something we could build on.

My return to the Leafs was just a start to a most incredible year, an incredible year that culminated in an incredible week in June 1992.

Earlier in this book, I wrote about my draft year, 1970, and how I was covered in sweat and cement dust and riding home from a day of building swimming pools in London when I heard on the radio that I belonged to the Toronto Maple Leafs. They don't do things like that in the NHL anymore—not by a long shot.

For the Sittler family and the 1992 NHL Entry Draft, it all started in the summer of 1991, in Japan of all places. It was an exciting summer for the family because Ryan was starting to get some attention for his hockey skills. If I thought my own hockey career was exciting, I don't think I was prepared for the feelings that came out as I saw my son develop and mature as a player. There never was any pressure from the family to excel and, for some years, Ryan was just a pudgy kid who played more for fun than advancement.

Then, almost by magic, the pudgy kid turned into a tall, lean athlete with shoulders out to here and a dream to do something with his abilities in the sport. Late in the spring of 1991, Ryan went to try-outs for the team that was going to represent Western New York in the Empire State Games. He also went to training camp for the United States under-17 team—he and his sisters have dual citizenship—and made it. Before we knew it, we were off the the under-17 world championships in Japan. The Ryan Sittler I saw playing against the Japanese, Canadians and Russians was a revelation. He scored twice against Canada in a 4-4 tie.

That was just the start of Ryan's international adventures. In the fall he returned to Nichols School and midget AAA hockey with the Buffalo Regals. He had been picked by Detroit of the Ontario Hockey League major junior during the midget draft and Jimmy Rutherford, a former NHL goalie, was trying hard to get Ryan. However, we were leaning to U.S. collegiate hockey and Ryan chose Nichols and midget, even though Detroit thought it might hurt his development.

Then came the second surprise. There had been an evaluation camp during the summer for the under-21 U.S. team and Ryan had not been invited, mainly because he was too young. However, when the time came for the final selections to go to Europe for the World Junior Championship, a couple of the selected players chose not to go and Ryan was invited to the team's final preparation camp in Albany prior to departure for Germany. It was explained to us that Ryan would be a fourth-line player, not get much ice time, but would benefit from the experience and this would put him in good stead for coming years. So, much against all expectations, the Sittlers spent the holidays in Europe and, as it turned out, Ryan got a lot more ice time than promised and acquitted himself well against the likes of Eric Lindros, Roman Hamrlik, Libor Polasek and Alexei Yashin.

When we returned home, the talk began of a first or second round pick at the June draft. By draft time, we had had almost six months of telephone calls and interviews with scouts, media speculation as to draft position and more attention than most people get in a lifetime. The crowning glory, so my son tells me, was when the hockey card companies began calling—in 1992, that's the real thing.

As a hockey father and a member of the front office of the Toronto Maple Leafs, I had a privileged glimpse of the entire draft process because I got to see our team's approach to the draft session. One thing I knew was, given the right circumstances, Ryan might end up with Toronto—the team had prepared a number of sweaters for the draft and one had the familiar Sittler on the back. But it would take the right circumstances. Cliff's main strategy was to get help on the blue line and some speed and finesse at center. The Leafs were looking at several possibilities, including Hamrlik, Darius Kasparaitis, Mike Rathje and Grant Marshall on defence, and at pivots like Yashin and Brandon Convery.

Cliff showed his experience and acumen during the first round of the draft. As a result, we ended up with the center and defenceman we were seeking, all with a couple deft moves. We had planned all along to take Convery with our first-round pick, No. 5 overall, but then we were stymied because we had no second round selection— our next player choice would be No. 53, a third-rounder. Now came the quandary, did we take Kasparaitis instead of Convery, the player we coveted all along; or did we find someone desperate for an offensive defenceman and trade down a few spots in Round One, but get a second round pick thrown in?

Cliff worked the telephones and called his good friend Bill Torrey. The New York Islanders sounded like the right mix, a team with a dozen or so defensive defencemen which could use a quarterback.

The Isles got Kasparaitis, the Flames and Flyers passed on Convery, and we got a second round pick, No. 32. That meant there was still a good chance that Marshall might be still around because he was rated a middle second rounder, even though he had been the highest scoring rearguard in the OHL last season. The question mark was a big one; the season before Marshall had suffered a broken neck when hit from behind into the boards and for the longest time there was a possibility that he might never walk again, let alone play hockey. So Marshall could ostensibly still be around by pick 32.

Then, it seemed, everybody started picking defencemen—David Cooper by Buffalo as No. 11, Sergei Gonchar by Washington No. 14, Sergei Bautin, Winnipeg 17, Jason Smith, New Jersey 18, and David Wilkie, Montreal 20. Our people got their heads together and concluded that Grant Marshall would not remain undrafted for 11 more picks.

Cliff called David Poile of Washington who had pick 23. He offered to swap No. 32, a fourth rounder and a fourth rounder in 1993 and Poile agreed. Marshall was ours.

You had to be at the Leafs table to feel the satisfaction of actually doing what we planned to do; of making the moves under pressure to get two hockey players the team wanted, rather than waiting passively for our next draft spot and the best available leftovers still there.

The first round of the 1992 Entry Draft—24 players in all—took a little over two hours, but for the Sittler family, it took a little under a week, and concluded an incredible roller coaster ride.

It began on Wednesday, June 17 for Ryan when he and his buddy Ethan Moreau of Niagara Falls Thunder, a first rounder in 1994, flew into Montreal. He came in early for a series of interviews with a variety of teams, among them Calgary and Washington.

Wendy, Meaghan, Ashley and I drove up first thing Thursday morning and immediately got into the swim of things, including attending a special hockey card show at a brand new 50-storey Montreal office building which is the first I've ever seen with a permanent ice rink at the lobby level. Each of the top-rated draft picks was introduced and skated out in his hockey shirt to have his picture taken. We sat in the audience and had a great time.

After that, on Friday, Ryan went one way, Wendy and the girls another, and I returned to our team meetings for the rest of the day. Later there was a press conference to announce the new inductees into the NHL Hall of Fame. They were Lanny McDonald, Marcel Dionne and Bob Gainey. Amazing—they couldn't have put this into a story, nobody would have believed it. My best buddy going into the Hall of Fame, alongside the two other guys with whom we had played on the 1976 Canada Cup team. My series-clinching overtime goal against the Czechs was assisted by Lanny and Marcel.

Quite a few of us had many sleepless moments that night and, although time seemed to drag, we found ourselves at the Forum about an hour before the scheduled commencement of the draft proceedings.

I had asked Cliff for permission to sit with my family until Ryan was selected and he was gracious about it. We agreed that shortly after Ryan was picked, I would return to the Leafs table.

Sitting next to us were Ardell and Lanny McDonald. There was a possibility that Ryan might be selected by the Flames and if that happened, I was thinking in the back of my mind that perhaps Lanny could present Ryan with the Flames sweater.

So there we all sat, Lanny and I discussing the Hall of Fame induction and what I would say as his presenter; Wendy and Ardell back together again; and Ryan anxiously awaiting The Word.

A year ago, Ryan would have been happy had someone in pro hockey known his name. Now, however, after many months of scouts, team interviews, international competition and media speculation, he had his sights set on the First Round. *The Hockey News*, the game's bible, had him projected as No. 4 pick, behind Todd Warriner, Mike Rathje and Roman Hamrlik. When Hamrlik (Tampa Bay), Yashin (Ottawa), Rathje (San Jose) and Warriner (Quebec) went, the Sittler-McDonald "bench" in Section 102 of the Forum became gripped with anticipation.

Toronto was up next, and it seemed that the 14,000-plus fans, and the thousand or so team and media types were all looking up at us, especially when Cliff Fletcher called time out.

Would the Leafs pick their second Sittler? I knew better, and I know that Cliff hurried to announce the swap with the Islanders to stop that kind of speculation. New York quickly selected Kasparaitis and then it was Calgary's turn. They wanted a playmaking center, a skilled passer who could feed some of their big wingers, and Cory Stillman, Todd Warriner's linemate at Windsor, fit the bill.

Then it was Philadelphia's turn. A week before the draft, the team had welcomed back Bob Clarke as Vice President, Hockey. We had left the team and the city under emotional circumstances and although I knew from talking to Bill Barber and others that they liked Ryan, I didn't think they had him tabbed for early first round. This all was before the Eric Lindros-Flyers- Rangers brouhaha.

We were sitting on tenterhooks when Wendy gave me an elbow. "Look at the Flyers table," she said.

President Jay Snider and general manager Russ Farwell were making their way to the stage with a Flyers sweater and cap in hand when I looked down.

Bill Barber and Inge Hammarström both had big grins and were giving us the "thumbs up."

And then I heard ... "The Philadelphia Flyers are proud to select, from Nichols School ... Ryan Sittler."

And then I couldn't see anymore.

The TSN cameras got the scene perfectly. Lanny hugging Ryan, Ryan hugging his Mom, and Dad the Hall of Famer blubbering away at 90 miles an hour.

When I was with the Leafs, I occasionally took Ryan out skating at Maple Leaf Gardens and I remember a picture of both of us in our blue-and-white with the 27 on the back appearing in a Toronto paper in 1980 or 1981.

However, Ryan really started playing hockey in Voorhees, N.J. in the Philadelphia suburbs and played most of his games at the

Coliseum, our practice facility out there. Ryan was a regular rink rat who would throw out the pucks to us at many of our practices.

And sitting at the Philadelphia table was Billy Barber, a close buddy. The Barber home in Cherry Hill, N.J. with Billy and Jenny as gracious hosts was my first home in Philly until I could get Wendy and the kids moved into Voorhees. Who knows? Maybe Ryan will get my room.

June 20, 1992 was just an amazing day. I was sitting in the Forum where I scored the Canada Cup goal in 1976. The four guys I played with and hung around with the most during that series were all there, and three of them were heading to the Hall of Fame. And the little tow-headed two-year-old who didn't understand what all the fuss was about way back in 1976 had just been drafted by a former team of mine. Who said "you can never go home again"?

Not only have I gone home, home is the many places where Darryl, Wendy, Ryan, Meaghan and Ashley Sittler have been over the years. "Home" is Toronto and the Leafs of 1992-93. It is East Amherst, N.Y., year-round and Ann Arbor, Michigan, while Ryan is playing college hockey at the university there. It may be Philadelphia and the Flyers in 1995 or 1996. It will be wherever Meaghan settles down to play for the U.S. women's Olympic hockey team in a couple of years. Or wherever Ashley decides to make her place in the world.

Regardless of location, as a family we believe home, finally, is where our hearts are—and our hearts belong to each other.

INDEX

BRETT
by Brett Hull and Kevin Allen
The NHL's most prolific goal-scorer, son of the great Bobby Hull, chronicles his own rise to hockey superstardom in this revealing autobiography.
0-7710-4271-X $6.99   24 pages b&w photos

THE HABS
An Oral History of the Montreal Canadiens: 1940-1980
by Dick Irvin
"A beautiful read." — *Hockey News*
"A wealth of hockey lore." — *The Toronto Star*
Veteran broadcaster Dick Irvin presents the vivid stories of more than one hundred players, coaches, officials and journalists as they recall the glory days of Canada's most successful sports franchise.
0-7710-4358-9 $6.99   16 pages b&w photos

SITTLER
by Darryl Sittler and Chrys Goyens with Allan Turowetz
"Sittler tells his story the way he played — bluntly and bravely." — Jim Proudfoot, *The Toronto Star*
Few Toronto Maple Leafs have been as beloved or respected as Hockey Hall-of-Famer Darryl Sittler. Here he provides an honest, occasionally painful look at his 15-season career in Canada's national sport.
0-7710-8080-8 $6.99   16 pages b&w photos

More Great Sports Titles from M&S Paperbacks...

AFTER THE APPLAUSE
by Colleen and Gordie Howe with Charles Wilkins
"A thoroughly enjoyable trip down memory lane." —*London Free Press*
Ten hockey greats — Phil Esposito, Boom Boom Geoffrion and Stan Mikita among them — and their wives talk about life in the limelight and in the post-career years. A national bestseller in hardcover.
0-7710-4227-2 $5.95   16 pages b&w photos

THE TALES OF AN ATHLETIC SUPPORTER
by Trent Frayne
"Hilarious, moving . . . Frayne writes with a playwright's ear for dialogue, and a sometimes poetic turn of phrase that make him the best sports columnist in Canada." — *Maclean's*
0-7710-3213-7 $6.99   8 pages b&w photos

MAPLE LEAF BLUES
Harold Ballard and the Life and Times of the Toronto Maple Leafs
by William Houston
"An incredible tale . . . Were it not for Houston's believable easy-reading journalistic style, one would think it came from the *National Enquirer*." — *The Winnipeg Free Press*
An up-to-date look at the team as well as a sharp account of irascible owner Harold Ballard.
0-7710-4242-6 $6.95   16 pages b&w photos

THE BOYS OF SATURDAY NIGHT
Inside Hockey Night in Canada
by Scott Young
"A well-reported history . . . a winner." — *Maclean's*
A behind-the-scenes look at Don Cherry, Ward Cornell, Dick Irvin and the others who have made Hockey Night in Canada this country's most successful broadcast institution.
0-7710-9097-8 $6.99   16 pages b&w photos